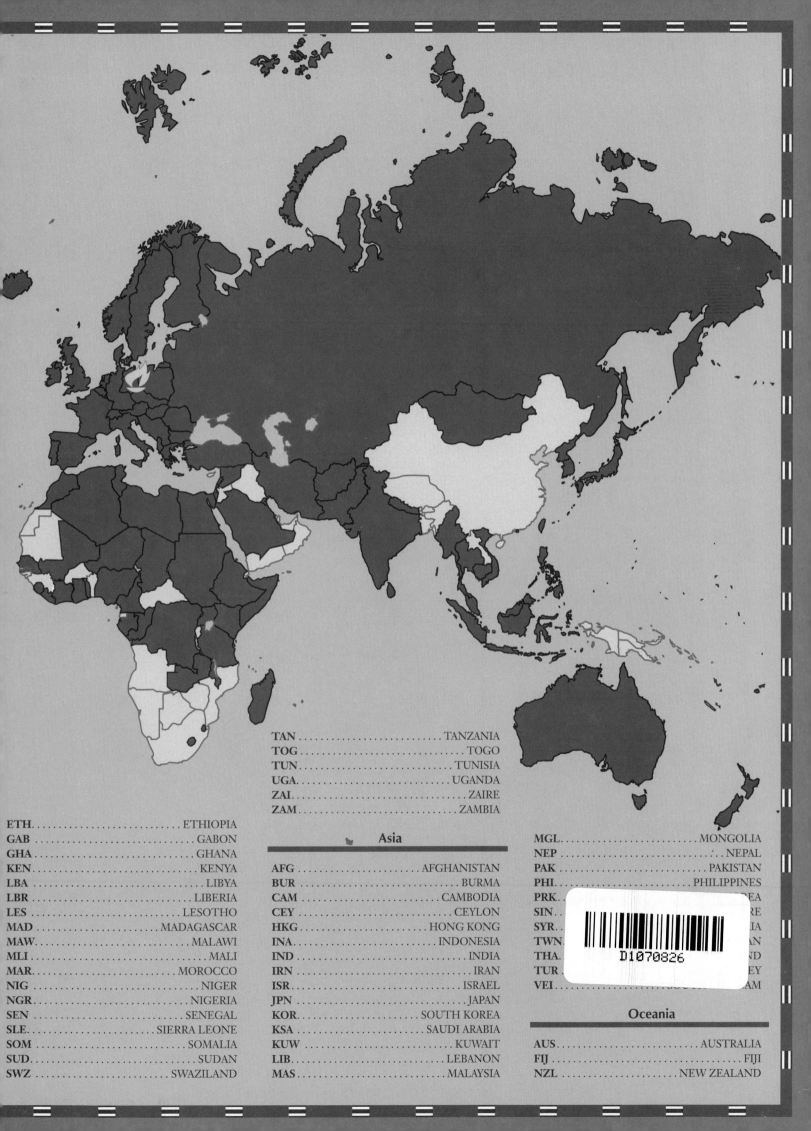

TAN . . . . TANZANIA
TOG . . . . TOGO
TUN . . . . TUNISIA
UGA . . . . UGANDA
ZAI . . . . ZAIRE
ZAM . . . . ZAMBIA

ETH . . . . ETHIOPIA
GAB . . . . GABON
GHA . . . . GHANA
KEN . . . . KENYA
LBA . . . . LIBYA
LBR . . . . LIBERIA
LES . . . . LESOTHO
MAD . . . . MADAGASCAR
MAW . . . . MALAWI
MLI . . . . MALI
MAR . . . . MOROCCO
NIG . . . . NIGER
NGR . . . . NIGERIA
SEN . . . . SENEGAL
SLE . . . . SIERRA LEONE
SOM . . . . SOMALIA
SUD . . . . SUDAN
SWZ . . . . SWAZILAND

Asia

AFG . . . . AFGHANISTAN
BUR . . . . BURMA
CAM . . . . CAMBODIA
CEY . . . . CEYLON
HKG . . . . HONG KONG
INA . . . . INDONESIA
IND . . . . INDIA
IRN . . . . IRAN
ISR . . . . ISRAEL
JPN . . . . JAPAN
KOR . . . . SOUTH KOREA
KSA . . . . SAUDI ARABIA
KUW . . . . KUWAIT
LIB . . . . LEBANON
MAS . . . . MALAYSIA

MGL . . . . MONGOLIA
NEP . . . . NEPAL
PAK . . . . PAKISTAN
PHI . . . . PHILIPPINES
PRK . . . . EA
SIN . . . . RE
SYR . . . . IA
TWN . . . . AN
THA . . . . ND
TUR . . . . EY
VEI . . . . AM

Oceania

AUS . . . . AUSTRALIA
FIJ . . . . FIJI
NZL . . . . NEW ZEALAND

THE OLYMPIC CENTURY
THE OFFICIAL 1ST CENTURY HISTORY OF THE MODERN OLYMPIC MOVEMENT

VOLUME 18

THE
XX OLYMPIAD

MUNICH 1972
INNSBRUCK 1976

BY

GEORGE G. DANIELS

WORLD SPORT RESEARCH & PUBLICATIONS INC.
LOS ANGELES

1996 © United States Olympic Committee

Published by:
World Sport Research & Publications Inc.
1424 North Highland Avenue
Los Angeles, California 90028
(213) 461-2900

1st Century Project
The 1st Century Project is an undertaking by World
Sport Research & Publications Inc. to commemorate the
100-year history of the Modern Olympic Movement.
Charles Gary Allison, Chairman

Publishers: C. Jay Halzle, Robert G. Rossi,
James A. Williamson

Senior Consultant: Dr. Dietrich Quanz (Germany)
Special Consultants: Walter Borgers (Germany), Ian
Buchanan (United Kingdom), Dr. Karl Lennartz
(Germany), Wolf Lyberg (Sweden), Dr. Norbert Müller
(Germany), Dr. Nicholas Yalouris (Greece)

Editor: Laura Foreman
Executive Editor: Christian Kinney
Editorial Board: George Constable, George G. Daniels,
Ellen Galford, Ellen Phillips, Carl A. Posey

Art Director: Christopher M. Register
Production Manager: Nicholas Pitt
Picture Editor: Debra Lemonds Hannah
Designers: Kimberley Davison, Diane Farenick
Staff Researchers: Mark Brewin (Canada), Diana
Fakiola (Greece), Brad Haynes (Australia), Alexandra
Hesse (Germany), Pauline Ploquin (France)
Copy Editor: Anthony K. Pordes
Proofing Editor: Harry Endrulat
Indexer and Stat Database Manager: Melinda Tate
Fact Verification: Carl and Liselott Diem Archives of the
German Sport University at Cologne, Germany
Statisticians: Bill Mallon, Walter Teutenberg
Memorabilia Consultants: Manfred Bergman, James D.
Greensfelder, John P. Kelly, Ingrid O'Neil
Staff Photographer: Theresa Halzle
Office Manager: Christopher Jason Waters
Office Staff: Chris C. Conlee, Brian M. Heath,
Edward J. Messler, Elsa Ramirez, Brian Rand

International Contributors: Jean Durry (France),
Dr. Antonio Lombardo (Italy), Dr. John A. MacAloon
(U.S.A.), Dr. Jujiro Narita (Japan), Dr. Roland Renson
(Belgium), Dr. James Walston (Ombudsman)
International Research and Assistance: John S. Baick
(New York), Matthieu Brocart (Paris), Alexander
Fakiolas (Athens), Bob Miyakawa (Tokyo), Rona Lester
(London), Dominic LoTempio (Columbia), George
Kostas Mazareas (Boston), Georgia McDonald
(Colorado Springs), Wendy Nolan (Princeton), Alexander
Ratner (Moscow), Jon Simon (Washington D.C.), Frank
Strasser (Cologne), Valéry Turco (Lausanne), Laura
Walden (Rome), Jorge Zocchi (Mexico City)

Map Compilation: Mapping Specialists Inc., Madison,
Wisconsin
Map Artwork: Dave Hader, Studio Conceptions,
Toronto
Film Production: Global Film Services, Toronto

Customer Service: 1-800-451-8030

Bookstore and Library Distribution:
Firefly Books Ltd.
3680 Victoria Park Avenue
Willowdale, ON M2H 3K1
(416) 499-8412

U.S. Offices
230 Fifth Avenue, #1607
New York, NY 10001

Printed and bound in the United States by R. R.
Donnelly Co.

The paper used in this publication meets the minimum
requirements of American National Standard for Information Sciences — Permanence of Paper for Printed
Library Materials. ANSI Z39.48-1984

ISBN 1-888383-00-3 (25-volume series)
ISBN 1-888383-18-6 (Volume 18)

Library of Congress Cataloging-in-Publication Data

Daniels, George G.
    The XX Olympiad : Munich 1972, Innsbruck 1976 / by George G.
Daniels.
        p.   cm. -- (The Olympic century ; v. 18)
    Includes bibliographical references (p. 172 - 173) and index.
    ISBN 1-888383-18-6 (alk. paper)
    1. Olympic Games (20th : 1972 : Munich, Germany) 2. Winter
Olympic Games (12th : 1976 : Innsbruck, Austria)   I. Title.
II. Series.
GV722 1972D36 1996
796.48--dc21   96-48959
                                                                        CIP

CONTENTS

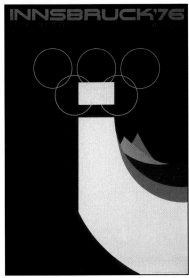

A BAVARIAN WELCOME

Restraint was the watchword for the Munich opening ceremony—a deliberate antidote to the forceful, nationalistic pageantry of the Berlin Games of 1936. The festivities began with 3,600 Munich children carrying decorated hoops and flowers, encircling the stadium track, and offering a greeting to spectators. A troupe from Mexico's famous Ballet Folklórico whirled onto the track in a brief salute to the previous Games at Mexico City.

Southern German culture came to the fore as 40 Bavarian shepherds, called *Goasslschnalzer*, entered, snapping bullwhips, followed by a cadre of lederhosen-clad *Schuhplattler*, or folk dancers. The final touch was the basso bleat of eight 15-foot-long alpenhorns that announced the start of the Parade of Nations.

Participating were a record-setting 122 delegations and nearly 7,000 athletes and administrators. Once they had all assembled on the field, they were welcomed by organizing committee president Willi Daume and IOC president Avery Brundage. Then came the official opening of the Games by German president Gustav Heinemann. Germany's gold medal winning eight-oared shell crew from the 1968 Mexico City Games *(left)* carried in the Olympic flag. Heidi Schüller, a German long jumper, took the athlete's oath, the first woman to have that honor.

Doves fluttered overhead as 18-year-old Günther Zahn, a middle-distance runner, entered the stadium with the Olympic torch. As he began a lap around the stadium, four athletes joined him: one each from the Americas, Africa, Australia, and Asia. Zahn broke away from the others when he reached a staircase leading to the cauldron. He climbed the steps, saluted the crowd, and lighted the flame. A *Böllerschützen*, a traditional Bavarian gun salute of three rounds from 20 guns, brought the charmingly understated ceremony to a close.

THE GAMES OF JOY

Munich had never claimed for itself the sort of lofty title that many big cities proclaim to the world—nothing comparable to Paris's supremely self-assured "City of Light" or New York's brassy "Big Apple." Munichers considered themselves gemütlich—cosmopolitan and tasteful, yet comfortable, indulgent, jovial, welcoming. Now and again they might agree that their city of a million people was *Weltstadt mit Herz*, the "Metropolis with a Heart." But mostly they eschewed hyperbole. When they thought about a motto, if they did, "Live and let live" seemed as good as any.

That was why everybody thought it such an excellent idea to hold the Games of the XX Olympiad in Munich. True, the Bavarian capital had been home to Adolf Hitler and his Nazis in the bleak years after World War I. And true that a street called Dachauerstrasse ran 11 miles from the city center to the place where some years later, 238,000 Jews died in concentration camp gas chambers. Yet that was the past—not forgotten, but of another, nightmarish era. In the decades following World War II, Munich had come to represent everything admirable about the New Germany, from the miracle of its reborn economy to its warm neighborliness and the vigor of its democratic institutions.

Here, in this prosperous town on the river Isar with the Alps for a backdrop, visitors would find treasures of art and architecture: the onion-domed church spires of the Marienplatz; the grand, leafy, statue-studded avenues and extravagant palaces with which seven centuries of Wittelsbach kings had memorialized themselves. All around were attractive houses and apartment buildings, many painted a delightful butter yellow and ocher with white trim, or mint green and white, or gentle peach, their dwellers riding soft blue and cream buses and trams to work and play.

Munich was prosperous, aswarm with BMWs, the Bavarian Motor Works' pistonlike, stainless steel headquarters

Marienplatz, Munich, 1972

Munich organizing committee president Willi Daume listens attentively at a May 1970 staff meeting. Daume was an IOC member from 1956 to 1991 and stood unsuccessfully for committee president in 1980. He died in 1996.

towers a monument to 20th-century industry. Munich was marvelous food and drink—seven breweries in the city proper (and more than a thousand others elsewhere in Bavaria); a delicatessen that rose up and up for seven astounding stories; a huge outdoor *Viktualienmarkt* of fountains, beer gardens, and red-awninged stalls overflowing with fruits and vegetables and hams and cheeses—enough, crooned one gastronome, "to make you go weak in the knees."

Munich was a students' town, filled with shaggy kids in black turtlenecks and sandals; an arty town, home to Europe's biggest movie studio complex; a town of Parisian chic, but somehow still homespun and Bavarian, some of the women dressing in traditional dirndls and puff-sleeved blouses. Describing the crowds of young and old hoisting two-liter beer mugs of an evening at the Pagoda in the vast riverside park called the Englischem Garten, an observer remarked that she had "never seen an argument or even anyone in a bad mood."

What better place to assuage the sour memories of Berlin 1936, where Hitler made a propaganda mockery of the Games of the XI Olympiad. Indeed, to Willi Daume, the industrialist who led the Munich Olympic Organizing Committee, the award of the 1972 Games to his

city represented nothing less than "the world gift of renewed trust in Germany."

The plans Daume and his colleagues outlined for the second German Olympics must have gladdened the heart of old Avery Brundage, soon to retire after 20 years at the helm of the International Olympic Committee. The organizers vowed to resist the gigantism, commercialism, and nationalism that Brundage found so odious. These Games were to be a commemoration of pure sport, smaller in scale and less ferociously expensive than the festivals of recent years—"an intimate affair," said Daume, "free of both false pathos and the fanatical pursuit of medals." They would be *"Die heiteren Spiele,"* the merry, carefree, happy, smiling Games—the Games of Joy—and Daume soon settled on a color scheme emblematic of that goal. Gone were all traces of Nazi brown, black, and red. "Red is the color of dictatorship and of totalitarianism, which we all abhor," he said. "We are using the colors of a May morning in Bavaria. Friendly colors: grass green, sky blue, cloudlike silver, and touches of flowery orange."

In the end, color would be virtually all that survived of Daume's initial plan. The momentum of the Olympics had grown too powerful to check. Too many important voices called for Germany to display its wealth and energy for these Games to be anything save another colossal spectacle. Munich 1972 would become the biggest pageant of sport ever held, with more athletes (7,123) from more nations (122) participating in more events (195)—and with more journalists (7,557) serving a larger audience (a billion people worldwide)—than the founders of the modern Olympics could possibly have imagined when they staged the first of the Games 76 years before. The astronomical cost, moreover, would have been incomprehensible to those Olympic fathers, as would the depth and breadth of dispute over professionalism, prejudice, and politics.

For example, the United States, which would

not have a particularly successful Olympics in anything except swimming, would complain with some justice of a concerted effort by Third World and Communist bloc officials to "get America." Munich also would see the sudden maturation of a Communist sports machine that was awesome in its efficiency, winning for the Soviet Union and its Eastern bloc satellites almost half of all medals, including 94 golds. The competition would nevertheless be so intense, the athletes from both sides of the Iron Curtain so extraordinary, that Olympic and world records would tumble by the scores. And for 10 magnificent days—from August 26 to the early morning hours of September 5—it seemed as though Munich would host not only the biggest of all Olympics, but also the very best.

So it seemed, at least, before the horror began,

the ultimate expression of how grotesquely politicized the Olympics had become. When it was over, lovely Munich would be a symbol of terror, and Olympism would be defiled and bloodstained forever. How bizarre, one grieving German would murmur, "to plan for light and earn darkness."

It was hard to believe, considering how much of the good life Munich had to offer, that the host city of the 1972 Games was practically without major sports facilities. With the Alps so close, Bavaria took naturally to winter sports, and for its "Olympic Summer," the Munich organizing committee in 1966 started more or less from scratch. When his city first acquired the Games, Willi Daume announced that Germany's hope for the future—hope that

WALDI

Organizers have always had unique ideas for promoting and financing the Games; traditionally, posters, stamps, and logos have been both symbols and moneymakers. But the Munich Games yielded something new: a mascot. The organizing committee set out to develop a culturally significant symbol that would also help publicize the Games and bring in licensing revenue. The result was Waldi.

Waldi was a dachshund modeled after Cherie von Birkenhof, a long-haired specimen of the breed with a pedigree that included a German champion and a canine Mr. World. Cherie was distinguished, but nowhere near as colorful as his alter ego: Waldi had a light blue head and tail, and his body shimmered with the rainbow stripes that mirrored the Games' color scheme. Designers counted Waldi's adorability factor as high,

especially with children, and licensed his image to souvenir makers. During the Games the striped dachshund appeared as a stuffed or wooden toy, on lighters, bottle openers, and pins. He was everywhere, and as forecast, visitors loved him.

Waldi's triumph invited imitation: Every Olympics since Munich has featured some sort of mascot. Most have taken the form of animals with national significance: a bear for Moscow 1980, an eagle for Los Angeles 1984, a beaver for Montreal 1976. But some have been more fanciful. Albertville 1992 generated Magique, an imp, and Atlanta 1996 concocted a computer-generated creature called Izzy. With varying degrees of success the mascots, real or fantastical, have delivered, adding color and revenue to the Games.

WHERE THE GAMES WERE PLAYED

Olympic Park Cycling Stadium

Olympic Stadium

Olympic Park Swimming Hall

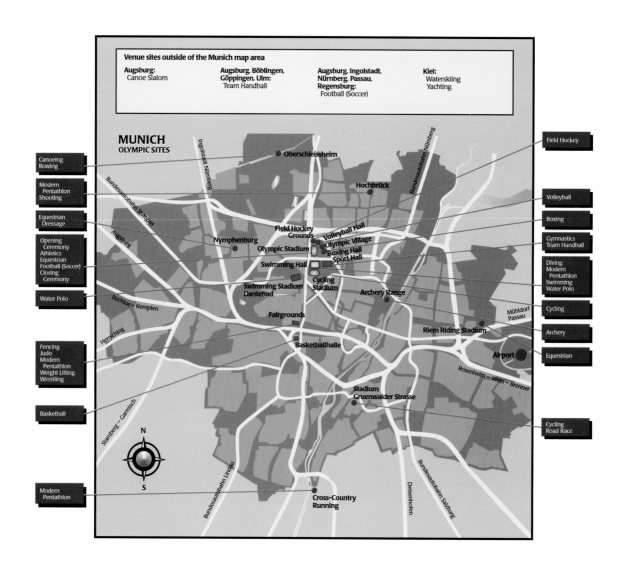

Venue sites outside of the Munich map area

Augsburg:
Canoe Slalom

Augsburg, Böblingen, Göppingen, Ulm:
Team Handball

Augsburg, Ingolstadt, Nürnberg, Passau, Regensburg:
Football (Soccer)

Kiel:
Waterskiing
Yachting

MUNICH OLYMPIC SITES

Canoeing
Rowing

Modern Pentathlon Shooting

Equestrian Dressage

Opening Ceremony
Athletics
Equestrian
Football (Soccer)
Closing Ceremony

Water Polo

Fencing
Judo
Modern Pentathlon
Weight Lifting
Wrestling

Basketball

Modern Pentathlon

Oberschleissheim

Hochbrück

Field Hockey Grounds

Nymphenburg

Olympic Stadium

Swimming Hall

Swimming Stadium Dantebad

Fairgrounds

Basketballhalle

Volleyball Hall

Olympic Village

Boxing Hall
Sport Hall

Cycling Stadium

Archery Range

Riem Riding Stadium

Stadium Gruenwalder Strasse

Cross-Country Running

Field Hockey

Volleyball

Boxing

Gymnastics Team Handball

Diving
Modern Pentathlon
Swimming
Water Polo

Cycling

Archery

Equestrian

Cycling Road Race

Airport

Mühldorf Passau

Ingolstadt Nürnberg

Bundesautobahn Nürnberg

Bundesautobahn Stuttgart

Augsburg

Buchloe – Kempten

Herrsching

Starnberg – Garmisch

Bundesautobahn Lindau

Rosenheim – Wein – Brenner

Deisenhofen

Bundesautobahn Salzburg

N
S

would find expression in the great Olympic celebration of youth—would rest on the ruins of the past. Circumstances made that literally true.

About two and a half miles northwest of the city center lay a 740-acre tract known as the Oberwiesenfeld. In times past, it had served Munich as an airport and as a drill field for soldiers of the Third Reich. More recently, part of it was a hill created by the dumping of rubble from the Allied air raids of World War II. A 950-foot TV tower and restaurant rose nearby, but the Oberwiesenfeld itself was unused and lifeless, except for hordes of rats and perhaps a few hoboes. This was the spot that Daume and chief architect Günter Behnisch would transform into the setting for what they liked to call "an Olympic Games in the Green."

As work progressed, there were constant contrasts between what was to be Munich 1972 and what had been Berlin 1936. The venues of Hitler's Reichssportfeld had been solemn and monumental, symbols of order, authority, Nazism. But the buildings of Behnisch and his colleagues aspired to airy lightheartedness, to accessibility, even to gaiety. Everybody spoke of the "human dimension." The Olympic Stadium, site of track and field, had room for 80,000 people, yet was designed so that the maximum distance between spectator and competitor was only 212 yards; everyone would have a good view. The nearby sports arena, where gymnasts and handball players would perform for 12,000 fans, was enclosed by glass walls for a sense of openness, as was the 9,182-seat swimming hall, with its five state-of-the-art pools, the edifice set partway into the ground so as not to appear overly massive.

Swooping overhead and connecting the three venues was the structure that would forever stand as the architectural symbol of Munich 1972: an immense, 800,000-square-foot roof of suspended acrylic panels, undulating across the landscape like some fantastic free-form circus tent. The

RETURN TO TRADITION

The Olympic torch relay was a German invention, inaugurated for the 1936 Berlin Games. With the Games back in Germany, Munich's organizers decided to honor that auspicious debut by imitating it. As with Berlin, the Munich relay traveled a completely overland route. It started on July 28 at Olympia and traveled through Greece, Bulgaria, Hungary, Yugoslavia, Austria, and West Germany. The only deviation from the 1936 path was a side trip through Turkey and Romania and the omission of Czechoslovakia, a country that declined to take part. There were ceremonies at border crossings and at larger cities along the way, just as there had been en route to Berlin 36 years earlier.

After nearly 6,000 runners had carried it 3,437 miles, the flame arrived in Munich on August 25 and rested at a city square called the Maximilianeum until the opening ceremony the next day. The streamlined aluminum torch (right), created by Germany's famous Krupp steel firm, entered the stadium on August 26 in the hands of Günther Zahn (above), Germany's junior champion 1,500-meter runner. Zahn, like his 1936 counterpart, Fritz Schilgen, won the honor as final torchbearer because of his graceful running style.

THE GAMES AT A GLANCE

	Aug 26	Aug 27	Aug 28	Aug 29	Aug 30	Aug 31	Sep 1	Sep 2	Sep 3	Sep 4	Sep 5	Sep 6	Sep 7	Sep 8	Sep 9	Sep 10	Sep 11
Opening Ceremony	■																
Archery												■	■	■	■		
Athletics (Track & Field)							■	■	■	■	■		■	■	■	■	
Basketball		■	■	■			■	■	■		■	■	■	■	■		
Boxing		■	■	■	■	■	■	■	■	■	■	■	■	■	■		■
Canoeing			■		■							■	■	■	■		
Cycling				■									■				
Diving	■	■					■	■	■								
Equestrian		■	■	■			■		■		■		■		■		
Fencing							■	■	■	■	■	■	■	■			
Field Hockey		■	■	■									■	■	■	■	
Football (Soccer)		■	■	■	■	■				■		■	■		■		
Gymnastics		■	■	■	■	■	■										
Team Handball							■		■		■	■	■	■	■	■	
Judo							■	■	■	■	■				■		
Modern Pentathlon		■	■	■													
Rowing		■			■	■	■										
Shooting		■	■	■	■	■	■										
Swimming		■	■	■	■	■	■	■									
Volleyball		■	■	■	■	■						■	■	■	■		
Water Polo		■	■	■	■	■	■	■									
Weight Lifting		■	■	■	■	■	■	■	■								
Wrestling		■	■	■	■							■	■	■	■	■	
Yachting			■	■	■	■						■	■	■	■		
Closing Ceremony																	■
Demonstration Sports																	
Badminton											■						
Waterskiing								■	■								

thing was a marvel of engineering as well as design: The translucent panels, each one nine feet square, were embedded in a series of cable nets carried aloft by immense steel masts, the biggest one measuring nine feet thick in places and rising 260 feet high. Architects compared it favorably with the visionary white shells of Australia's new Sydney Opera House half a world away. The only sour note was price: The 18.6 acre roof would end up costing more than $120 million.

But Daume's organizing committee wasn't inclined to button its billfold in panic. Armies of landscapers were hired to turn the littered Oberwiesenfeld into a verdant Olympic Park, its centerpiece a lake where a mighty fountain sent clouds of water 100 feet skyward. The park was intended as a place for people to enjoy as they pleased—to loll on the grass, play with their children, picnic and barbecue, go swimming and boating, or simply sit and chat on comfortable semicircular benches. Down its center ran a *Spielstrasse*, a "play street," with refreshment booths, pantomimists, painters, puppet shows, oompah bands, and folk dancers.

In the Olympic Park was a stadium for cycling. Within walking distance or a short bus ride were an arena for volleyball, one for boxing and judo, and an outdoor area for field hockey, along with an exhibition area for fencing, wrestling, and weight lifting. There was also a hall for basketball, although it accommodated only about 3,000 spectators. An appropriate site for archery,

Members of London's Dogg's Troupe perform an improvisational play at Olympic Park's Spielstrasse. The street-level stage was intended to facilitate interaction between performers and spectators.

returning to the Games after almost 50 years, was laid out in the city proper, amid the emerald tranquillity of the Englischem Garten. Rowing and canoeing, however, required heroic measures: the excavation of 81 million cubic feet of earth five miles from town to create a spring-fed, 2.23-kilometer course with grandstands for 41,000 spectators. Always thoughtful, everlastingly human, the organizers saw to it that each venue was equipped with small "cosmetic cabins" near the victors' podium so that "lady athletes"—or gentlemen, for that matter—could appear "as fresh as a daisy for the medal ceremony."

In Augsburg, west of Munich, an artificial canal was created for canoe slaloms, white-water races for kayaks. And as at the 1936 Games, yachting was slated for a sailing center near the north German city of Kiel.

Year after year, millions of marks poured forth to modernize and expand Munich's transportation system, to build a press city, a radio-TV center, and a vast Olympic Village—later to become condominiums—with every conceivable amenity for the 12,000 athletes and their coaches and trainers. The organizers recruited armies of young people and clothed them in pastel orange and blue coveralls—no jackboots or brown shirts for these Olympics—to assist participants and visitors who inevitably got lost despite the groves of multihued signs pointing the way to the various sports sites.

All told, perhaps 200,000 people wound up attending the Games themselves, and those who shared in Munich's Olympic Summer at one time or another numbered about two million, three-quarters of a million of them non-Germans. Athletics aside, the guests found a city of good New Germans yearning to remind the world of the role the good Old Germans had played in pre-Hitler European society. The months leading up to the Games saw continuous celebrations of theater and ballet, symphony and opera. Art lovers discovered major

displays of German painting and sculpture amid the other treasures housed in Munich's renowned museums. As for the Olympic cause, the Deutsches Museum mounted an exhibit entitled *One Hundred Years of German Excavation in Olympia*, for essentially all archeological work at the site of the ancient Greek Games had been financed by Germany.

A fountain erupts from the middle of a man-made lake near the center of Munich's Olympic Park. The stadiums in the park were connected to areas where visitors could relax, picnic, or simply enjoy a walk in the sun.

Surging in the 200-meter butterfly, Mark Spitz *(leading)* begins to show his superiority. Although he had set a record, Spitz wasn't that impressed with his time in the race. "If it had been do or die," he told a reporter, "I could have broken 2 minutes."

No one ever calculated the cost of it all. The construction and administration of Olympic facilities alone consumed five million worker hours and 1.9 billion deutsche marks, equivalent to $640 million, almost three times the cost of the Mexico City Games four years earlier. Half of the sum was underwritten by the West German government, with Munich and the state of Bavaria splitting the other half. Willi Daume counted it a worthwhile investment. When the receipts were totted up from TV rights, from the 4,435,583 admissions—filling 89.6 percent of all seats—from lotteries, concessions, and the like, the sponsors recouped nearly two-thirds of their outlay. The remaining $200 million or so bought Munich, Bavaria, and Germany a sports complex and leisure center with few equals in the world. Indeed, Daume would later report that within five years after the Games, no fewer than 30 million people had visited the Olympic site, either as tourists, spectators, or athletes. By any reckoning, that represented success.

Schwimmhalle Olympic Park, 5:30 p.m., August 28, the second day of competition: The final of the 200-meter butterfly was coming up, and eight young men stood at the head of the 50-meter racing pool. There were two West Germans, an East German, a

Hungarian, an Ecuadorian, and three Americans. All eyes in the overflow crowd of 9,000—some of whom had paid scalpers $50 a seat—were on the darkly handsome, mustachioed American fidgeting nervously on the starting block in lane 4. He was Mark Spitz, 22, the California superswimmer who had been setting world records in butterfly and freestyle sprints since he was 16. Four of his individual world marks still stood, rating Spitz, on paper at least, as the greatest swimmer who ever lived. But people wondered about his grace under this sort of pressure. Four years earlier, as a bumptious teenager at Mexico City, Spitz had let everybody know that he figured himself for a potful of gold. He was wrong: Among other embarrassments was a last-place finish in this very event, the 200-meter butterfly, regarded as the strongest of his specialties. If Mexico City 1968 had produced a goat, Mark Spitz was it.

Spitz had since matured. He stood an inch taller and 15 pounds heavier now at 6 feet and 170 pounds. He was cooler—and at least a little wiser. "I'm prepared," was all he would say to hounding newsmen. "I'm making no predictions. I'll just swim my best."

At the gun, Spitz hit the water in a perfect start and spurted into the lead, limber legs whipping up and down in the prescribed dolphin kick, broad shoulders powering his arms up and around in the paddle-wheel stroke acknowledged to be the toughest and most spectacular in swimming. No one even came close to him. After four stunning laps, Spitz slapped the electronic touchboard more than 2 seconds ahead of teammate Gary Hall. Time: 2:00.70, almost a second better than his own world record.

A huge grin splitting his face, Spitz leaped from the pool and clasped his hands over his head in triumph as a thunder of applause shook the Schwimmhalle. He rested for perhaps 40 minutes. Then more cheers erupted when Spitz, swimming freestyle now, anchored the U.S. 4 x 100-meter relay team to a world-record victory. This clocking—3:26.42—eclipsed by almost 2.5 seconds the old mark, also held by the United States. The second-place Soviets were 23 feet behind.

Two up, two golds. It was not lost on German swim fans that the word *Spitze* means "peak" in their language. At Munich that afternoon, Mark Andrew Spitz began the climb that would bring him to a Mt. Olympus never before scaled by any athlete in the 76-year history of the modern Games.

It had already been a very long journey. To all intents and purposes, Spitz's childhood ended at age eight and a half, when his father enrolled him in the swimming program at a Sacramento YMCA. Arnold Spitz knew what he was doing. The family had just returned from six years in Hawaii, where Mark had shown exceptional talent in the water. The lad himself preferred basketball, but "father"—never "dad"—was an aggressive, ambitious scrap metal executive, the sort who boasted, "In business I'm known as a forceful individual." A frustrated competition swimmer himself, the elder Spitz decided what his son's sport would be. And in a few months, with just a little coaching, Mark was champion of the Y, winning not only his age group but also shellacking much older boys. Obviously, he needed to move up and out of the Y. But there was a problem.

The Spitzes were Jewish, and in the United States of the 1950s and 1960s, elite competitive swimming was the nearly exclusive preserve of white Anglo-Saxon Protestants. WASP kids got their start at country clubs, in tony private prep schools and a few upper-echelon public schools—places where usually it was not good enough just to be white: A person had to be a certain kind of white—non-Jewish white.

But Arnold Spitz was lucky. He found his solution in Sherman Chavoor, owner, manager, and

Proud parents Arnold and Lenore Spitz congratulate son Mark. A German official was so taken by Mark's feats at Munich that he had the Spitzes flown in from nearby Garmisch by chartered helicopter to ensure that they wouldn't miss the last of their son's record-setting races.

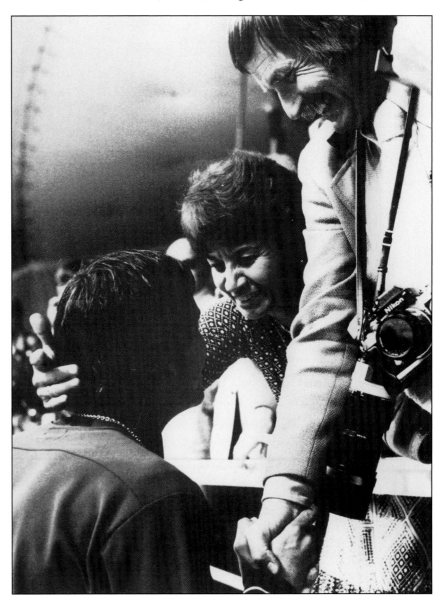

Stopwatch in hand, Sherman Chavoor monitors the progress of his charges during a workout at the Munich pool. Chavoor had trained Mark Spitz as a teenager but was in Munich as the U.S. women's swimming coach. In a career that lasted 32 years, Chavoor trained swimmers who set 83 world records and won 16 gold medals.

demigod coach of suburban Sacramento's Arden Hills Swim Club. Chavoor numbered Amateur Athletic Union and Olympic champions among "my boys and girls" and would reel off their world and American records by the scores. He also catered to Jews; 35 Jewish families swam and played tennis alongside the 600 or so Christians who enjoyed membership at Arden Hills.

Chavoor saw something remarkable in 10-year-old Mark. The boy was not especially big for his age, but he had a body purpose-built for swimming: wiry, with long arms ending in huge, scooplike hands; large feet on legs so supple that they could even bend slightly forward at the knee—which meant that he could kick 6 to 12 inches deeper than other boys. All this was married to flawless coordination. In the pool, Spitz glided effortlessly, never battling the water, every movement focused on forward progress.

He had the right attitude, too. Father had seen to that from the start. "Who plays to lose?" the older Spitz once told a newsman. "I'm not out to lose. I never said to him, 'You're second. That's great.'" Arnold Spitz and his boy had a dialogue they repeated over and over:

"Mark, how many lanes in a pool?"

"Six, father."

"And how many lanes win?"

"One, only one."

The father's ambition blazed from the eyes of the son. Sherm Chavoor put Mark in with a couple of his teenage stars, big, strong, older boys who at first beat Spitz easily. But Mark never gave up. "You'd think they were going for the Olympic gold medal even then—in the early-morning mists with nobody watching," Chavoor recalled. "In a matter of weeks, he was swimming nearly head to head with the other two."

In Chavoor's world, the world of real competitive swimming, pain was the currency of success. Along with most top coaches, he believed that conditioning was 90 percent of the game, and he worked his swimmers without mercy six days a week, 11 months a year. Youngsters pumped iron to develop arm, stomach, and back muscles, did squats for their legs—and swam sometimes to the point of unconsciousness. Even the eight-year-olds did 3,000 to 5,000 meters a day, while the older swimmers started with 8,000 meters and worked up to almost double that. Chavoor put them on kickboards to churn 1,000 meters without using their arms, then immobilized their legs with thick rubber bands while they concentrated on strokes.

Chavoor practiced his own special brand of interval training. He might order a series of ten 100-meter sprints, giving his swimmers about 10 minutes' rest between sprints. Then he successively cut the rest interval to a minute, to 45 seconds, 30 seconds, and finally 10 seconds. Trainers at first worried about inflicting physical damage with such a brutal regimen. But it built up the kind of endurance that kept the muscles functioning even after the athlete's exhausted lungs could no longer supply adequate oxygen. And that, insisted Chavoor, "will give him the edge over any other swimmer who *hasn't* punished himself with interval training."

Mark Spitz didn't talk much about the rigors of this conditioning, but another of Chavoor's stars did. Said Debbie Meyer, who won three

WHITE-WATER WILES

The sport of canoeing joined the Olympic Games at Berlin 1936, but its most exciting event, white-water slalom, didn't appear on the program until Munich. In 1972 there were four slalom races: kayak singles for both men and women, and for men only, Canadian singles and pairs.

The delay in including slalom canoeing as an Olympic event stemmed from the logistical problem of providing a suitable river. Munich didn't have one, but organizers weren't fazed: They built one. The world's first artificial rapids took form near the flat-water canoe course at Augsburg, a city 40 miles west of Munich. The man-made waterway was a 2,165-foot (660-meter) sluice of frothing water replete with dangerous boulders, challenging whirlpools, and 30 gates for paddlers to navigate. The course, whose water flow could be varied to accommodate changing conditions, was a technological marvel.

The host country hoped the new canal would carry its paddlers to gold medals, but the East Germans had other ideas, reading in the rushing waters a great chance to show up their capitalist neighbors. Socialist officials were so intent on victory that they had a replica of the course built in Leipzig. Months of practice there before the Games yielded all four gold medals to East Germany. The West Germans, who had never known about the Leipzig course, finished second in the Canadian pairs and singles and were left wondering what had gone wrong.

East Germany's Siegbert Horn navigates a gate during the kayak slalom finals. After its debut at Munich, white-water canoeing was dropped from the Olympic program until Barcelona 1992.

indi-vidual golds at Mexico City: "It starts in the legs. First they feel numb and itch from the lack of oxygen. Then the numbness turns into a searing ache. It spreads from the legs into the midsection and then into the lungs. Every breath becomes torture. Then the pain moves into the arms and you almost wish they'd drop off." Added Don Schollander, who captured four golds at Tokyo 1964: "It is right there, at the pain barrier, that the great competitors separate from the rest."

Some measure of Spitz's competitiveness could be seen in the 17 national age-group records he set before he reached 11. But father told him: "I don't care about winning age groups, I care for world records."

Those started to fall in 1967. By then the family was living in California's Bay Area, and Mark had been training for three years under George Haines, guru of the celebrated Santa Clara Swim Club. Every bit as tough and dedicated as Chavoor, Haines had turned Santa Clara's team into the best in the country, perhaps the best in the world; his team won every Amateur Athletic Union national championship from 1963 to 1968. And here came Spitz, able to qualify for AAU meets at 14, piling up the points for Santa Clara as a freestyle and butterfly sprinter. He could swim the distances, too. In 1966 he came within 0.40 of a second of breaking the world 1,500-yard freestyle record, and a year later he set his first world mark with a 4:10.60 clocking in the 400-meter freestyle. That brought everything together; the critical mass was there. Before 1967 ended, Mark Spitz had nuked another four world marks and had been named World Swimmer of the Year by *Swimming World* magazine.

None of this brought huzzahs from his Santa Clara teammates. Although everybody acknowledged the teenager's brilliance, Spitz had a way of pushing his peers' faces in it, always talking about himself and how great he was, always hotdogging it in practice and trying to show them up. Don Schollander, who swam for Yale during the school year and for Santa Clara in the summer, found Spitz distinctly obnoxious. "He was a cocky kid, a showboat," said the Olympic hero. "We ignored him. Just dismissed him as a jerk." Arnold Spitz charged that his son, far from being dismissed, was being persecuted. "So I told Mark to shove it down their throats with times," said the elder Spitz. "Let them talk, but beat the hell out of them in the pool." How much Spitz's unpopularity might have owed to anti-Semitism—or how much his youthful arrogance was a defense against shyness, fear, and self-doubt—is anybody's guess. The fact remains that he was a braggart and a loner, and if he needed friends, he didn't have them.

So at Mexico City in October 1968, 18-year-old Mark Spitz was under pressure—to please his father, to throw his teammates' taunts back in their faces, to prove that he was as good as he said he was, as good as everybody said he was. Santa Clara's George Haines had been named coach of the U.S. men's swim team, and he confidently predicted six golds for his superstar: the 100- and 200-meter butterflies, the 100-meter freestyle, and three relays. It was a reasonable assessment; by then Spitz had set eight world records, three of which still stood. But the boast, splashed all over the newspapers, was sometimes made to sound as if Spitz himself were mouthing off again. Relations with his teammates worsened to the point where some of them started calling him "Jew-boy" in public.

Diploma

Jeux
de la XXe Olympiade
Munich
du 26 août
au 10 septembre
1972

Games
of the XXth Olympiad
Munich
from 26th August
to 10th September
1972

Spiele
der XX. Olympiade
München
vom 26. August
bis 10. September
1972

Officiel
Official
Offizieller

Dr. Giorgio de Stefani

Der Präsident
des
Organisationskomitees
für die Spiele
der XX. Olympiade
München 1972

Der Generalsekretär
des
Organisationskomitees
für die Spiele
der XX. Olympiade
München 1972

The front of the Munich winners' medals used the time-honored image of the goddess Victory triumphantly holding an olive wreath. Gerhard Marcks, a former Bauhaus master, designed the back, using the mythological twins Castor and Pollux as symbols of sport and friendship. The top six finishers in every event received diplomas with rainbow stripes.

Spitz's spirits seemed to collapse under the weight of it all. He complained of a cold, had a run-in with the team manager, grew silent and withdrawn. He struggled to a third-place finish in the 100-meter freestyle, managed a second in the 100-meter butterfly (in which he held the world record), then hit his nadir in the 200-meter butterfly—eighth and dead last, with a time that was almost 8 seconds off his world record. Only by swimming legs on the victorious U.S. 4 x 100-meter and 4 x 200-meter relay teams did he salvage anything from his first Olympic Games. "I had the worst meet of my life," was all he could say, and the agony was still there years later. "I just can't forget losing," he said. "I never will."

Meanwhile, the Spitz family's association with George Haines was ending in acrimony. Arnold Spitz had long resented any suggestion that Mark's accomplishments were due to his coach. "If George Haines is naive or foolish enough to think that he created Mark, he's crazy," Spitz *père* told a *Sports Illustrated* reporter. "This is what *I* created. He's a gorgeous human being, he's a beautiful person." Arnold Spitz stopped and thought a moment. "You think I created a monster?" he asked, and then repeated, "He's beautiful, he's exceptional."

In the summer of 1969, Mark refused to swim for Santa Clara in the AAU national championships, partly because he had just returned from the Maccabean Games in Israel, but largely because of a philosophical difference with his coach. "George was mainly interested in getting points for the team," he said. "So was I. But I was interested in Mark Spitz, too. I had to be.

The whole idea is to win, not take second." Without him, Santa Clara failed for the first time in six years to win the national championship. The Spitzes got a letter from George Haines summarily severing the relationship.

Spitz went back to Sherm Chavoor, who had already introduced him to one of the premier college coaches in the country. He was James E. "Doc" Counsilman of Indiana University, perennial Big Ten and National Collegiate Athletic Association swimming power. Though Spitz's grades were on the low side of mediocre, Counsilman got him a full four-year scholarship at Indiana, plus a guarantee of dental school afterward. Those gifts were small, though, compared with the coach's ultimate coup: He helped Mark Spitz mature socially. Counsilman asked his swimmers to give Spitz a break, and because they revered their coach,

19

they did. "Frankly, Doc really hasn't helped me that much with my strokes," Spitz told *Sports Illustrated* in 1970. That was fair enough; by then his style needed little improvement. But Spitz continued: "What Doc has done for me is to make me more friendly. I think I've really grown up in that way."

At Indiana, Spitz led the Hoosiers to four NCAA championships in a row. He also got along well enough to be elected team cocaptain his final year. The summers of his college years were spent at Arden Hills, following Chavoor's arduous path to fitness. By the end of August 1971, Spitz was in his best shape ever. At the AAU championships in Houston, he put on what Chavoor acclaimed as "the greatest one-man show in the history of American swimming." Spitz won the 100- and 200-meter freestyles and the 100- and 200-meter butterflies. He set two more world records, trounced the class of the country, and was scarcely breathing hard. Never before had anyone taken four individual golds in the AAU outdoor national championships. But the success seemed bane as well as tonic: Spitz wandered off the road to good guyhood. "This pool here in Houston is one of the worst I've ever competed in," he carped to the press after his victories. The next morning, Houstonians agreed that for all his prowess, he was still a twerp.

Spitz's churlishness was all too characteristic, even if he was only saying publicly what other swimmers griped about in private. Nothing kills speed more than a big backwash from the gutters of a pool, and as the Olympics approached, the athletes of water sport wondered what Munich would be like. They found perfection. As usual, the organizers had thought of everything. The Schwimmhalle's 50-meter racing pool was equipped with revolutionary gutters that carried away the wash, while an injection system replaced lost volume; the depth was a uniform seven feet, exactly right to buffer vertical waves bouncing off the bottom; the plastic lane floats

were designed with ripple-smothering perforations all around; and softening agents removed limestone salts from the water, making it more slippery. Spitz spoke for all when he favored reporters with a rare laudatory comment: "This is the finest pool I've ever competed in. It's *made* for world records." He would prove the point.

The final of the 200-meter freestyle was slated for 5:30 p.m. on August 29, the day after Spitz's double victory in the 200-meter butterfly and the 4 x 100 freestyle relay. He hadn't swum the 200-meter freestyle at Mexico City, but now he held the world record for the event, and only two men were credited with any chance to beat him. One was Australia's Mike Wenden, back to defend his 200-meter title from the Mexico City Games. The other was America's Steve Genter. Wenden had lost his edge and wouldn't have much luck. Ordinarily, Genter would have been a long shot. Although he had swum well in the Olympic trials, he had no major championships to his credit. What he did have was strong motivation: He had a score to settle with Mark Spitz.

A week earlier, Genter had undergone minor surgery to reinflate a collapsed lung, and while German doctors recommended that he not compete, U.S. sports surgeons felt that he would heal in time to swim. At any rate, Spitz reportedly commented: "This may sound terrible, but now I don't have to worry about *him*." It did sound terrible, and it sounded worse later when Spitz suggested to Genter that he ought to withdraw before he hurt himself again.

Competitors understood that big-time swimming meant big-time psych. Genter, for one, shaved his head and body to be seal-sleek in the water and worked up an emotional frenzy with a jiggling, mumbo jumbo dance on the starting block. Spitz took the opposite, who-needs-that-junk tack of growing a moustache and letting his hair get long. All's fair among the studs of swimming. However, Genter thought Spitz had overstepped the bounds with his display of phony

A long, powerful freestyle stroke and a booming kick helped make Mark Spitz unbeatable at Munich. But coaches observing him often found his competitiveness even more impressive than his form.

concern. "He was trying to psych me out," said Genter. "But I'm going to race. I think I can beat him."

Steve Genter gave it the shot of his life. He felt the stitches tugging in his chest as soon as he hit the water, but he kept driving and had a slight lead on Spitz as they flipped off the third turn. Then came Spitz, sweeping past just as Genter felt his own lungs tighten in the last half-dozen strokes. Spitz's victory margin of 0.95 of a second represented about 3 feet over the courageous Genter, who at least had the satisfaction of pushing his rival to a 1:52.78 world record.

That made it three races, three records for the superstar—and the marvel of Mark Spitz in that marvelous pool would continue. Two days later, Spitz blasted through the 100-meter butterfly to win by 6 feet in 54.27. World record No. 4. An hour later, he anchored the U.S. 4 x 200-meter freestyle relay team to a 30-foot victory over the West Germans. Time: 7:35.78. World record

No. 5, an amazing 7.52 seconds better than the old standard, to which Spitz had also contributed.

Only two events remained for the California prodigy: the 100-meter freestyle and the 4 x 100 medley relay. Now the demons of doubt started to gnaw away at Spitz's resolve. After Mexico City, he had vowed never to lose again—never even to *risk* losing again, if he could help it. He had five for five at Munich. He had surpassed the mighty Don Schollander's four golds at Tokyo, had eclipsed every swimmer in history. Why not ease off? Why expose himself to embarrassment? Spitz complained of a sore back and told Coach Chavoor that he would swim in the medley but might drop out of the 100-meter freestyle. "I've done what I wanted to do," he said. "I'd rather win six out of six, or even four out of four, than six out of seven. It's reached a point where my self-esteem comes into it. I just don't want to lose."

Chavoor refused to let him quit. "I'll break his

Teammates parade Mark Spitz through the swimming hall after his record-smashing performance at Munich. East Germany's Kristen Otto is the only Olympic swimmer to come close to Spitz's amassing of seven gold medals at one Games. She would win six at Seoul 1988. Unlike Spitz, however, Otto would not set world records in each event.

him. Desperately, Spitz surged and slammed the touchplate half a stroke ahead.

The scoreboard flashed 51.22 as the crowd shrieked. Spitz had his sixth gold and sixth world record. The next day, the U.S. 4 x 100 medley relay team, with Spitz swimming a fine butterfly leg, made it seven and seven. He had done it. Mark Spitz, the hotdogging brat, the reviled "Jew-boy," the Mexico City also-ran, the slowly maturing loner, the greatest swimmer ever, had achieved his peak and entered the Olympic pantheon. No athlete had ever captured seven gold medals in a single Games before, much less set seven world records. Most likely, no one else ever would. Henceforth, people would bracket the name Mark Spitz with those of Jim Thorpe, Paavo Nurmi, Jesse Owens. Spitz started to say something about how the world had been "ready to write me off," how he felt vindicated. Then he stopped, fell silent for a moment, and almost whispered, "I am in a bit of a trance."

To one degree or another, the same trance might well have affected quite a few other swimmers at Munich. Mark Spitz was in a class by himself, certainly. Yet at these Games, 13 other swimmers broke 16 individual world records and matched three more, while individual Olympic standards were rewritten an astonishing 70 times. At the end, the fans were hoarse from screaming, officials scratching their heads with wonder, athletes in a daze of delight. That admirable pool had a lot to do with it, in that it gave all comers a rare chance to realize the very best in themselves.

The heroine of the competition was a long-legged youngster still a few weeks shy of her 16th birthday, an Australian girl as naturally modest and charming as Mark Spitz was sometimes boastful and boorish. Shane Gould arrived in Munich after a meteoric rise that saw her demolish six world records during nine months of the previous year. Her specialty was freestyle,

damn neck," he growled to a friend, and on Sunday afternoon, September 3, Spitz stood ready for the final of the 100-meter freestyle. The man who worried him was teammate Jerry Heidenreich, a powerhouse who on a good day could match him stroke for stroke and in fact had beaten Spitz in the semifinals. At the gun, Spitz came off the block like a torpedo squirting out of its tube. By 50 meters he had a 1-meter lead. He hit the turn perfectly and maintained his edge as he charged for home. Heidenreich started inching up. Something distracted Spitz at 85 meters; he faltered, lost his rhythm. Heidenreich was with but she could swim any stroke, at any distance. Because of her versatility, admirers called her the greatest female swimmer who ever lived. Some thought she bore favorable comparison with Spitz himself. As it happened, she didn't achieve everything hoped for her at Munich, but she left with her head high, her reputation solidly intact, and a cluster of gold around her neck.

Shane's mother reported fondly, if perhaps apocryphally, that her waterbaby "cried when bath time ended; she crawled down the beach straight into the waves of Sydney Harbour; she bobbed in a rubber tyre, smiling with satisfaction, before she was a year old." Whatever. Shane's father was an airline executive, and where the family lived—Sydney, Fiji, Brisbane, Sydney again—always gave the girl all the open water she needed to become a champion swimmer. Her training didn't start in earnest, however, until 1970, when she started working with Australia's highly regarded Forbes Carlile.

Like Chavoor and other first-rate coaches, Carlile was a bear for conditioning; he had Shane swimming upwards of 10,000 meters a day. But he didn't tamper with her unorthodox style; from using flippers as a child, she had developed an extremely slow kick, only two beats per arm cycle as opposed to the six-beat flutter then in vogue. Gould's kick remained the same whether she was sprinting or going for distance. Her speed came from her arms and her size: A big girl at 5 feet 7 ½ inches and 129 pounds, she generated tremendous power. That was evident in 1971 and early 1972, when she smashed every women's freestyle record from 100 to 1,500 meters. Her 58.50 for 100 meters erased the oldest swimming record on the books, set in 1964 by Australia's legendary Dawn Fraser. Gould's 1,500 meters was more impressive still: Her 17:00.60 clocking redid the world record by 18.60 seconds and would have won her the *men's* Olympic gold in 1956, 1960, and 1964.

There was no women's 1,500-meter freestyle

on the Olympic program, so Gould entered the 200-meter medley and the four freestyles from 100 to 800 meters. Favored in all five races, she had the American women so worried that they went the psych route with T-shirts emblazoned "All That Glitters Is Not Gould." The ploy probably had no effect on Gould, but it may have given the U.S. swimmers some extra zing. The Aussie ace was upset in the 100 meters by a very determined Sandra Neilson and Shirley Babashoff—after which Gould showed her class by warmly congratulating the two Americans. And she had to settle for silver when America's

Australia's Shane Gould hangs on to a lane marker while catching her breath after a race. Gould owned two world records going into Munich and set two more at the Games. In spite of her success, she would retire in 1973 at the age of 16.

Keena Rothhammer drove to a world-record 8:53.68 in the 800 meters.

But Gould owned the medley and the 200- and 400-meter freestyles, setting world records in both. Babashoff and Rothhammer chased her so closely in the 200 that she clipped 1.65 seconds off the record, with both American women beating the mark as well. Some Australian newsmen sniffed at Gould's "failure" to win every race—an unaccountably ridiculous criticism. Her three golds and three records, and her five individual medals overall, placed Shane Gould on her own Olympic pinnacle, alongside Spitz and apart from any other woman swimmer in history.

When she was in the pool, it was hard to believe that Gould was only 15 years old. The truth was easier to credit when she stood on the winners' podium, happily waving a treasured toy kangaroo and flashing the pretty teeth that had been freed from their braces just for the Olympics. She had begged her dentist for the temporary reprieve; thinking that she might win a race or two, she wanted to look her nicest.

Even without the heroics of Spitz and Gould, the swimming program at Munich 1972 was a testament to sport's endless capacity for drama and surprise. Here was 18-year-old Beverly Whitfield, hitherto just a supernumerary on the Australian squad, suddenly touched by a greatness that took her from last to an Olympic-record victory in the

Olympische Spiele München 1972

Munich organizers solicited young artists to create posters to help promote the Games. West Germany's Paul Wunderlich, creator of this torso, was one of 28 painters from 11 countries whose works contributed to the push for an improved balance between sport and art.

200-meter breaststroke. "I can't believe it," she squealed as she leaped from the pool and into Shane Gould's arms. Then both young ladies dissolved into tears. Here was Melissa Belote—an unsung 15-year-old Virginian who liked the backstroke because it kept the pool chlorine out of her eyes—leading from start to finish in both the 100- and 200-meter backstroke events, setting an Olympic record in one and a world record in the other. Belote then helped set another world record in the 4 x 100 medley relay. She was the star of the American women's team.

So many young Americans and Australians were mounting the podium that Munich looked at times like a dual meet between the two countries. But that was an illusion. The Communist sports machine was coming on fast, led by East Germany's 22-year-old Roland Matthes, undefeated in the backstroke since 1967. At Munich, Matthes again proved himself greatly gifted, winning two more golds—and setting fresh Olympic records—at 100 and 200 meters. Superb in all strokes, he then led the G.D.R. men's relay teams to a silver and a bronze. East German women captured a bronze and four silvers—losing a gold by 0.36 of a second to the United States in a 4 x 100 freestyle relay that saw both teams clip 3 seconds from the world record. East Germany's young Fräuleins would soon astonish the world by sweeping every swimming record on the books in a breathless rush to the top of a sport long dominated by the West.

There was glory as well for Sweden, which carried off its first gold in swimming since 1928: Big, blond Gunnar Larsson defeated America's Tim McKee in both the 200- and 400-meter medleys. The 200-meter was pure delight, one of those special races where the first four finishers—McKee and two other Americans chasing hard after Larsson—broke the world record. But the 400-meter ended sourly; Larsson and McKee appeared to hit the electronic touchboard simultaneously, so close

together that both were clocked in an Olympic-record 4:31.98. Ordinarily, with times taken to the nearest 0.01 of a second, it would have been a dead heat. But then officials discovered that the superprecise electronic gadget had registered Larsson in 4:31.981, McKee in 4:31.983. Thus Larsson got the gold by 0.002 of a second. A lot of people argued that variations in lane conditions made it absurd to measure that microscopically. In time that view would prevail, but Tim McKee would never see the gold medal he might rightfully have expected to share with Larsson.

Yet McKee's disappointment was nothing compared with the anguish of another U.S. swimmer whose life's achievement was stripped away. At 16, Rick DeMont was the youngest member of the American swim team. He was given a good chance in both the 400- and 1,500-meter freestyles. He had, in fact, set a world-record 15:52.91 in the 1,500 at the Olympic trials, and many expected a close race between the kid and teammate Mike Burton, the 25-year-old defending Olympic champion.

The 400 came first. Finishing with a phenomenal drive, DeMont slapped home in an Olympic-record 4:00.26, just 0.01 of a second ahead of Australia's Brad Cooper. The following urine test for drugs was routine. The result was not. Two days later, DeMont learned that his urine contained ephedrine, widely used as a decongestant but banned for its ability to enhance lung capacity. The youngster was flabbergasted. He had taken ephedrine for asthma since he was four years old, and he had fully reported that fact on his Olympic medical form. But U.S. team doctors apparently did not spot the problem on the forms, never alerted DeMont to it, and never came up with a substitute for ephedrine, as physicians for other national teams did.

On the day of the 400-meter, DeMont had awakened wheezing at 1 a.m., had taken a Marax

SPRINGING BACK

Comebacks abounded in the springboard diving at Munich. America's Micki King *(below)* had been a hard-luck story at Mexico City four years earlier. There she had led the field at the eighth of 10 dives, but her ninth, a one-and-a-half layout, went horribly awry. She struck the board and broke her arm. In pain, the Air Force lieutenant gamely took her last dive but missed badly and wound up fourth.

The finals at Munich seemed eerily familiar. King, now 28, moved into first with two dives remaining. But this time there was no lapse of concentration. Two seamless dives helped the American hold off Sweden's Ulrika Knape, the platform champion, and earned King the gold medal.

On the men's side there was less drama, but the comeback motif nevertheless prevailed. The Soviet Union's Vladimir Vasin had competed at Tokyo and Mexico City, finishing no better than eighth. But Munich would be different. The ninth dive in the series was pivotal, as Vasin faced a challenge from Italy's Franco Cagnotto. Cagnotto faltered, while the veteran Vasin ripped the best dive of the day. At his third Games, Vasin finally triumphed.

A dejected Rick DeMont gets sympathy from his mother after learning about his disqualification from the Games for using a banned substance. Feeling unjustly punished—American doctors had neglected to warn him against using a prescription decongestant—DeMont continued to campaign for his lost gold medal, asking the IOC to reconsider as recently as 1996. It refused to reopen the case.

tablet as usual, swallowed another at 8 a.m. and a third at 2 p.m., four hours before the final—not imagining that he was doing anything illegal. But rules were rules, and DeMont was banned from the 1,500-meter final. When the ageless Mike Burton swept to victory in 15:52.58, erasing De-Mont's record, the teenager was there at poolside to congratulate Burton through his tears.

Then came a series of hearings, with doctors, officials, and coaches all pointing accusatory fingers at one another. When all was said and done, the IOC decided that banishment from the 1,500 meters hadn't been punishment enough for Rick DeMont. He would also be stripped of his gold medal in the 400-meter freestyle. Years later, DeMont was still asking himself: "Why did this happen to me?"

Including DeMont's victory—and there was no reason not to—U.S. swimmers wound up winning 18 of 29 events and harvesting another 23 silver and bronze medals. It was a fabulous performance. Yet the totals represented more than half the gold medals and almost half of all the awards earned by the entire 431-athlete U.S. contingent at Munich. In a number of other sports long dominated by Americans, Murphy's

Law, with corollary, seemed to dog the U.S. squad. Murphy, as everyone knew, was the fellow who decreed: "If something can go wrong, it will go wrong." The unknown author of the corollary suggested that "Murphy was an optimist." Americans could only mutter "amen" to that.

The most eagerly anticipated single event in track and field, the shoot-out the world wanted to see, was supposed to match the cream of the United States against the hero of the USSR in the 100-meter dash, the winner to claim the traditional title of "fastest man in the world."

At the starting line in the final, compact and muscular in his red CCCP jersey, was Valery Borzov, paradigm of Soviet sports. On his right, looking lanky in his white U.S.A. shirt, was Robert Taylor. There was a saying among track coaches: "Sprinters are born, not made." Taylor, all agreed, had been born with the talent and the lithe, leggy body suited to his craft. Borzov, on the other hand, was made—insofar as that could be said of any world-class athlete.

A Ukrainian by birth, Borzov was geared into the Soviet sports scheme as a long jumper when he showed talent in a children's sports school. By 14 he was jumping 20 feet (6 meters), but what really impressed his mentors was

A cauldron handle *(far right)* dating from the eighth century BC was probably left behind by a spectator at the ancient Games. It was common for visitors to stay for weeks at the festival, combining enjoyment of sports with worship of their gods. A figure of the sun god Apollo *(right)* was prominent in the frieze that adorned the pediment over the west entrance of the Temple of Zeus at Olympia.

EXCAVATING ANTIQUITY

The cultural program at Munich, like those before it, held a successful series of concerts, exhibitions, and theater productions. But what set it apart from other Olympic art celebrations was an exhibit that spoke directly to the origins of Olympism: *One Hundred Years of German Excavation in Olympia.*

Earthquakes and floods in the Peloponnesian peninsula of southern Greece had obliterated Olympia from maps for centuries—so long that stories about the sacred home of the ancient Games were regarded by many as mythical. But in 1766, the site was discovered by Richard Chandler, an English theologian and classics scholar. Wars and the Greek independence movement undermined efforts to develop Chandler's find until 1875, when German scholars finally convinced the Greek monarchy of the value of excavating the site.

The Germans' most active work at Olympia occurred during two phases, from 1875 to 1881 and from 1936 to 1966. The digs produced information and artifacts that account for much of what is now known about the Games of antiquity, their nature and significance, and their athletes.

The popular 1972 exhibition, held at Munich's Deutsches Museum, celebrated Germany's contributions to archeology by displaying some of the treasures of Olympia. Artifacts in the exhibit ranged from ancient sports equipment and primitive handicrafts to the sublime art of Greece's classical period. The featured piece was the reconstruction of the west pediment frieze of the Temple of Zeus, classical Olympia's most impressive structure.

Scores of laborers pause from their excavation work at Olympia for this 1875 photograph. Ruins and artifacts from the original home of the Olympics have combined with written accounts to delineate a portrait of the ancient Games.

Ideal form out of the blocks propels the Soviet Union's Valery Borzov in the 100-meter dash. Borzov had been unbeaten in the 100 since the 1969 track season. Despite his record, he earned little respect from American coaches and sprinters.

his runway acceleration. They moved him into sprint training. At 17, Borzov was in Kiev's Physical Education Institute and under the wing of bioscience professor Valentin Petrovsky. "We had to determine what we wanted to build and what it would take to mold the possible 'ideal' sprinter," recalled Petrovsky. "An entire team of scientists undertook to study all possible factors related to speed: We calculated the angle of thrust during a race, the position of the body at the start, reaction time, and many other factors."

The researchers studied slow-motion movies of the great sprinters and applied their techniques to the model. They devised charts and graphs indicating how fast their pupil should do 30 meters and 60 meters for the desired result at 100 meters; every segment was programmed. Petrovsky likened the work to that of designers producing an aircraft from a set of theories. Borzov wasn't fond of such similes. "I don't want to be a living toy in the hands of the coach," he once protested, arguing that while Petrovsky and Company provided the essentials, the refinements were his.

There was credit enough for all. Borzov had neither a rocket start nor a breathtaking final burst, but he was strong and smooth throughout—throughout the 200 meters as well as the 100, in fact.

The Soviet dash man started winning races on the international circuit as a 20-year-old in 1969. And though he never touched the world

Olympische Spiele München 1972

marks of 9.90 for 100 meters and 19.83 for 200, he had been undefeated since 1970. The string included victories against half a dozen top U.S. sprinters. Borzov had to rate as the favorite at Munich, but he had never run against the trio of Yanks he now faced. At the U.S. Olympic trials in Eugene, Oregon, both Eddie Hart and Rey Robinson had matched the world-record 9.90 in the 100, while Robert Taylor did a 10-flat that matched Borzov's best.

In Munich, all four of the front-runners breezed through the first heats, which began shortly after 11 a.m. on August 31. The Americans returned to the Olympic Village to relax and maybe nap a bit. Sprint coach Stan Wright told them that the next round, the quarterfinals, would start at 7 p.m. A little after 4 that afternoon, the trio wandered into ABC-TV headquarters before catching the bus back to the stadium. On the TV monitors, some sprinters were settling into the blocks. "What's that? A rerun of the heats this morning?" asked Robinson. "Rerun nothing," came the reply. "That's live."

Breaking into a cold sweat, Robinson realized that he was watching the start of his quarterfinal heat. Wright had got it horribly, unbelievably wrong; he had been reading a preliminary schedule that was 15 months old. The quarters were scheduled for 4:15, not 7—and here were America's brightest hopes, three-quarters of a mile away. An ABC driver raced them to the

Victor Vasarely's gift to the Munich Games poster project was a complex pattern of squares, triangles, and parallelograms. The Hungarian artist is one of the world's best-known practitioners of geometric painting.

Assured of victory, America's Gerald Tinker pumps a fist after handing the baton to 4 x 100-meter teammate Eddie Hart. But U.S. domination of the dashes was challenged at Munich: Americans won only two gold medals in 10 sprints.

track. But it was too late for Hart and Robinson; they were out of it. Taylor just managed to shrug off his warm-up suit, jump into his spikes, and take second to Borzov.

Wright was anguished, the runners furious. "He can say he's sorry," seethed Rey Robinson. "What about three years? What about torn ligaments, pulled muscles, a broken leg?" He added bitingly: "He can go on being a coach. What can I go on being?"

The rest was anticlimax. Rob Taylor met Valery Borzov in the final, and Borzov, leading for the last 70 meters, triumphed by 0.10 of a second in the unexciting time of 10.14. The Soviet Union's first sprint champion in Olympic history shrugged off the absence of Hart and Robinson. "I gave 90 percent of what I had to give," he told reporters, clearly suggesting that he would have beaten the Americans anyway.

Borzov later reduced his effort ratio to "maybe 70 percent," which drew catcalls from the U.S. press. Yet much of the world was inclined to take him at his word, especially after he won the 200 in 20-flat four days later. That triumph made Valery Borzov the first athlete to be crowned king of both glamour dashes since America's Bobby Morrow at Melbourne 1956.

For all his laurels, though, the Soviet star could not overcome Eddie Hart at anchor in the 4 x 100 relay. The determined Hart started with a 1.5-meter lead, doubled it, and blazed to a 38.19 victory that topped the world record set by another U.S. sprint quartet at Mexico City four years earlier.

The smudge of doubt about Borzov remained. Those who argued for his greatness called him a master tactician who ran just fast enough to win; they contended that he had never been pushed to a record. The champion himself liked to say, "My chief opponent was, is, and always will be the stopwatch." If so, why the unexceptional times?

Borzov disappeared from the track scene in 1973, reportedly suffering from depression, but came back a year later to reclaim his 100-meter European title. His last hurrah was a third-place bronze in the 100 at Montreal 1976, after which he got married and took a place in Kiev's sports hierarchy. Valery Borzov might have been Professor Petrovsky's "ideal sprinter," the ultimate triumph of Soviet man and method. But no one would ever be sure.

Murphy, whoever he was, must have been nodding grimly to himself as the U.S. continued to suffer misfortune. Consider the pole vault, which American athletes had won in every Olympic Games since London 1908. Bob Seagren, the reigning

Olympic champion and world-record holder at 18 feet 5 ¾ inches (5.63 meters), was strongly favored to repeat at Munich—until politics and bureaucracy conspired to make a hash of the competition. Seagren and most other top vaulters had been using a new, lightweight "Cata-pole"—but not Wolfgang Nordwig, East Germany's bronze medalist at Mexico City. Nordwig had trouble getting the hang of the new pole, had stayed with an older model, and in recent months had not bettered 17 feet 8 ½ inches (5.40 meters).

The protests began a couple of months before the Munich Games. The East Germans claimed that the Cata-poles contained illegal carbon fiber (not illegal and not true, anyway) and that the new poles had not been universally available at least a year prior to the Games. A month before Munich, the International Amateur Athletic Federation, governing body for track and field, bowed to pressure and banned the Cata-poles. The IAAF reconsidered and reversed itself on August 27, four days before the start of competition. The reversal brought more wails from the G.D.R., with the result that officials confiscated all Cata-poles on the evening of August 31, twelve hours before the qualifying round.

The ensuing competition was such a shambles that only 10 men cleared the 16 feet 8 ¾ inches (5.10 meters) required to qualify; officials filled out the field with four who had vaulted only 16 feet 4 ¾ inches. Furious and demoralized, using a type of pole he had long since discarded, Seagren battled Nordwig up to 17 feet 10 ½ inches (5.45 meters) before missing three times. That left it to Nordwig, and with the best effort of his career, he slipped over the bar at 18 feet ½ inch (5.50 meters). The vault was 5 ¼ inches short of Seagren's record, not remotely comparable, but it won the gold. "A fair competition was insured by the decision not to allow the new poles," smirked Nordwig.

Leaving the pit, Seagren fairly hurled his pole

at Holland's Adriaan Paulen, an IAAF official who had played a major role in the charade. Some East German reporters got on him about that. "The pole Mr. Paulen chose for me to jump with really wasn't my pole," retorted Seagren. "So I gave it back to him—and I didn't charge him for it, either." Back home, Seagren considered suing the IAAF, but his father talked him out of it, wisely advising that whether he won or lost the lawsuit, he would be marked for life as a sorehead. As for the controversial Cata-poles, the IAAF declared them legal three weeks after the Games were over.

The extreme arc of Bob Seagren's vaulting pole appears ready to lift him to great heights. Seagren and Sweden's Kjell Isaksson had pushed each other over the 18-foot barrier and to world records during the 1972 track season, but an equipment dispute kept them from posting lofty marks at the Games.

Yet not all was bitter for American trackmen that first week of Munich 1972. Experts had all but conceded the 800-meter run to the Soviet Union's Yevgeny Arzhanov, undefeated in the metric half-mile over the past four years. But that was before Ohio's Dave Wottle popped into contention. Recently turned 22, just married and finishing up college at Bowling Green, Wottle was a skinny 6-foot-tall 140-pounder with an unruly shock of blond hair and an engaging grin. He had started doing distances in high school, he explained, when his coach threw a paternal

arm around his shoulders and said, "'Dave, I'm going to send you where I send everybody else who has no talent. I'm going to put you with the distance runners.'"

So Wottle became a miler and clicked with a 3:59 mile his sophomore year at Bowling Green. He liked to hang back, conserving energy for what developed into a blazing kick at the finish. Yet his legs, for all their power, were fragile: He had to sit out seven months beginning late in 1970 with stress fractures in both fibulae. The next year, however, he won the NCAA 1,500-meter and the AAU 800-meter titles. At the 1972 Olympic trials, Wottle was serious only about the 1,500 meters, and he entered the 800 merely for a lark. "I'm just getting myself ready for the 1,500," he said. "I'm not a half-miler. I don't have any idea what I'm doing. I don't have the quarter speed to go with those guys in Europe. Can't a guy just have some fun?"

Just having fun, running with his trademark dirty white golf cap clamped on his head, Wottle outkicked everybody to win the 800 in 1:44.30—and grab a share of the world record held by New Zealand's fabled Peter Snell and Australia's Ralph Doubell. Wottle qualified for the 1,500, too, still believing that would be his race.

At Munich, Wottle's fortunes appeared to fizzle. Although he qualified for the 800-meter final, an attack of tendinitis made his legs ache, sapping any confidence he may have felt in facing the unbeaten Arzhanov and a couple of jackrabbit Kenyans, Michael Boit and Robert Ouko. For the first lap, half the race, Wottle lagged eighth and last, as far as 10 meters behind the pack. The pace slowed some at 400 meters, allowing Wottle to catch up. He glided along for another 100 meters or so, until Arzhanov charged into the lead, prompting Wottle to make what he would later describe as "a little move, to about fifth or sixth spot. I didn't want to start my all-out kick just yet."

At the top of the stretch, Arzhanov had opened

An angry Bob Seagren thrusts his substitute vaulting pole at Adriaan Paulen, the International Amateur Athletic Federation technical committee president who banned his pole from competition. Seagren derided the decision as "100 percent politics."

a 7-meter gap and seemed unbeatable. Wottle was fourth, thinking about a bronze medal. He kicked past Ouko and zeroed in on Boit. Now a new goal presented itself. "I want to be a silver medalist," went through his head. Wottle sprinted past Boit. Five meters from the finish he reconsidered again. Maybe, just maybe, he might have a shot at Arzhanov. "He was faltering," said Wottle. "I think he noticed me coming up on his shoulder." Wottle saw the Soviet star try to gather speed, pumping his arms, commanding his leaden legs. "His upper body was saying yes, but his legs were saying no," recalled Wottle. In desperation, Arzhanov dived for the finish line as Wottle charged across, arms held high in victory. Time: 1:45.86 for Wottle, 1:45.89 for Arzhanov, a difference of only 0.03 of a second. "I think I won by the bill of my cap," marveled the new gold medalist.

On the victory dais, Dave Wottle placed his right hand over his heart in the civilian salute as "The Star-Spangled Banner" rolled across the stadium. But he didn't remove the grungy golf hat; to his mortification, he had forgotten all about it. What was the protest? inquired an Australian newsman at the ritual press conference. No protest, replied Wottle, tears streaming down his face. "I'm very embarrassed. I'm going to apologize to the American people. Right now, and again, and again." Back home, however, few of his proud compatriots thought it necessary.

As stirring as Dave Wottle's victory was, it shouldn't have come as any great shock to the experts or to the 80,000 fans jamming Munich's Olympiastadion: The Olympics were so often the Games of upset, of hail and farewell to old champions and welcome to new. At Munich, in the 35 track and field events for men and women, only one of 1968's gold

A surging John Akii-Bua leads by a comfortable margin in the final of the 400-meter hurdles. Akii-Bua was Uganda's first Olympic champion. His country's boycott of Montreal 1976 would deprive the world-record holder of the chance to win a second title.

The Soviet Union's Yevgeny Arzhanov dives at the finish of the 800-meter final as America's Dave Wottle continues to kick. Wottle's signature was a remarkable acceleration that could carry him from the back of a pack to the front in the homestretch of a race.

medalists accepted a second bright laurel. He was Viktor Saneyev, the Soviet Union's wizard of the triple jump, who would go on to yet another two Olympics. Otherwise, with four years between Games and the norms of track and field climbing giddily, the heroes and heroines all wore fresh new faces.

Among the newcomers was John Akii-Bua, one of 43 children presented by eight wives to a local chieftain in northern Uganda. Akii-Bua enjoyed relating how as a barefoot lad he had chased zebras through the brush, trying to catch one by the tail. His fleet-footed father could actually catch them, said John, but he and his brothers could not. He did, however, grow up big and strong enough at 6 feet 2 inches and 170 pounds to become an officer of the law with access to the athletic facilities at the Kampala police academy. Since he had spent his youth jumping over logs and bushes in his quest for zebras, he naturally gravitated to the hurdles.

The first the track world heard of Akii-Bua was at the 1970 Commonwealth Games, where the 20-year-old finished fourth in the 400-meter hurdles. Fourth place was unremarkable—except that the Ugandan had only been practicing a few months. The next year he set an African record 49.70 for the 400-meter hurdles and followed that with a 49-flat victory in a U.S.-Africa meet in Durham, North Carolina.

Training for the Olympics, young Akii-Bua worked on both speed and endurance, running from four to 10 miles daily, sometimes in heavy shoes and a weighted vest. A visiting writer asked if he believed in interval training as a stamina builder. "I don't do interval training," replied Akii-Bua. "Of course, I don't know what interval training is." But he did have the benefit of tutoring in technique from Malcolm Arnold, a Britisher coaching in Uganda. Akii-Bua absorbed everything he could learn about Great Britain's David Hemery, the 1968 Olympic

champion hurdler whose 48.10 world record still stood. "Hemery was almost his god, certainly his main spur," said Arnold. "There was nothing written about David that John didn't read."

Hemery, trying for a repeat, was the favorite at Munich in the 400-meter hurdles. Second seed went to America's Ralph Mann, who had posted an excellent 48.60. The stars drew the preferred lanes, 5 and 6, with Akii-Bua in the dreaded, tightly curving lane 1. "When you are in lane 1, you are always the loser," he groaned. For 200 meters, the plaint seemed prophetic: Hemery and Mann held a slight lead over the red-suited Ugandan. But Akii-Bua caught them at the fifth hurdle and powered away, pumping vigorously, holding his form, skimming a hurdle every 15 strides. At the finish, he had better than 2 meters on Mann and the fading Hemery.

Shrieks rose from the Olympiastadion when the scoreboard flashed 47.82, announcing a new world record by 0.28 of a second. John Akii-Bua held his hands to his mouth in astonishment, then raced off down the track, laughing and leaping imaginary hurdles until officials finally collared him for the medals ceremony.

How sweet it was, that very first Olympic medal for tiny Uganda, among the smallest of African nations. And how sweet it was next day, September 3, when little Finland at long last resumed its place of honor among the Olympic giants. In the Games from 1912 to 1936, Finnish runners had won 20 gold medals, 19 silvers, and 9 bronzes at distances of 1,500 meters and beyond—since then nothing, save a third in the marathon at Melbourne 1956.

Finland's instrument of renewal was another policeman: Lasse Viren, a tall, skinny 23-year-old whose massive heart beat only 32 times a minute, pumping vast amounts of oxygen-bearing blood. Viren hadn't grown up trying to catch reindeer by the tail, but he loved running—at all hours of the day and night. Since he was the sort who did things totally, he left mechanical trade school at 18 to immerse himself in distance running. In time he became a cop, but running remained his life. Seeking a mentor, he presented himself to Finland's respected Rolf Haikkola, a man who understood talent when he saw it. What impressed Haikkola was Viren's economy of effort; when everyone else was running at the limit, Viren just floated along, that mighty heart booming the freshened blood round and round.

For the Munich Games, Haikkola entered Viren in both the 10,000-meter run, scheduled for September 3, and the 5,000 meters, slated for September 9 in the concluding crescendo of events. The bearded young Finn was known for superior times at every distance from 3,000 meters up, but the field at Munich was daunting. No fewer than 50 aspirants entered the 10,000 meters, requiring three heats—the most since 1920—to winnow the field. Viren came in fourth in his very fast heat with a time of 28:04.40, putting him sixth among 15 qualifiers, every one of whom had bettered the Olympic mark. The defending champion, Naftali Temu of Kenya, suffered the indignity of being lapped in the first heat; he failed to qualify.

The race itself went down as one of the most exciting on record. Great Britain's Dave Bedford, the second-swiftest qualifier, scattered the pack with a sizzling 59.90 first lap. At 2,000 meters he continued to run well ahead of world-record pace. At 4,000 meters Bedford still clung to the lead, continuing a killing cadence, but 10 of his rivals were now running with him. Lasse Viren was one of them.

The formation shifted at 4,500 meters, on the backstretch of the 12th lap. Bedford's pursuers were all in a bunch. Running on the inside, Viren collided with Tunisia's Mohamed Gammoudi, winner of the last Olympic 5,000. Their legs got entangled, and Viren sprawled heavily to the track. He lay there for perhaps as long as a second before bounding up and sprinting after the pack. Gammoudi, knocked momentarily unconscious,

took longer to regain his feet; he continued for another 600 meters, then gave up.

The pitiless pace was dropping quickly. Bedford still led at 6,000 meters, but he was 2.70 seconds off the record. Within another 1,000 meters, he had to relinquish the lead. Viren pushed to the fore. At 9,000 meters the serious running began. With the Finn were Belgium's Emiel Puttemans, the fastest qualifier, and Ethiopia's Miruts Yifter, who had won the third heat. The pace had now fallen 10.20 seconds behind the record, but all

three front-runners looked strong as they swapped the lead back and forth.

Viren lit off his kick 600 meters from the finish, and with a lap to go he led Puttemans by 3 meters, Yifter by another 10. On he flew, with his beautiful stride and boundless endurance, sprinting the final 400 meters in an unheard-of 56.40 seconds.

As Viren flashed across the finish line, the scoreboard signaled 27:38.40. Not only had the Finns returned, but Viren had clipped a full second off the world mark set seven years earlier by Australia's renowned Ron Clarke. There would be more for Lasse Viren, and before the Munich Games were over, a second Finn would mount the podium in triumph.

For the hundreds of British fans who had cheered themselves hoarse at Dave Bedford's early speed, there was keen disappointment in his sixth-place finish, 33 seconds and half a lap behind. Yet Britons everywhere found solace—lots of it—in Mary Peters.

Late in the 10,000-meter race, Finland's Lasse Viren leads the fastest field ever assembled for the event. Viren had run only three 10,000-meter races before Munich but had posted times that made observers think he could challenge the world record.

Ireland's Mary Peters *(center)* happily embraces West Germany's Heidemarie Rosendahl *(left)* and East Germany's Burglinde Pollak during the pentathlon medal ceremony. The pentathlon became the heptathlon at Los Angeles 1984.

A hard-working secretary from Belfast, Northern Ireland, the 33-year-old Peters was competing for the third time in an Olympic pentathlon. Even friends thought she was overdue for retirement. Peters had finished a respectable fourth at Tokyo 1964, then dropped to a depressing ninth at Mexico City. Now here she was, facing both middle age and awesome opposition. The favorites were West Germany's Heidemarie Rosendahl, who held the world record for the long jump, and East Germany's Burglinde Pollak, world-record holder in the pentathlon itself.

Big, blonde, beaming Mary Peters just shrugged and went out to give it a try. Carrying 158 pounds on a 5-foot-8-inch frame, she was really too husky for a runner. But on the first day of competition, she managed a lifetime best 13.29 in the 100-meter hurdles to take second in the opening event. She then won the shot put with another personal best—53 feet 5 ¼ inches (16.29 meters). That evening under the floodlights, with 50,000 fans chanting her name, she managed 5 feet 11 ½ inches (1.82 meters) in the high jump—yet another personal best and another victory.

By the end of the first day, Peters was 97 points ahead of East Germany's Pollak and 301 points ahead of West Germany's Rosendahl. But the final two events—the long jump and 200-meter dash—were Heide Rosendahl's best and Mary Peters' worst. Lean and leggy, Rosendahl was superlative in the long jump, lofting out 22 feet

5 inches (6.83 meters) to within a whisker of her world record. Peters could only heave herself 19 feet 7 ½ inches (5.98 meters). In one swoop, Rosendahl had narrowed the gap to 121 points. And Pollak, with a jump of 20 feet 4 inches (6.20 meters), had drawn to within 47 points. All depended on the 200-meter dash.

Out came the calculators. Peters and Pollak were more or less equal in the dash. Rosendahl posed the threat. If she could match her top time of 23.10, then Peters also must achieve her ultimate—24.20—to eke out victory. Her British teammates sought to comfort her. "What are you worried about?" one of them said. "You're certain of a medal anyway." Peters found zero consolation in that. She shook her head. "*Any* medal's no good," she said. "It's got to be the gold."

Rosendahl flew out of the blocks. At 80 meters she had a 3-meter lead over Pollak and Peters. By 130 meters, the struggling Peters felt as if a switch had been thrown; her power suddenly drained away. Still she kept pumping, arms almost dragging her aging legs to the finish. The scoreboard flashed 22.96 for Rosendahl, her finest time ever. Had she done it? The board blinked, then finally registered 24.08 for Peters, also a career best.

Mary Peters stood in an exhausted trance, unable to calculate the result. Then someone put an arm around her. It was Heide Rosendahl. The answer was written all over the German woman's smiling young face. Mary Peters' 24.08 had given her victory by 0.10 of a second and 10 points—4,801 to 4,791. She had set a world record, too. And all at the age of 33.

Improbability might not have been the rule at Munich, but there was more than enough of it to give an oddsmaker dyspepsia. Rowing, for example, had never commanded much enthusiasm in New Zealand; a statistician commented—undoubtedly after the event—that only about 1,000 active oarsmen plied their sport in the entire country. But among them were enough tall, brawny young men for coach Rusty Robinson to proceed with his design.

In competitive rowing, traditional style called for a long, graceful lean forward and sweep back. Robinson regarded that as a waste of energy and devised a more upright style featuring faster, deeper strokes; it was awkward and man-killing, but a superbly conditioned crew could use it to drive a shell at a very fast clip.

Robinson's top crews—an eight with coxswain, a coxless four—put aside jobs, family, everything, for the three intensive months their training demanded. They dug into their savings, held raffles, and otherwise scrambled to raise $45,000 for food, lodging, and plane tickets to Munich. When they got to Europe, Robinson's radically stroking eight lost badly in a preliminary meet with the United States and West Germany. But the Kiwis were just warming up.

In the eight-oared final, most prestigious of Olympic rowing events, the black-shirted New Zealanders jumped away from the starting pontoon at 45 deep, hard pulls to the minute; grabbed the lead; and were never headed. By the halfway mark on the 2,000-meter course, Robinson's men had daylight between themselves and the nearest pursuer. The Americans, the West and East Germans, the Russians all made a run,

New Zealand's shell comfortably glides in first at the finish of the eights competition at Munich's Oberschleissheim course. The Kiwi victory at Munich did not signal the rise of a new rowing power. New Zealand has won only one Olympic championship since its Munich title.

but none could come within half a boat length as the Kiwis swept across the finish in 6:08.94. The United States crew was 2.67 seconds back, shading East Germany by 0.60 of a second.

A fluke? Not bloody likely, since in the fours without cox, New Zealand's rowers came within an ace of beating one of the greatest quartet of oarsmen ever assembled. The East Germans from Dresden's Club Einheit had won their first world championship in 1966 and hadn't lost a major competition in six years. At Munich, the New Zealanders boldly attacked, and with 500 meters to go led the highly favored East Germans by nearly a boat length—an enormous edge at that point in a world-class event. But Dresden's champions found their reserves; they started creeping up and caught the gutsy New Zealanders five strokes from the finish for a 1.37-second victory.

Olympic chroniclers would note that 34 countries had taken part in the rowing competitions, and 11 of them had won medals. Aside from the New Zealanders, however, the stars of the show were all Communist bloc athletes, big, strong, and perfectly honed. Of the seven rowing events at Munich, East Germans won three and Soviet oarsmen two, with another seven silvers and bronzes going to Eastern bloc rowers. The Big Red Sports Machine, as Western journalists had come to call it, was rolling right along.

Like the fans who filled the grandstands for the rowing events, the 100,000 spectators who visited Munich's Ringerhalle during the 10 days of Olympic wrestling never found it boring; the skills of the athletes were far too spectacular. But, as in rowing, wrestling yielded a familiar sameness to the victory announcements: East Europeans had long been outstanding wrestlers, and the Soviets and their socialist friends dominated

ON TARGET

Archery is an ancient and ubiquitous sport, a fact suggesting that surely it has always been part of the Olympic program. Not so. Archery was included in four of the first six modern Olympic Games but was dropped after Antwerp 1920. Its problem as an Olympic event was, ironically, its widespread popularity. Almost every country in the Olympic movement had its own set of rules for archery competition, and lacking a common tradition, officials found it impossible to establish a program for the Games.

The sport's international governing body, the Fédération Internationale de Tir l'Arc (FITA), developed acceptable guidelines and won approval for an Olympic return in 1967. The decision came too late for the Mexico City Games, so archery's comeback had to wait until 1972.

The competition took place at Munich's English Garden with individual events for both men and women. Men shot two rounds of 36 arrows each at targets from distances of 90, 70, 50, and 30 meters; women from 70, 60, 50, and 30 meters. Targets for the longer distances were 4 feet in diameter with a 4.8-inch bull's-eye; for the shorter distances the target was a little more than 2.5 feet across with a bull's-eye 3.2 inches wide. Americans won both titles and set world records: John Williams, an 18-year-old army private, was the men's gold medalist, and America's Doreen Wilbur, a 42-year-old homemaker, took the women's competition.

the Greco-Roman competition. Soviet grapplers captured four of the 10 events—with all six of the remaining titles gathered in by their Eastern bloc comrades. In the freestyle program, the USSR clamped on another armlock, winning five of the 10 golds, along with two silvers and a bronze. What serious competition the Soviets faced came from a handful of surprising Japanese and Americans.

There was scant reason to hope that America's Chris Taylor would defeat Soviet hero Aleksandr Medved in the first round of the super heavyweight class. The 23-year-old Taylor was gargantuan—at 6 feet 5 and 412 pounds by far the heftiest athlete at Munich—but he was amazingly nimble for his bulk; no one discounted his abilities. The 6-foot-6 Medved was 181 pounds lighter than Taylor and a dozen years older; still, he was the consummate wrestler, twice an Olympic gold medalist, seven times world champion. Moreover, he had beaten Taylor all three times they had met.

At Munich, though, Taylor was putting up a pretty good scrap—until the bout was made a farce by the Turkish referee. Again and again, the official penalized Taylor for passivity. Later, after Medved had been awarded a 3-1 decision, the chief referee questioned the Turk's judgment.

"Well," said the Turk, pointing at Taylor, "he weighs 400 pounds and the Russian only weighs 225 pounds. I thought such an advantage was unfair."

"Get out," barked the head referee, "and don't come back."

Medved went on to defeat five more opponents for his third Olympic gold. Taylor had to settle for a bronze, but he did have the satisfaction of seeing some of his teammates medal.

America's John Williams inspects his target as a sheaf of arrows protrudes from the bull's-eye. Williams set two world records at Munich en route to a gold medal.

Rodney Pattisson *(right)* checks a line tied by crew member Christopher Davies. During a three-Games career, Pattisson, a tough taskmaster, teamed with three different shipmates.

CAPTAIN PATTISSON

A love of the ocean was a foregone conclusion for Great Britain's Rodney Pattisson. He was born in the seaside village of Campbelltown, Scotland, and his father, an avid yachtsman, set his brood to sailing. A passion became a profession when Rodney earned a commission in the Royal Navy. Instead of following the usual shore-leave pursuits, the young submarine torpedo officer raced yachts in his spare time and developed into a superior helmsman. But in his first push for the Olympic Games he failed to make the team. That was in 1964. During the next four years he became, by some accounts, the best yachtsman in the world. That assessment would receive some confirmation at Acapulco, the 1968 Olympic yachting venue, when Pattisson and his crew won the Flying Dutchman class gold medal.

One taste of victory was not enough. To prepare for Munich, Pattisson resigned his naval commission in order to train full-time. His obsessive dedication cost him crewmen, who couldn't endure his constant badgering, but by the Games he had settled with Chris Davies, a naval officer from Hampshire. Sailing *Superdoso*, Pattisson was again the class of the field, winning four of the first six starts and a second gold medal. A push for a third title fell short; Pattisson could manage only a silver at Montreal 1976.

Lightweight Dan Gable, who had trained an incredible seven hours a day—every day—since 1969, pinned three men and handily decisioned three others for top honors in his division. Welterweight Wayne Wells and light heavyweight Ben Peterson also grappled their way to gold, while Ben's brother John brought home the middleweight silver medal.

Finally, in another smile from fortune, Rick Sanders—a long-haired, free-spirited sometime bartender from Portland, Oregon—came within 2 points of winning the 125 ½-pound bantamweight division. He lost out to Japan's Hideaki Yanagida, and there were those who groused that the brilliantly innovative Sanders would have won in a breeze had he trained even one-tenth as hard as Dan Gable. Maybe yes, maybe no. In any case, Sanders contributed to the most robust showing by American wrestlers since Paris 1924.

Among the many splendid things about the Munich Games—about most Olympic Games, for that matter—was the variety of competitions that afforded a share of limelight to athletes in many disciplines. The wrestlers had reveled in their combative sport. Now, from the opposite end of the spectrum, came the gymnasts, equally athletic, yet all harmony, fluidity, and grace. Here again, Eastern bloc athletes set out to prove socialist superiority in all things. They made their point with emphasis—and more than a little charm—in the women's competition. The men's exercises were another matter.

At Helsinki 1952, the Soviets had celebrated their first Olympics by displacing the Germans, Swiss, and Finns as the world's top male gymnasts: Moscow's men had won the team and all-around gold medals, as well as three of six golds in individual events. They repeated at Melbourne four years later. But in the 1960 Games at Rome, the compact, muscular Japanese had asserted mastery on the bars, horse, and rings, and in the acrobatic floor exercises. Japan's male gymnasts hadn't lost an Olympics since.

At Munich, crowds overflowed the Olympic Park's 12,000-seat Sporthalle for the six days of gymnastics. The fans watched in wonder as Japan's six-man team, including three holdovers from the Mexico City champions, raked in medals: 12 of 18 on the individual apparatus; the team gold by the wide margin of 7.20 points; the gold, silver, and bronze in the all-around competition. The winner of the all-around, 25-year-old Sawao Kato, had also carried away the gold at Mexico City; at Munich he became only the third man in Olympic annals to defend the all-around title successfully.

Unlike some products of the Big Red Machine, the Japanese gymnasts were no robots, no automatons mechanically performing safe, standard routines. They were inventive and daring, genuine artist-athletes. In winning the silver—to Kato's gold—on the horizontal bar, 24-year-old Mitsuo Tsukahara performed a sensational dismount that involved a double twist with a one-and-one-half back somersault. Executed perfectly, it earned him a near-perfect 9.90 from the judges and warm approval from the crowd.

But no one, no other athlete in the Games of the XX Olympiad, captured the imagination of the spectators—and a whole world of TV watchers—the way Olga Korbut did. She was the sixth and lowest-ranked member of the Soviet women's gymnastic squad, an alternate who got to compete only because one of her teammates was injured. Korbut was 17 years old, almost a woman, but she looked like a child of perhaps 12, a sticklike pixie in pigtails, standing 4 feet 11 inches tall and weighing barely 84

Aleksandr Medved grabs West Germany's Wilfried Dietrich's foot in an attempt to break him down during a super heavyweight freestyle wrestling match. Dietrich, a champion at Rome 1960 and a five-time Olympic medalist, lost to the Soviet, who would win his third consecutive gold medal at Munich.

Sawao Kato somersaults in the floor exercises during his successful defense of his all-around title. The 1970s were an era of domination for Japan's male gymnasts, who would win 10 Olympic gold medals during the decade.

pounds. What she had in giant measure, however, was personality.

Among the USSR's women gymnasts, personality ran counter to type. They were matchless at their craft; indeed, Soviet women had dominated gymnastics for two decades with their balletic precision and finesse. Yet they often struck observers as aloof and if not joyless, then somewhat stoic in their performances. Not Korbut. "Medals and titles don't do anything for me anymore," she insisted. "I don't need them. I need the love of the public, and I fight for it." In competition, she flirted with spectators, strutting and prancing, tossing her blonde head, winking, and flashing a smile that enveloped the entire lower half of her face.

Furthermore, there were steel springs in her waif's body, and they would uncoil in routines of breathtaking complexity and originality—loops, backflips, and somersaults on the bars and balance beam that no one had ever witnessed in competition before. Some credited Korbut's early coach, Reynald Knysch, with inventing routines specifically designed to take advantage of her flexible, short-waisted body. If so, Knysch found an apt and dedicated pupil; it was said that she practiced one difficult and dangerous half back somersault on the uneven parallel bars 20,000 times over a period of two years. Yet while she excelled at the most demanding maneuvers, she sometimes

Olympische Spiele München 1972

botched the simple compulsory exercises. And that was why Olga Korbut arrived in Munich as an alternate.

But things were going well for her. At the end of the team exercises, in which the Soviet women handily defeated the East Germans and Hungarians, Korbut was third in the individual rankings and was already everyone's delight. "Oh my—wow!" exclaimed an expert TV commentator after she pulled off her upward back somersault on the uneven bars. She looked a cinch for a medal, possibly even the gold as champion all-around gymnast.

The problems started the next day. Korbut had moved into the lead for the all-around title, but then she experienced a bad 30 seconds on the uneven bars. Swinging up onto a bar, her feet hit the floor; then as she continued, a hand momentarily slipped. Beginner's mistakes. Down she dropped to seventh place. In tears she fled to her coach and sat crying while her teammate, Lyudmila Tourischeva, outdid East Germany's Karin Janz for the most coveted of gymnastics awards. At one point a matronly woman—no one ever learned who—left the stands with a bunch of flowers in her hand, waved away a guard, and gave the bouquet to the weeping girl. The woman said something sympathetic and returned to her seat. The TV cameras beamed it all to 400 million people on seven continents: Little Olga in tears was irresistible.

Angular runners grimace at the finish of a relay race in Jacob Lawrence's poster for Munich 1972. The social progress of blacks in America is a frequent subject for Lawrence's paintings, and this work evokes the importance of sports in African-American society.

45

Focusing on her catch after releasing for a back flip, Olga Korbut shows her agility on the uneven parallel bars. The Munich Games were the first major international event for Korbut, yet she contended for a gold medal in the all-around competition.

Her final night was TV fare as well. Fighting for love, if not gold, Korbut won both. She took a fifth in the side horse vault, never a strong event for her. But returning to the fateful uneven bars, she performed a flawless half back somersault that sent the crowd into raptures—and then outrage when it earned only a 9.80 from the judges. The fans demanded a perfect 10 and rocked the Sporthalle with boos and whistles. For 10 minutes the jeering continued while the judges reconferred. In the end, the mark stood. Korbut came in second to the G.D.R.'s Janz. More howls of anger. The judges were not deaf and certainly were not fools. As Olga continued to perform well, the crowd screeched its adoration, and the scoring improved markedly. Korbut won an individual gold with a tremendous backward somersault on the balance beam and followed with a second triumph in the floor exercises.

Those two golds and the silver, plus the gold for her part in the team championship, did not make Olga Korbut the premier woman gymnast at Munich. Some experts felt that she had been overmarked; most agreed that all-around champion Lyudmila Tourischeva had the stronger technical skills and that she, not Korbut, should have won the floor exercises. How Tourischeva herself felt might have been reflected in the televised image of the medal ceremony after the floor exercises: Tourischeva standing rigid and stony-faced while Korbut danced on the top step, smiling and waving.

The elf, the impish alternate, had become the sweetheart star of Munich—and the role model for a world of young girls who would immediately take up gymnastics. More than just popularizing her sport, however, Korbut had changed its character forever. People no longer yearned to see young women in graceful balletic routines. They wanted tiny Olga Korbut or her counterparts to take their breath away with aerial attacks on the apparatus. They would get everything they wanted four years later at Montreal when a 14-year-old Romanian girl would become the new queen of the gymnasts.

Meantime, Olga Korbut had nothing to regret.

As ABC-TV's able Jim McKay commented: "Everyone should have a perfect moment in life, even if it is in part illusory. This was Olga's. She had seen triumph, then disaster, then total victory. In a few short days, she'd seen it all."

Not quite. Tragically, Olga Korbut and all the other golden young athletes at Munich were about to see how fragile a perfect moment can be. They would learn soon enough that peace and amity can be as fleeting and illusory as glory, and disaster can be final and very real.

The Soviet Union's Lyudmila Tourischeva demonstrates strength and control on the balance beam. The beam was Tourischeva's worst apparatus. She had fallen off it at important meets in three of the four previous seasons, but she kept her poise at Munich.

THE GAMES OF TERROR

MUNICH 1972

Nothing projected the German vision of the Munich Games quite so powerfully as the Olympic Village. If joy radiated color, then the Olympisches Dorf, built to house 12,000 athletes and team personnel, was the apotheosis of Willi Daume's dream for a Games of Joy. He had promised a bright palette, and the Village was a stunning kaleidoscope of prairie greens and apple greens, sky blues and turquoise blues, purples, mauves, and taupes, fields of yellows and oranges. The profusion of color lent life and gaiety to the apartment blocks and social centers, to the inlaid pedestrian promenades and the underground roadways, to the winding multihued canals, tumbling little waterfalls, and graceful fountains with their phosphorescent rainbow sprays.

Mood followed color. In this vibrant village, the rules were few and the company exciting. Munich beckoned to its youthful visitors, and athletes returning in the small hours had no trouble getting to their beds without the bother of guards or identification checks. A chain-link fence encircled both the men's and women's quarters. Its gates were closed at midnight and guarded by gatekeepers. But the fence was only six and a half feet high and not topped with anything so unfriendly as barbed wire. A vigorous young man—or woman, for that matter—had merely to put toe to link and swing up and over. It happened all the time.

And so, at 4 a.m. in the pinkening dawn of Tuesday, September 5, the two Bavarian civil servants on their way to work—a mailman and a telephone lineman—were not in the least surprised by the scene at the southern edge of the men's compound. There, four young men were lifting heavy sports bags and long, thin objects wrapped in canvas over the fence to a couple of companions. All six men wore sweat suits bearing the names of Islamic nations participating in the Games—Libya and Saudi Arabia stood out—and they were being very careful with their belongings.

A terrorist on a balcony in the Olympic Village, Munich, September 5, 1972

49

The lineman thought the long, thin things might be fishing rods. But the mailman shook his head—guns probably, he said. The shooting competitions had ended, and these marksmen must be turning in their equipment after a night of celebration.

The Bavarian was partly right about the packages: They did contain guns—Soviet- and Czech-made assault rifles, with enough ammunition in the duffels to equip a company of assault troops. But the mailman was altogether wrong about the six men. They weren't athletes. They were self-styled *fedayeen* (fighters for the faith), members of the Black September arm of the Palestine Liberation Organization, also known as El-Fatah and headed by the implacable, Israel-detesting Yasir Arafat.

Black September had announced itself to the world 10 months before with the assassination of Jordanian prime minister Wasfi Tal, who was visiting Cairo. The Jordanian statesman had averted war with neighboring Israel by driving El-Fatah from his land; death was the Palestinians' response. Now, on this September night, the fedayeen were laying their sights on a new target: Block 31, Connollystrasse, the cheerfully painted apartment building that housed the bulk of Israel's 28-member delegation to the Games of Joy.

Three of the Israelis were away at Kiel for the yachting. Two more, members of the Israeli Olympic committee, were living at a Munich hotel. Another two were women, a swimmer and a hurdler, both lodged in the women's quarters. The remaining 21 members of the Israeli

At peak capacity during the Games, Munich's Olympic Village housed 10,047 athletes and officials. The arrow points to the building at 31 Connollystrasse that was home to most of the Israeli delegation. Some nations housed security personnel with their delegations. The Israelis did not.

contingent—three wrestlers, three weight lifters, two fencers, two marksmen, a race walker, along with 10 coaches, judges, doctors, and the delegation head—lived at 31 Connollystrasse.

The terrorists had changed clothes and donned various masks, hoods, and other disguises by the time they reached the building. It was then about 4:30 a.m. Their number had grown to eight with the addition of two inside men. These two turned out to be the leaders, known to their fellows as Issa and Tony. Issa, the chief, may have been Mohammed Mahmud Essafadi, in his late twenties, a wiry, German-educated Lebanese engineer who had wangled a construction job at the Olympic site. Tony, taller and equally lean, was a cook at one of the Village cafeterias, but little else has ever been authenticated about him or the other six. In the shadow world of terrorism, passports are lies and the past evanescent.

Six Israelis were asleep in Apartment 1, the apartment the athletes called the Big Wheel's Inn because it housed the coaches and judges. Ordinarily, the sleeping men might not have heard the key—a carefully made copy—when it scraped in the lock on the apartment door. But the lock proved stubborn, and 40-year-old Josef Gotfreund, a wrestling referee, woke to the rattling of the doorknob. He slipped from his bed, reaching the door just as it swung ajar to reveal the men with guns. "Terrorists! Danger, you guys! Danger!" bellowed Gotfreund, hurling his 275-pound bulk at the door.

The desperate, grunting struggle lasted 20 seconds. But it was eight against one. The terrorists burst in and rammed the muzzles of their Kalashnikov AK-47s into Gotfreund.

A crash of breaking glass alerted the Arabs to the escape of Gotfreund's roommate, wrestling coach Tuvia Sokolovsky, who shattered a French door and dashed for sanctuary among the nearby South Koreans. Two guerrillas sent futile bursts of fire after Sokolovsky, while four more

raced up the circular stairs to the other bedrooms. There they leveled their weapons at four sleepy Israelis: fencing master Andre Spitzer, 30; rifle coach Kehat Shorr, 53; weight-lifting judge Yacov Springer, 52; and track coach Amitzur Shapira, 40.

Scarcely three minutes into the raid, the fedayeen had five prisoners. They slapped them around, then trussed and gagged them, then went hunting other victims in the apartments at 31 Connollystrasse.

For all the terrorists' obvious planning, and for all the visibility of their prey—each apartment entrance in the Village displayed a printed list of occupants—the invaders didn't score particularly well. After a half hour punctuated by shots and yells, they were back in Apartment 1, standing over four more Israelis: weight lifters Zeev Friedman, 28, and David Marc Berger, 28, and wrestlers Eliezer Halfin, 24, and Mark Slavin, 18. Two other Israelis had resisted. National wrestling coach Moshe Weinberg, 33, had hammered a huge fist into one Arab's face. Weight lifter Josef Romano, 32, hoping to launch a breakout, had slashed another attacker on the nose. The enraged terrorists shot them to ribbons.

The Palestinians failed, however, to bring down another weight lifter, Gad Tsobari, who escaped in a hail of bullets. And they hadn't found eight Israelis hiding in the apartment complex, all of whom would eventually run to freedom, including delegation chief Shmuel Lalkin.

On Munich police records, the initial alert came at 4:47 a.m. from a cleaning woman. She phoned to say that she had been passing by the Village and had heard gunfire at 31 Connollystrasse. Soon reports were flooding in. The first officer at the scene saw a hooded man—an Arab, he thought, with an automatic weapon—standing in the doorway of 31 Connollystrasse; the gunman motioned the cop to stop reporting into his walkie-talkie. A few minutes later, the

Members of the Israeli weight-lifting team *(from left to right)*: Zeev Friedman, David Berger, Josef Romano, and coach Tuvia Sokolovsky. Friedman finished 12th in the bantamweight division. Romano, a middleweight, stood in 25th place before an injury forced him from competition. Berger, a naturalized Israeli from Cleveland, was disqualified on a technicality during a light heavyweight bout. All three athletes were killed. Sokolovsky eluded the terrorists and survived.

Josef Gotfreund, a wrestling referee, became the terrorists' first captive after they invaded the Israeli apartments. Much admired in wrestling circles, Gotfreund would die at the hands of his captors. Officials and judges, along with athletes, made up the Israeli delegation at Munich. Amitzur Shapira was the coach of the two Israeli track competitors. The Romanian-born Andre Spitzer had the two-man Israeli fencing team in his charge. Yacov Springer, attending the Games as a weight-lifting judge, had been an Olympian for his native Poland at London 1948. All were killed during the crisis.

nature of the horror became clear when escaped wrestler Gad Tsobari, calling from a police box, informed authorities that terrorists had invaded the Israeli quarters.

The ultimatum arrived at 5:08. Terrorist leader Issa appeared in a second-floor window. His face was darkened with charcoal. Big sunglasses hid his eyes, and a white beach hat was jammed down on his head. He dropped a message from the window. It was typed in English and began, "The revolutionary organization Black September demands that by 9 a.m. the Israeli military regime free the 236 revolutionary prisoners whose names are listed herewith." There followed a roll call of the worst terrorist killers and bombers in Israeli jails, along with Ulrike Meinhof and Andreas Bader, two murdering ultraradicals in West German hands.

On the release of these criminals, the message said, the Palestinians would fly off to a sanctuary of their choice and there release the hostages.

A quarter of an hour passed, and Issa came down to talk with a police officer. The two argued briefly. Suddenly, Issa screamed: "We'll show you a corpse!" He snapped his fingers, and out flew a body from the doorway of Apartment 1. It was Moshe Weinberg, his head half shot away, his lungs a viscous pulp visible through a tear in his shirt. "*Verstehen Sie mich?*"—"Understand?" Issa snarled in German. "We'll kill them all, starting at 9 o'clock. One each hour. And we'll throw their bodies into the street!"

She came strolling down Connollystrasse at 5:40, a pretty young blonde woman wearing rose-tinted glasses. She walked as casually as if she hadn't a care in the world. She wore the turquoise uniform of the women's Olympic security service, but in fact she was a lieutenant in Munich's criminal division. Fräulein Graes, they called her. Her real name was a secret. She specialized in Arab languages and affairs. Over the next hours, she would be the primary liaison with the terrorists. Now she met Issa and seemed to have a calming effect on him. He came to the doorway, where they talked quietly for a few minutes.

The police were in the process of sealing off the

Gotfreund

Shapira

Spitzer

Springer

area and setting up a *Krisenstab*, a crisis command, in a nearby administrative building. Heading the command was Bruno Merk, Bavaria's interior minister, backed by his federal counterpart, Hans-Dietrich Genscher. Overseeing them both, and in operational control of the crisis team, was Munich's tough-minded *Polizeipräsident*, the police commissioner, Manfred Schreiber. Willi Daume represented the Munich Olympic Organizing Committee, while 84-year-old Avery Brundage, just six days away from retirement, decided to speak for the IOC.

The first meeting of these principals took place at 7:15 a.m. Everyone agreed that it was crucial to negotiate and play for time; the use of force to free the hostages would be a last resort. The Israeli government had been notified of the Black September demands, and while awaiting a reply, the Munich team's first priority was to get the 9 a.m. deadline extended.

Fräulein Graes was back at Apartment 1 by 8:45, tapping lightly on the door with her fingertips. Issa answered, and after a few words Graes motioned for a delegation from the Krisenstab to join her. Accompanying these officials was A. D. Touny, an Egyptian member of the IOC and an important personage in the Arab world. Issa had no interest in the proposal that five high-ranking Germans, including Ministers Merk and Genscher and Police Commissioner Schreiber, trade

places with the Israeli hostages. "No," he snapped. "You are not our enemies. The Israelis are." But the white-hatted little Lebanese did listen to his fellow Arab when Touny argued that the Israelis had only just received the demands and that no one had yet been able to reach Prime Minister Golda Meir. Issa decreed a new deadline: noon. Graes and her companions left.

The Israeli reply at 10:45 a.m. Munich time surprised nobody. In a phone conversation with West German chancellor Willy Brandt, Golda Meir stated her government's firm position that "under no conditions will Israel make the slightest concession to terrorist blackmail." Brandt pleaded for some gesture, however small, and said that he would release the captured killers Andreas Bader and Ulrike Meinhof. Meir agreed to consult her cabinet, but she told Brandt that she was irrevocably against any compromise.

Meanwhile, Fräulein Graes had returned to Apartment 1 at 9:15 to inform Issa that atmospheric conditions were making a hash of communications with Jerusalem. "Let's hope for the hostages' sake that they quickly improve," he hissed.

Graes nodded and started walking away from the apartment in her usual relaxed way—to perform an act of personal defiance and bravery. Two Israelis—the team doctors—were known to be hiding in Apartment 4. As Graes

Kehat Shorr was the coach of the two-man Israeli shooting team. A former national pistol-shooting champion of Romania, Shorr had fought with resistance forces during World War II. He had immigrated to Israel in 1963. He died at Fürstenfeldbruck. Israel had hoped Munich would be a learning experience for its young wrestlers. Eliezer Halfin, a lightweight freestyler, was eliminated in the third round of the tournament. Mark Slavin, at 18 one of the youngest in the Israeli delegation, was a Greco-Roman wrestler whose first bout was scheduled for September 5. Wrestling coach Moshe Weinberg was the terrorists' first victim. Halfin and Slavin would also die.

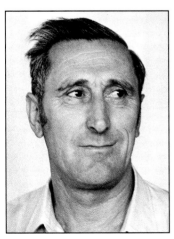   

Shorr **Halfin** **Slavin** **Weinberg**

53

The terrorist leader known as Issa was a Lebanese national whose real name was Mohammed Mahmud Essafadi. After the ill-starred Games, officials learned that Essafadi and two of his accomplices had infiltrated the Munich Olympic organization by taking jobs in the Olympic Village.

passed by that apartment, she looked up at the windows and began thrusting her purse up and out from her body, a signal for "flee," while silently mouthing in English, "Go! Go! Out! Now! Go!"

The doctors understood. They flung open the French doors to the garden and dashed out. A terrorist on the rear balcony of Apartment 1 screamed "Halt!" But they were gone before he could draw a bead. Graes, too, was unharmed; apparently the Arabs had not seen her lifesaving signal.

It was now late morning, and most of Munich was aware of an incident involving the Israelis at the Olympic Village. The first curiosity seekers were collecting at the fence. Newsmen besieged the Village, clamoring for

details and demanding to know if the Games were being canceled or suspended. That issue had been debated at the 10:15 Krisenstab meeting, and while neither Daume nor Brundage objected to a postponement, Police Commissioner Schreiber did. Tens of thousands of suddenly idle people would come crushing around the Village, hindering authorities and vastly upping the odds for a catastrophic incident. Schreiber's logic won out.

The program of dressage, volleyball, boxing, basketball, canoeing, handball, soccer, and a few track and field events continued. A bizarre sort of normalcy settled over Olympic Park. The endlessly training distance runners cut through the cordons of police on their way out of the Village for cross-country jaunts. The sausage sellers along the Spielstrasse were as busy as ever. The puppet masters, mimes, and jugglers went on with their routines, while the rock, jazz, and blues bands drowned out the TV announcers explaining about the armored cars in the nearby Village plaza.

Israel's Ambassador H. E. Eliashiv Ben-Horin arrived from Bonn at 11 a.m., bringing a message that formalized his government's already-stated position: Israel did not negotiate with terrorists; there would be no exchange of the 234 prisoners. Responsibility for concluding the affair rested with West Germany—though Israel would understand if the Germans agreed to free their two jailed terrorists on behalf of the hostages.

"Is this an irrevocable decision?" asked Bavaria's Bruno Merk.

"I believe so," Ben-Horin answered.

That meant force, unless the terrorists should somehow collapse or relent. On the odd chance, the Germans pretended that negotiations were continuing. At 11:55, Issa, holding a live grenade, walked out to talk with a delegation from the Krisenstab, again including Egyptian IOC member Touny. Connections with Jerusalem remained poor, they said; the entire Israeli cabinet was involved. Issa agreed to another hour, until 1 p.m., but warned that if by then Israel had not freed the 234, "we will execute two hostages right here in this street, for the world press and television."

Police Commissioner Schreiber took the terrorist at his word and asked Ambassador Ben-Horin to convey his opinion that the Black Septembrists were fanatics ready to kill and die. "If Israel refuses to negotiate, we will attack," Schreiber said, "but it will take a miracle to keep the hostages from suffering terrible losses." Minister Merk added that to hold down their own casualties, the police would have to use overwhelming force, making it even riskier for the captives.

None of this moved the Israelis to alter their decision. The negotiations continued nonetheless, with Fräulein Graes translating when Issa chose to talk. He seemed to feel comfortable with her, and at one point he offered her a cigarette; she amiably accepted, and he lit it like a gentleman. Her benign presence may have helped persuade the terrorists to extend the deadline twice more—first to 3 p.m., then to 5.

But Issa and his fedayeen showed no weakening of resolve. Rather, they imposed a new demand: They were tired of waiting for the Israelis to make up their minds and had decided to fly to Cairo with the hostages. "When we land in Cairo," said Issa, "we expect to find waiting for us each and every one of the prisoners whose release we demanded. If not, before getting out of the plane we will execute all of the hostages, without exception." It was now a little after 4:30 in the afternoon. Issa gave the Germans until 7 to produce an aircraft.

The new ultimatum was, of course, impossible for West Germany to accept; no civilized nation could abandon guests kidnapped on its soil. The Krisenstab continued to play along and got the deadline extended to 10 p.m.—while working on the only remaining alternative: rescue by force.

A critical question was how many of the Israelis

were still alive, and in what condition. Issa had two of the hostages—Andre Spitzer and Eliezer Halfin—brought to a second-floor window. Spitzer called down: "All hostages who survived the dawn attack are still alive." He was not allowed to say more. The Germans demanded to see with their own eyes, and at 5:15 Bonn's Hans-Dietrich Genscher climbed the stairs of Apartment 1.

There, in a blood-splattered, bullet-pocked bedroom, he found nine living Israelis bound hand and foot; a number of them showed the marks of savage beatings. Josef Romano's body

A masked terrorist peers down from a balcony at 31 Connollystrasse. The eight instigators of the Munich massacre belonged to Black September, a group that took its name after the month in 1970 when radical Palestinians were expelled from Jordan.

lay in the middle of the floor, so chopped up by slugs that it would later break in half when medics went to remove it.

Did the Israelis agree to leave Germany? asked Genscher.

Yes, replied Kehat Shorr, the oldest, speaking for them all, but they assumed that in doing so, "our government would meet the demands of the terrorists"—he spat out the term—"for otherwise we would all be shot."

Genscher put it another way: "In other words, if your government did not agree to the exchange, you would not be willing to leave German territory."

"Naturally," said Shorr. "In that case there'd be no point to it."

The message was perfectly clear. All Israelis knew that their leaders would not, could not, cave in to terrorist pressure. The hostages were putting themselves in German hands, come what may.

"You will not be abandoned," said Genscher.

Meantime, a fire smoldered within the IOC. Since the first phone call at 6 a.m., Avery Brundage had figured prominently in all Krisenstab decisions. At 3:51 in the afternoon, he had acted for the IOC by canceling the remainder of the day's sports program; he scheduled a memorial service for the murdered Moshe Weinberg for 10 the next morning, September 6, after which the Games would resume at 4 p.m. Later that first afternoon, when the terrorists demanded a plane to Cairo, Brundage had stormed that the IOC would not tolerate participants in its Games being carried off to their doom.

In none of this had the IOC's lame-duck president consulted his colleagues, or even communicated with them. Lord Killanin, first vice president and Brundage's imminent successor, was away at Kiel for the yachting, along with two other Executive Committee members. Brundage not only failed to inform Killanin of developments but actively stood in the way of his speedy return.

The IOC's longtime leader obviously felt that he alone was best able to steer a path for the Olympic establishment in this unprecedented and fast-developing situation. And there was some truth to that. But his autocracy angered many IOC members, notably the second vice president, Count Jean de Beaumont. "To Brundage, *he* is the IOC—no one else, just him," raged the French nobleman to reporters. "One week before he goes out of office, and he's playing pope without cardinals, when the very

Conferring with negotiators, Essafadi motions to a window in the apartment where the hostages are held. The Israeli captives were confined at 31 Connollystrasse a little more than 17 hours before being transported to the Fürstenfeldbruck airfield. Food was brought for them twice during that time. The terrorists refused to eat.

A German sharpshooter dressed as an athlete moves into position near the Israeli apartments in the Olympic Village. But authorities held back on ordering an attack, regarding an assault as a last resort in case negotiations failed or the hostages appeared to be in imminent danger.

Police hold back throngs of onlookers as word of the terrorist attack spreads. Lacking detailed information from authorities, news reports throughout the crisis tended to be erroneous or misleading.

A helicopter dispatched by the Munich crisis team swoops over the Olympic Village shortly before the transfer of the hostages. Crisis team members argued whether it would be better to ambush the terrorists during the hostage transfer at the Village or at Fürstenfeldbruck. They decided that an attack at the Village, still populated by thousands of athletes, posed too great a risk.

existence of the organization and movement he is the head of is at stake!"

Killanin finally returned from Kiel late in the afternoon and called an emergency Executive Board meeting for 7 p.m. To a man, the eight members—other than Brundage—felt that their president should not have involved the IOC in the Krisenstab, that the terrorist crisis and its resolution was entirely a German affair. Yet what was done was done—and the IOC did not wash its dirty linen in public. The Executive Committee endorsed Brundage's plan for a commemorative service the next morning. And its members were of one mind that the Games must not be canceled, that they must not surrender to crime and horror, that the principles

they stood for must seem invincible. Meeting at 10 that evening, all the IOC members who had managed to convene unanimously ratified their leaders' decisions.

The curtain rose on the final act just as the IOC members began their meeting. After hours of discussion, of strategies examined and discarded, Police Commissioner Manfred Schreiber and his colleagues had decided to ambush the terrorists and try to liberate the hostages at the military airfield of Fürstenfeldbruck, 22 kilometers west of Munich.

Knowing Israel's adamant position, the Germans had blandly lied to the Black Septembrists: Negotiations were continuing with Jerusalem, they reported. The responsible authorities had all agreed to the Cairo transfer, a Lufthansa Airlines Boeing 727 would be waiting at Fürstenfeldbruck, the terrorists and their prisoners would be transported there by helicopter. There was one condition: no taking of German hostages, meaning the helicopter pilots and Lufthansa crew. "You have my word," said Issa.

Schreiber ordered his second-in-command, Georg Wolf, to start deploying forces at the airfield. The plan was to illuminate the ramp brilliantly, giving expert marksmen (the best available, at any rate; neither Munich nor Germany had any specially trained sharpshooters at the time) the best possible shot as the terrorists hustled their hostages toward the trijet 727. Executed swiftly enough, the strategy might succeed. In case the trap failed and a fight developed, the snipers would have backup from nearly 150 men with overwhelming weaponry; it was essential to protect the police officers out in the open posing as mechanics, crew members, and ramp agents. A squadron of light armored cars and another 200 men would be standing by in Munich as reinforcements.

The first chilling flaw in the scenario became evident when Issa and his band led their captives from Apartment 1. Despite the six men observed by the postal and telephone workers at dawn, authorities subsequently could account for only five Arabs. The officials convinced themselves that there were no more; everything was predicated on that. Five snipers waited at Fürstenfeldbruck, one for each enemy; that in itself was odd, since standard tactics in such matters called for two sharpshooters per target. Now, as the terrorists prodded their prisoners into a military

bus for the short ride to the helicopters, Bavaria's minister Merk exclaimed, "Eight! There are eight of them!" Eight terrorists, and no chance of taking them all out simultaneously unless more crack shots could be rounded up immediately. Schreiber assumed that was being taken care of.

The two gray-green helicopters—15-passenger Bell Iroquois marked D-HAQO and D-HADU—squatted on the grass like prehistoric dragonflies. A large crowd had gathered behind the lines of police. The throng watched in fascinated silence as Issa jumped from the bus and inspected D-HAQO minutely. Then he signaled with a flashlight. Down from the bus, AK-47s jabbing into their backs, half-hopping on hobbled legs, came Shapira, Shorr, Berger, Slavin, and Spitzer. The terrorists loaded them into D-HAQO. Issa's second-in-command, Tony, and three other Arabs, their duffels bulging with ammunition, would ride in that machine. Issa

An army bus carries the hostages from 31 Connollystrasse to helicopters waiting at another part of the Olympic Village. The terrorists had originally intended to exit with the captives through underground passages. Plans changed after an inspection made their leader fearful of an ambush.

turned his attention to D-HADU. Gotfreund, Friedman, Springer, and Halfin went in, then Issa and the last three terrorists. The four pilots, two for each chopper, spooled up their jets and lifted off. It was 10:18. Scarcely 60 seconds later, Schreiber and other members of the Krisenstab took off for Fürstenfeldbruck in a third helicopter.

Schreiber's chopper landed at 10:29, well in advance of the other two. On orders, the pilots were stooging around at low speed until Tony in D-HADU got suspicious and screamed: "If we're not down in five minutes, I'm shooting one of you." The D-HADU pilot hit his throttles. His colleague in D-HAQO quickly followed suit.

Meanwhile, Schreiber met Wolf at the base of the field's control tower.

"Some lousy thing to happen at the last minute, eh? We sure never expected that, did we?" said Schreiber.

"What lousy thing?" asked Wolf.

"Why, that there are eight of them."

"What? Of who? You don't mean there are eight Arabs?"

Schreiber was aghast. "You mean you're just finding that out from me?"

The 24 minutes since the Arabs had left Apartment 1 would have been ample time to bring in additional sharpshooters. But no one had thought of it—or even informed Wolf.

"*Verdammt*," growled Schreiber. Then, "Well, never mind. We can still make up for it." They went over the positions of their five snipers: Three were above them on a terrace of the control tower; one was under a fire truck, another behind a parapet on the field. Backup machine gunners were with the snipers.

D-HAQO flared for a landing at 10:35, followed seconds later by D-HADU. In the tower 40 meters away, Schreiber phoned Munich for the armored cars and other reinforcements to "proceed at full speed ahead." On the field, the four pilots shut down their birds, then stepped

Fürstenfeldbruck airport was a military installation 13.6 miles west of Munich. The crisis staff chose it as the site for the ambush because it was relatively isolated from populated areas. If shooting started there, they reasoned, casualties could be kept to a minimum.

out and according to plan started slowly walking away. "Halt!" came the shout. And now there were 13 hostages instead of nine.

At 10:36 Issa and a comrade went to inspect the Lufthansa 727. They started back toward the choppers four minutes later. Two other Arabs were in the open. Whatever else happened, Wolf could not let the terrorist leader return to the German helicopter pilots; Issa would discover soon enough that the 727 was not going anywhere, and he was a proven killer. Wolf gave the order to fire.

Five Zeiss scopes zeroed in on the targets at ranges of 55 to 100 meters. Five fingers squeezed the triggers of five Heckler & Koch G-3 semiautomatic carbines. Five shots shattered the night. Two terrorists were killed instantly. But three shots missed. The marksmen fired again, and yet again. In another half second, the machine gunners opened up. A third terrorist was mortally wounded. But not Issa. Head down, running in little zigzags, he raced through the storm of bullets to dive unhurt beneath helicopter D-HAQO.

Tony and three others were on the concrete by now, Kalashnikovs ripping. Within 15 seconds, the banks of floodlights had been shot out; the ramp was in darkness. The chopper pilots saw a chance and ran to the four winds, the Arabs furiously spraying fire after them. One pilot made it to safety without a scratch. Another was hit in the chest, but not fatally; somehow he kept going until he reached a police vehicle. With bullets ricocheting all around, the other two pilots flopped to the concrete and lay motionless, playing dead. The Arabs turned back to the tower. A police brigadier edged out from the building to draw a bead on Tony. The terrorist shot first. His burst tore off the top of the officer's head.

The firing lasted four minutes. Then came silence, the eerie quiet of waiting enemies. Five minutes became 10, then 30, then more than an hour. During that time, a series of news bulletins

electrified Munich: The hostage crisis was over, the Israelis rescued, the terrorists either dead or captured. At 11:45, Willi Daume left the IOC meeting to take a phone call. He returned flashing the V-for-victory sign and shouting, "We have won!"

But they had not. At the airfield, Wolf had ordered the terrorists to throw down their weapons and surrender. They ignored him. Thus far, none of the hostages had been harmed; Issa was certain that the Germans would ask again to negotiate and that he would eventually fly out with his captives. Possibly that was why the Arabs did not shoot one of the pilots when he started crawling, ever so slowly, to safety 40 yards away. Issa was not stupid; why totally enrage the Germans?

The terrorist leader must have realized his fate when the six armored cars arrived at 11:55 and almost immediately went into action. Their mission above all was to reach the remaining German pilot, lying on the ramp near the helicopters. Then they and a flying squad of 23 men were to surround and capture the terrorists.

An armored personnel carrier moves into position at Fürstenfeldbruck. After shooting at the airfield stopped, three of these vehicles tried to flush the terrorists from their hiding places beneath the helicopters. The tactic failed; soldiers feared that firing on their quarry might cause an explosion and kill the hostages.

"Forward!" ordered the commander at 11:59. The Black Septembrists started firing two minutes later as the armored cars, lights ablaze, approached D-HAQO and D-HADU. Through the open doors, the hostages could be seen tied to their benches, the Arabs crouching up against their legs, emptying magazines as fast as they could load and reload. The bullets merely bounced off the armored cars' sides.

Suddenly Issa and two others leaped from D-HAQO; the leader's slight silhouette was clear. He had a Kalashnikov in one hand, a fragmentation grenade in the other. Issa stooped and pulled the pin. Then he stood and carefully lobbed the grenade at the feet of the five hostages in D-HAQO.

It was done; the worst had happened.

The explosion ignited the chopper's fuel tanks, and in less than a second, a hissing, roaring crematorium of flame enveloped the Israelis: Shapira, Shorr, Berger, Slavin, Spitzer. The mercy was that they surely died instantly. And now, by the lights of the oncoming armored cars, Tony and another terrorist could be seen in helicopter D-HADU, their bodies swaying as they emptied AK-47s into Gotfreund, Friedman, Halfin, Springer. These Israelis, too, probably died at once: Autopsy doctors would find an average of four slugs in each of their bodies.

Amid the oily clouds and scorching heat, the motionless heap that was the fourth helicopter pilot suddenly sprang to life. The terrorists aimed burst after burst at the desperately sprinting flyer. But their eyes were smarting from the smoke, and they failed to bring him down. In five seconds the pilot was nearing the tower, where Georg Wolf himself rushed out to shield the last yards with his own body.

It was 12:05, and the end was coming at last for Issa and his killers. A huge, red Luftwaffe fire truck braked to a stop by the burning chopper. Two firemen in silvery asbestos suits—with

Confused orders during the airport siege put Anton Fliegerbauer, a Munich police brigadier, in the line of terrorist gunfire. Originally set to back up police sharpshooters, he was dispatched to a runway to attack terrorists who were inspecting a 727 that they thought would be their getaway plane. Three Germans were wounded at Fürstenfeldbruck. Fliegerbauer was killed.

bulletproof vests beneath—started spraying foam. Suddenly Issa and two Arabs popped from the foam, shooting wildly. Massed police fire drove them back into the suffocating whiteness and out the other side. Two of the Arabs collapsed. Issa dashed for D-HADU, where Tony and the fifth terrorist were frenziedly working their weapons.

Tony lowered a rope to his chief. Issa grabbed it—and as he sought to scramble up into the helicopter, a probing searchlight from one of the armored cars caught him full in its beam. On the control tower terrace, the three sharpshooters took precise aim. Then they shot Issa dead. He jerked—once, twice, three times—as each 7.62-millimeter slug slammed into his body.

The Arab with Tony dropped to the concrete and lay still. The police made a rush, Schreiber and Wolf running up with their men. The Arab had either fainted or was playing dead. Wolf yanked his hair; that brought him painfully back to life. Schreiber climbed into D-HADU. The police commissioner took one look—and in a forlorn gesture, he started removing the hostages' blindfolds. "The four Israelis seemed to be asleep, peacefully," he said. "Their heads were bent and they leaned against each other."

Back on the ramp, the police collared the two other Arabs who had crumpled. They were unhurt. Like the one with Tony, they had either fainted or were suddenly overwhelmed, frozen with fear.

But not tough Tony. Issa had chosen his second well. The lanky killer had leaped from D-HADU, darted for the nearby airfield fence, and taken cover on a railroad track under a train of tank cars. It took police with dogs and tear gas 40 minutes to locate him, flush him out, corner him in a parking lot, and in a last furious gun battle, riddle him with machine-pistol bullets.

All the while, the ecstatic bulletins of victory over the terrorists had been circling the

A day after the abortive airport ambush, photographers got a look at the helicopters that had carried the doomed Israelis and their captors to Fürstenfeldbruck. The damage to the helicopter at left came when terrorist leader Essafadi lobbed a hand grenade into it, killing five hostages. The stained interior of the second helicopter *(below)* showed bloody reminders that its occupants died from machine-gun fire.

globe. In Israel at 1 a.m., Golda Meir drank a champagne toast to success and went gratefully to bed. Not until 3:17 did Reuters flash the terrible truth: "All the Israeli hostages were killed during the shoot-out at the air base, according to an announcement made tonight by a West German military spokesman."

The memorial service began at 10 a.m., 80,000 silently bereaved people filling the Olympiastadion as Munich's Philharmonic commenced the funeral march from Beethoven's *Eroica*. The athletes sat on the field, facing the speakers' stand. No Arab nation had sent a single representative, nor had the Soviets. The Israeli delegation—what was left of it, 17 out of 28 souls—sat up front, leaving 11 empty seats for everyone to stare at.

Willi Daume escorted Moshe Weinberg's mother, trembling in her grief; she had come to Munich a few days earlier, planning to enjoy the Games and have supper this very evening with her son. The music ended, and Daume, his voice thick with emotion, spoke briefly of this "day of immense mourning," of the murder and dehumanization visited on "this great and fine celebration of the peoples of the world, this celebration that had been dedicated to peace."

IOC president Avery Brundage speaks during the Munich memorial service for the slain Israelis. His IOC colleagues accused Brundage of abusing his authority at the beginning of the crisis, but they were unanimously behind him when he announced that the Games would continue.

Reporters noted that he said nothing about the continuation of the Munich Games. The IOC's decision of the previous evening was known to all, but nothing official had yet been announced. Daume left that to Avery Brundage.

The IOC's retiring president had never been known as an eloquent speaker—or as a particularly sensitive one. He spoke for less than a minute and made a botch of it, linking as though they were somehow equally horrible a threatened black African boycott of white-ruled Rhodesia to the slaughter of the Israelis. That sent shivers through the crowd. Yet no one could doubt the old Olympian's strength and passion, and he received a standing ovation when he declared: "We cannot allow a handful of terrorists to destroy this nucleus of international cooperation and goodwill we have in the Olympic movement. The Games must go on, and we must continue our efforts to keep them clean, pure, and honest."

The Israelis carried home their dead the next morning. At the airfield, a woman dressed in black stood alone beside the ramp while 11 coffins were loaded into the jetliner. She was Fräulein Graes, come to say farewell. She buried her face in her hands as the last coffin went into the hold and the survivors marched on board.

Leaders of the hostage rescue team (from left to right) Hans-Dietrich Genscher, Bruno Merk, and Manfred Schreiber face reporters after their failed attempt to save the Israelis. In spite of the bloodbath at Fürstenfeldbruck, there was little political fallout for any of the officials.

At the Tel Aviv airport, mourners crowd the flower-strewn coffins of the murdered athletes. A state funeral was held at the airport for all the victims. Individual rites followed in the hometowns of the slain.

THE
AFTERMATH

Just after the massacre, a sorrowing German educator and sports historian named Dietrich Quanz wrote to Munich's Olympic organizing committee to offer a suggestion: A table covered with black cloth should be set up in the Olympiastadion, and every medal-winning athlete should have the opportunity to come forward and deposit his or her trophy on the tablecloth. Each man and woman would sign a book and receive a document attesting to the gift. Quanz hoped and believed that there would be many, many medals—their gold, silver, and bronze all to be fused into a gleaming sculpture that would forever memorialize both the slain Olympians and those who lived on in triumph.

Nothing came of Quanz's idea. Willi Daume and his organizing committee were swamped, in the throes of revising schedules and arrangements so that the Games could continue after 24 hours of mourning. In any case, the professor's plan would almost surely have met resistance from various athletes and

from the politically supercharged delegations from the Arab and Communist worlds.

Yet it was the most Olympic of proposals, speaking directly to the ancient Greek belief that life and death were part of a divine cycle. Just as the still, brown earth gave birth to eager green shoots, so the young Greek athletes testified in their magnificence to the eternal renewal of the species. Sport was life, the Olympics the symbol of regeneration. One spirit passed and was gone; four years later another rose in its place. On they came, the Games of resurrection, following one after another in an unbroken chain.

This is what the founders of the modern Games had so devoutly believed, a faith the West Germans made certain to emphasize at the memorial service on the morning of September 6. "The Olympic Idea lives on. Our commitment to it is stronger than ever," vowed *Bundespräsident* Gustav Heinemann. And it was a faith the Israelis reiterated through their heartbreak and anger.

Flags at half-mast, Munich, September 6, 1972

They were leaving now, but they would return. "This abominable crime notwithstanding," said delegation head Shmuel Lalkin, "we have decided to participate in future Olympic Games in a spirit of brotherhood and honesty."

Munich 1972 had five more days to run. They would see the athletes erect their own memorials—to the Israelis, to themselves, to their countries, to the Games, to sport, to rebirth, to life.

For the first time, East Germany had the satisfaction of competing under its own banner as a separate and distinct nation. On rejoining the Summer Olympics at Helsinki 1952 after a postwar hiatus, Germany, now divided into two nations, had bowed to IOC wishes by putting aside political differences and fielding a joint team. (That was in theory, at least; in fact, most of the team's members were West German.) Now the German Democratic Republic, as the Soviet satellite wished to be known, insisted on its own identity. The Easterners had been working religiously to construct a sports machine that would glorify communism; sport, if nothing else in that blighted land, would prove socialist superiority. Much of the effort was modeled on Moscow's program that had produced the spectacular likes of Valery Borzov. Yet not even the Soviets could match their German comrades' obsession with victory. Aside from swimming, the G.D.R.'s primary target among the headline sports was women's track and field. And at Munich, the athletes in blue and white dazzled the world.

So overwhelming were the East German women that the United States, foremost at Mexico

Shmuel Lalkin, head of the Israeli delegation at Munich, speaks during the September 6 memorial ceremony for his slain compatriots. Lalkin, along with five other Israelis, was in the Connollystrasse apartments at the time of the terrorist attack but managed to evade capture.

City 1968, suffered the ignominy of precisely one silver and two bronzes out of 42 medals available. The G.D.R.'s only significant competition came from a gutsy Australian in the glamour dashes, and overall from the kindred West Germans. Even then, the East German women raced away with five of eight golds in the running events and added another in the javelin; four silvers and three bronzes brought the medal haul to 13. Had Munich been an ordinary track meet with the usual point scores, advised *Track & Field News*, the young ladies from the G.D.R. would have amassed 133 points, almost twice the total of the runner-up West Germans.

Inevitably, there were those who sought to diminish the achievement. Australian Olympic track coach Ken Stewart sounded a loud raspberry by publicly accusing "European" female runners of pumping themselves up with illegal anabolic steroids. Heretofore, steroids had been associated only with field events: the shot put, discus, hammer, javelin. Stewart had no doubt that they would also improve performance in the "explosive events," as he called the dashes. "After all, anabolic steroids simply make an athlete's muscle fibers stronger," said the Australian coach, adding that "among certain European countries there were no lean women sprinters, hurdlers, or long jumpers. Whether short or tall, they all had heavy buttocks."

Stewart carefully avoided naming countries and individuals. Yet everybody knew whom he meant when he told Sydney newspapers that one massively muscled European speedster weighed in at 11 stone four pounds, or 158 pounds, the biggest woman sprinter he had ever seen. As it happened, 158 pounds was exactly the weight of the superstar of the whole show: East Germany's 22-year-old Renate Stecher, who had powered her 5-foot-7 ¼-inch frame to victory in both the 100-meter and 200-meter dashes.

Unfair! Sour grapes! snapped the East Germans. They acidly pointed out that in winning her championships, Stecher had twice beaten Stewart's own star, Raelene Boyle. Moreover, nothing whatsoever had turned up in the postrace drug tests. That defense didn't quiet the critics; the suggestions of East German drug use would persist and multiply over the coming years. After the fall of the Communist East German regime, light filtering into the recesses of the vaunted sports machine would, in fact, reveal a systematic and long-term practice of dosing many athletes with steroids. But at the time of the Munich Games, no one offered proof, and the tremendous performances of Renate Stecher and her teammates would stand on their own merits.

For Stecher, Munich was the ultimate reward after nine very long years of training. G.D.R. sports scouts had discovered her when, at 13, she zipped through a school-meet 100 meters in 12.90 seconds—a time that would have earned her an Olympic berth at Amsterdam 1928. As she developed, Stecher turned out to lack the breathtaking acceleration of most great sprinters. However, she was smart and diligent enough to become, like Borzov, a supreme technician—those big, beautifully conditioned muscles erupting off the blocks, devouring the distance with flowing, flawless strides.

Going into Munich, Stecher hadn't been defeated in either the 100 meters or 200 meters since 1970. Twice she had run a world-record-equaling 11.00 for 100 yards. And when the 100-meter final came, early in the program, before the terrorist horror, Stecher had made it look easy. The husky East German had the lead over slender Raelene Boyle within 50 meters and drove on to win by 2 full meters. Her time brought a whoop from the stadium's knowledgeable crowd: 11:07 seconds, 0.01 of a second better than the world mark set by America's Wyomia Tyus at Mexico City.

The experts looked for a tougher test at 200 meters after the Games resumed on September 6. Here was Poland's Irena Szewinska, the

THE EAST GERMAN SPORTS MACHINE

An East German diver poises for an exercise under the watchful eye of a scientist at Leipzig's Forschungsinstitut für Körperkultur und Sport, or Research Institute for Physical Culture and Sport. The sole purpose of the Leipzig facility was to turn elite athletes into Olympic champions.

East Germany officially took part in the Olympic Games from 1972 to 1988. In that brief span it generated Olympic champions in numbers wholly out of proportion to its population. In the span of five Olympiads, East Germany, with a population of 16 million, produced 182 gold medalists. By comparison, the United States, with 250 million people, produced 204.

In a country whose very national identity depended in large part on fielding athletic champions, sport for all was a governmental imperative, though the ideal fell short of reality. There were hundreds of public sports facilities throughout the country, but the best of these concentrated less on the masses than on developing athletic prodigies. In these establishments, coaches nurtured promising charges with sophisticated training techniques and the best equipment.

But beyond fine coaching and excellent gear, East German athletes benefited from the most advanced sports medicine system in the world. Pioneers in biomechanics, the nation's sports doctors were expert in making their athletes faster and stronger. Precise regimens combining medicine and physical therapy not only created better athletes but precisely defined training limits to maximize potential and minimize burnout and injury.

Unfortunately, this medical expertise had a dark side. Long-held suspicions that doping was endemic among East German athletes were confirmed when, after Germany's reunification, a number of doctors from the East admitted that their athletes were routinely dosed with steroids and other dubious substances. Tragic in human terms, drugs also tainted a sports system whose success was otherwise undeniable.

Rows of children *(above)* keep soccer balls flying in an exercise to develop teamwork. In socialist East Germany, the importance of the collective was a concept ingrained from birth.

An overflowing stadium in Leipzig shows enthusiasm for the Spartakiade, a national sports festival in East Germany. The annual competition promoted patriotism and provided a stage for future world champion athletes.

East Germany's Renate Stecher leads the field by a stride in the women's 100-meter dash. Like the Soviets' Valery Borzov, the men's 100-meter champion, Stecher was not blessed with explosive speed but was a technically flawless runner. She became the first woman since America's Wilma Rudolph in 1960 to win both the Olympic 100- and 200-meter dashes.

defending champion and onetime world-record holder, now 26 and recently a mother, yet running well despite a bothersome ankle. Here again was Raelene Boyle, who at 17 had won the silver at Mexico City, just 0.15 of a second behind Szewinska. The 200 was Boyle's best race, and after the 100, she was alight with competitive fire.

The distance was Renate Stecher's favorite as well. "It gives you a better opportunity to fight," she said, and in the final she met Boyle's furious challenge. Blazing out of the turn, the Aussie ace came up on Stecher. Down the straight they flew, shoulder to shoulder—until at last Stecher's great power prevailed. They hit the finish line in the blink of an eye: 22:40 and a share of the world record for Stecher, 22:45 for Boyle. Suffering

pain from her ankle, Szewinska barely edged out another East German for third.

In the glow of victory, Renate Stecher told the press: "Szewinska was my nightmare all the weeks before the Games—and she will be again in the next seasons." It sounded less like a confession than a polite nod to a past champion. But with sure intuition, Stecher knew it to be true. For there would be a postscript to the dashes at Munich, one of those priceless epilogues that sportswriters live for.

Renate Stecher kept on winning and winning until by 1974 she had piled up an astounding 90 consecutive victories at 100 and 200 meters. Then in August 1974, at the European championships in Rome, she finally met defeat over both distances—at the hands of Irena Szewinska, who earlier in 1974, at the advanced age of 28, had reclaimed her world record for 200 meters. There was more: Trying her limber legs and enormous will at the most demanding of sprints, Szewinska capped her year by ripping through 400 meters in 49.90 seconds, thereby lopping an unbelievable 1.10 seconds off that world record. The handsome Polish woman, by now a grande dame of sport, would still be running magnificently two years hence at the Montreal Games—where she would add to Olympic legend with yet another lustrous world record.

Meanwhile, at Munich 1972, the high-stepping, drum-rolling, cymbal-crashing East German parade to the victory stand was in full swing. Pretty Monika Zehrt, not quite 20 and no horse at 5 feet 6 ¼ inches and 123 pounds, took off like a thoroughbred to set an Olympic-record 51.08 for 400 meters. A world record toppled when teammate Annelie Erhardt, 22, glided over the 100-meter hurdles in 12.59 seconds, so dominating the field that one expert called her the "only real hurdler" among the

women at Munich. And then there was the women's 4 x 400 relay, held for the first time as an Olympic event. With Monika Zehrt incomparable at anchor, the East Germans demolished their own world record by almost 6 seconds in 3:23.00. *Track & Field News* declared the feat "staggering"—and remarked on a field so outstanding that the next five finishers all either beat or equaled the old record.

The West Germans placed third after the United States in that relay. The sun had been shining for them as well as their sisters behind the Berlin Wall. Early in the Games, Hildegard Falck had set an Olympic record in the 800 meters. The next day, as in a fairy tale, an unknown 16-year-old high jumper named Ulrike Meyfarth became the youngest person of either sex to win an individual gold in track and field. The happy-go-lucky youngster had never jumped higher than her own considerable 6-foot-½-inch height and had finished only third in the West German trials. But with the championship at stake, she cleared the bar at a world-record-equaling 6 feet 3 ½ inches (1.92 meters). The

Monika Zehrt has a comfortable lead as she takes the baton from Helga Seidler. The East Germans set a world record during the 4 x 400-meter relay that stood until a new East German team broke it four years later at Montreal.

sound in the jam-packed Olympiastadion was akin to that of a bomb exploding.

Yet the leading lady for Munich's hosts had to be Heidemarie Rosendahl, the 25-year-old physical education teacher at West Germany's

Falling toward the landing pad, West German schoolgirl Ulrike Meyfarth has just cleared 6 feet 3 ½ inches (1.92 meters) for a gold medal. Meyfarth and Bulgaria's Yordanka Blagoyeva had matched each other at six consecutive heights before Blagoyeva missed at 6 feet 2 ¾ inches (1.89 meters).

Sports University at Cologne who had come within 10 points of besting Britain's Mary Peters in the pentathlon. Even a one-woman track team has to have a specialty, and for Rosendahl it was the long jump—world-record holder since 1970 at 22 feet 5 ¼ inches (6.84 meters), undefeated in 1972. Scheduling officials were so confident of victory that they held the long jump on the first day of competition. Rosendahl didn't disappoint her nation of fans, though a young Bulgarian named Diana Yorgova threw a scare into everybody by coming within half an inch of Rosendahl's winning leap.

The long-jump victory was the Bundesrepublik's very first Olympic championship, and throughout the Games, wherever the tall, lovely Heide went, people clustered around her to touch the sleeve of her pale lilac track suit, pat her shoulder, say hello and *danke, danke schön!*

Now, on September 10, the festival of sport was winding down, and all attention focused on the 4 x 100 relay—West Germany against East, their two teams the class of the field. The West's hopes rode with Rosendahl; along with other assets, she had to her credit an excellent 11.30 for 100 meters. Still, the Easterners were strongly favored; they had to be, with Renate Stecher at anchor. And, they had in fact won both the European championships and a preliminary Munich heat. But sport is like the weather; the computer has yet to be invented that can predict the outcome with certainty.

Going into the final 100 meters, Rosendahl's three teammates had built up a 5-foot lead. The baton pass was impeccable, and off she raced, streaming auburn hair, Stecher pounding desperately in her wake. Accounts differ: Some say the East German champion made up a foot or two, others that Stecher didn't gain an inch, still others that the flying Rosendahl added substantially to her team's lead. It all was academic as the West German ace streaked across the finish to a crescendo of cheers. Time: 42.81, shattering the

world and Olympic records set by a U.S. quartet at Mexico City.

"That's my most wonderful medal!" beamed the heroine of the hour, and every West German joined in a joyful chorus of cheers. The underdog had triumphed totally—and against those big, scary cousins to the east.

As for the rest of the women's competition, the Soviets could applaud record-breaking heavyweight victories in the shot put and discus for Nadezhda Chizhova and Faina Melnik, respectively. They found a heroine of their own in Lyudmila Bragina, a slight but steely 29-year-old who made a private game of the first Olympic 1,500-meter event for women. Three races for the unbeatable Bragina—two heats and the final—three world records, the times tumbling by 5.50 seconds to 4:01.40.

Otherwise, excepting Britain's magnificent Mary Peters, women's track and field at Munich

1972 was an all-German affair. Between them, the two Germanys had won almost half of all the medals, including 10 of the 14 golds, while setting or equaling nine world and Olympic records. *Fräuleins über alles*. Absolutely.

Jesse Abramson could only scratch his head in wonder at what continued to befall the United States at Munich. Writing in the *International Herald Tribune*, the veteran reporter of every Olympics since Paris 1924 was compelled to say that "no country previously had met with such misfortunes, of their own making or otherwise." The size and athletic tradition of the U.S. guaranteed numerous stellar performances. And Abramson, adding up the total track and field medals at the end of the Games, made a case that America, though tied 6-6 with the Soviet Union in golds, had really triumphed over its great rival with 19 medals to 13. Yet anyone with eyes must

West Germany's Heidemarie Rosendahl springs in front of Renate Stecher at the finish of the 4 x 100-meter relay. Rosendahl's dramatic finish, combined with the two medals she had already won, made her West Germany's heroine of the Games.

have thought that for Team U.S.A., Murphy's Law had gone into turbodrive.

Consider the 400 meters. American stars had little trouble winning the race. The heavily favored John Smith pulled up with a recurrent thigh injury coming out of the first turn. But teammates Vince Matthews, a 25-year-old New York City youth worker, and Wayne Collett, 23 and a UCLA law student, blasted home one-two in 44.80 seconds—a good enough time, though 0.80 seconds off the world record. The finish was to be expected, since in 17 modern Olympics U.S. sprinters had won 12 golds, 7 silvers, and 7 bronzes. What nobody expected was the behavior of the two African-American athletes at the ceremony.

From their appearance, they might have been in the locker room—sweatshirts hanging open, Matthews showing a dirty gray T-shirt underneath, Collett in his running shorts, barefoot and holding his spikes. When Matthews mounted the podium's top step, Collett hopped up there with him. At the anthem, they did not acknowledge the U.S. flag, but stood at an angle, Collett with hands on hips, Matthews scratching his chin, both of them looking around and chatting. As he

Preparing to fling the javelin, Ruth Fuchs is about to demonstrate East German superiority in field events. Fuchs set an Olympic record in winning the javelin gold, though she didn't add to her world record. She would hold the world mark from 1972 to 1977 and again from 1979 to 1980.

stepped down, Matthews twirled his medal around his finger like a watch fob.

The heavily German crowd hated it, hated this further debasement of their Games, this nose-thumbing at tradition and the Olympic spirit. An avalanche of whistles and boos swept down from the stands and followed the pair as they left the field.

Was this another Black Power demonstration like the one that had caused such consternation at Mexico City four years earlier? Christopher Brasher, the British Olympic champion (steeple-chase, 1956) turned chronicler of the Games,

thought not—for Matthews anyway. "Poor Vince Matthews, who is as thick as a pair of gum boots, did not really know what was going on," wrote Brasher. Collett was another matter. Brasher recalled that the law student had given the howling crowd a raised-fist Black Power salute just before leaving the stadium via the ath-letes' tunnel.

In view of the events a few days before and the bleak mood of Olympic officialdom, nothing short of an abject apology—possibly not even that—would have set matters right. Neither runner was inclined to apologize in any case,

The Soviet Union's **Lyudmila Bragina** heads a tight pack of finalists in the 1,500 meters, a race making its Olympic debut for women. The front was a familiar spot for Bragina, who lowered the world record for the distance every time she ran it at Munich.

A shoeless Wayne Collett stands idly next to an equally inattentive Vince Matthews during the medal ceremony of the 400-meter dash. Matthews, who had competed alongside the fist-pumping African-American medalists at Mexico City 1968, used his moment at Munich to convey the impression that race relations in America hadn't improved in four years.

Matthews fumbling around with such further aggravations as "I'm an athlete, not a politician. I never stand at attention." The IOC reacted by laying on the bullwhip. In a furious letter to the U.S. Olympic Committee, Avery Brundage summarily banned Matthews and Collett from all Olympic competition for life.

Some thought the punishment overkill. "It's ludicrous," snapped U.S. marathoner Kenny Moore. "Those crotchety old men haven't been getting their sleep." But the ban stood—and its effect was to inflict yet another calamity on America.

Smith, Matthews, and Collett were the heart of a 4 x 400 relay team that had been as safe a bet for the gold as anything at Munich. With Smith injured and the other two disqualified, there was no team, and no way to cobble one together. "Your four 200-meter men could have won the 4 x 400 relay," sympathized the IAAF's

Adriaan Paulen. But substitutions weren't allowed under the IAAF rules then in effect. The United States sat out the race, and a quartet of Kenyans ran off with the gold in 2:59.80, almost 4 seconds off the world mark set four years earlier by Vince Matthews and three other Yanks.

Americans could take pride in a world-record-equaling performance by peerless Rod Milburn in the 110-meter high hurdles. Nor did anything bad happen to 18-year-old long jumper Randy Williams—undoubtedly because he kept his good-luck teddy bear with him at all times. Mr. Bear and a strong pair of legs propelled Williams to a prodigious 27 feet 4 ½ inches (8.34 meters) in the qualifying round, fifth-longest jump in history. After that, the American youngster took the gold with 27 feet ½ inch (8.24 meters) in the finals. However, the gremlins returned to bedevil George Woods, a 70-foot shot-putter heavily favored in his event. In the first round, Poland's 32-year-old Wladyslaw Komar, ninth in 1964, sixth in 1968, uncorked the greatest heave of his life: 69 feet 6 inches

(21.18 meters), 7 ¼ inches better than his previous best. In two tries, Woods came within half an inch. Then, on his last put, the 16-pound ball actually hit the marker that indicated Komar's distance—bending the marker's shaft high enough up for observers to believe that it was the winning put. Amazingly, officials ruled that the put measured only 69 feet ¾ inch. Woods argued that at the very least he deserved another put. But no, the head official ruled that it was a valid put. End of competition. Gold to Komar, silver to Woods.

Then there was Jim Ryun. Again, officialdom had a hand in America's travail. Determined to reverse his 1,500-meter loss to Kenya's Kipchoge Keino at Mexico City 1968, Ryun had been training hard and running impressively. U.S. coaches submitted his superb 3:52.80 mile to those arranging the heat lineups. But somehow Ryun's time for the mile got interpreted as a 1,500-meter clocking. Quite mediocre. So the computer dumped Ryun into a preliminary heat with Keino. And here were the two favorites

Out of sync with his slower rivals, America's Rod Milburn *(foreground)* already has a step on the field in the 110-meter hurdles. Milburn was unbeatable in the 1970 and 1971 seasons, at one point winning 27 straight races.

Airborne during a jump in the steeplechase, Kip Keino contends for the lead. The talented Kenyan had hardly trained for the race, yet he won it for his second career Olympic gold medal.

head-to-head at the very start on September 8.

Preliminary heat or no, the race was getting interesting 550 meters from the end, Keino out front, Ryun coming up fast, trying to squeeze between two fading runners. He didn't make it through, colliding with a Ghanaian runner. To an Agence France Presse reporter, it looked as if Ryun had been violently elbowed into the Ghanaian. "The blow Ryun received in the side looked like something out of a karate exhibition," wrote the French newsman. Ryun went down in a sprawl, bruising his hip and straining an ankle. Stunned, he lost at least 75 yards before scrambling to his feet and chasing after the field. The crowd roared him on, but it was hopeless. Ryun filed two appeals claiming foul. The judges turned them both down, ruling that the collision was his fault. Thus ended the Olympic career of one of history's greatest middle-distance runners.

Kipchoge Keino didn't win the final two days later. The victor was a Finn, 24-year-old Pekka Vasala, who had been stricken with stomach troubles at Mexico City and had finished last in his heat. Nevertheless, the Olympic experience had so moved Vasala that he promised himself, "Someday, somewhere, I would accomplish something great." At Munich, he had but one plan: stay with Keino. And at 600 meters, when Kenya's champion made his move, Vasala was at his shoulder, matching stride for stride as Keino accelerated. Into the homestretch they went—the young Finn reaching deep for his reserves and outkicking Keino to win by 3 meters in 3:36.30, no record but still the sixth-fastest metric mile ever. The emotion of it overwhelmed Vasala when he reached the dressing room. "All became misty and I was crying uncontrollably," he recalled later. "I had completely lost control of myself."

The great Kip could still beam broadly, for he had performed a tour de force in another event, one that was totally foreign to him. A major goal for Keino in the years between Games had been

to repair his 1968 loss to Tunisia's Mohamed Gammoudi at 5,000 meters. It was not to be: The Munich organizers had planned both the 1,500- and 5,000-meter finals for the same afternoon. Swallowing his disappointment like the sportsman he was, Keino scanned the schedule for another challenge. Ah! The 3,000-meter steeplechase was slated for September 4, quite early enough. So, with only four practice runs back

Kip Keino (No. 576) stays in front of Finland's Pekka Vasala in the 1,500-meter race. Keino was attempting to win a second consecutive 1,500 meters, having won the event at Mexico City in 1968, but he fell short, settling for the silver.

home, the 32-year-old superstar raced away from the field, displaying atrocious form at the barriers but doing everything fast enough to set an Olympic record: 8:23.60. "I don't enjoy the jumps," Keino smiled, saying that he took them "like an animal. But the running in between, I love it."

Lasse Viren takes a celebratory lap of honor, reviving memories of Finland's domination of distance running in earlier days. Viren didn't win as many races as his legendary countryman Paavo Nurmi had in the 1920s, but he did achieve something Nurmi never had: back-to-back distance doubles, at Munich and Montreal.

The 5,000 meters, when it came on the last day, brought further glory to Finland and Lasse Viren, he of the remarkable heartbeat and world-record 10,000 meters. Unlike the earlier race, this one had no rabbity pacesetter for everyone to chase. The race proceeded methodically, no one making a move until four laps from the end. Then America's Steve Prefontaine, who had cockily promised to run the last mile in less than 4 minutes, charged off in pursuit of that goal, and the field gave chase.

At the bell signaling the last lap, Prefontaine had distanced most of the competition. Only three men still dogged the chunky, leg-pumping American: Viren, Tunisia's defending champion Mohamed Gammoudi, and Britain's Ian Stewart. Prefontaine was tiring, though, and the race came down to a duel between the tall, lanky Viren and the wiry little Gammoudi. The Tunisian ace led briefly going into the backstretch. Then came Viren, his silky stride skimming the track, surging past Gammoudi to win by 3 meters in an Olympic-record 13:26.40. With his splendid double victory, the quiet Finnish policeman took his place beside Czechoslovakia's Emil Zatopek and the Soviet Union's Vladimir Kuts in the Olympic pantheon of long-distance heroes.

The program called for one final distance race on that September 10, the last day of the Games. It was the marathon—at 42,195 meters, or 26 miles 385 yards, the longest, cruelest, and most Olympian of events. There is no evidence that the ancients ever ran such a race, their longest distance being between 4,000 and 5,000 meters. But when the organizers of the first modern Games decided to include an ultimate test of endurance, they seized on the legend of Pheidippides, the runner who was fabled to have died of exhaustion after speeding the 26-plus miles to Athens with news of victory over the Persians at Marathon in 490 BC. Tracing that course so appealed to the planners that they considered it the most important competition of the 1896 Athens

HEAVYWEIGHT

Of the 50 Soviet champions at Munich, none was as popular as Vassily Alekseyev. The 6-foot-1 ½-inch, 337-pound weight lifter had come to prominence in 1970 when he set the first of 79 career world records for combined weight in the sport's lifts: press, snatch, and clean and jerk. Later that same year he would become the first man to surpass the 600-kilogram (1,322.8-pound) barrier and the first to jerk 500 pounds (227 kilograms). He would also win in 1970 the first of eight consecutive world championships.

Alekseyev's weight-lifting records had the media jostling for a moment with him at Munich. Reporters observed, among other things, that he was capable of gluttony seldom matched since the eating orgies of ancient Rome. Alekseyev's main competition at the Games was West Germany's Rudolf Mang. But the Russian showed that he had no peer: He outlifted Mang by 66 pounds (30 kilograms).

At Montreal 1976, Alekseyev's celebrity had grown like his waistline (he had swelled to 345 pounds), and he was still the king: He beat his closest competitor by 77 pounds (35 kilograms). Injuries derailed him after the 1977 season, though he would make it to Moscow 1980. But he wasn't his old self. He failed to make the finals on his home turf and retired after the Games.

Games. Nor had the magic of the marathon, as the distance came to be known, paled in the years since—partly because athletes of so many nations had excelled in the contest.

Greeks had finished 1-2 and 4-8 in the first marathon. Subsequently, runners from Luxembourg, Canada, South Africa, Finland, France, Argentina, and Korea had earned the gold. The incomparable Zatopek had won for Czechoslovakia in 1952; Americans had succeeded twice, but not since London 1908. Ethiopians had come closest to dominance, victors in each of

the last three Games: Abebe Bikila, supreme at Rome 1960 and Tokyo 1964, and Mamo Wolde, champion at Mexico City.

Now aged 40, yet lean and leather-tough as ever, Wolde was at Munich to defend his title. But the experts discounted him for younger men. Prime among them were Belgium's 23-year-old Karel Lismont, new to the marathon yet winner of his only three outings, and America's Frank Shorter, 25, who had placed fifth in the 10,000 meters at Munich and was seeded No. 1 marathoner at the end of 1971 on the strength of two impressive victories that year.

At the gun, 69 athletes from 36 nations loped twice around the Olympiastadion track and then ran out through a tunnel and into the Munich suburbs. The pace was a relaxed 15:51 for the first 5 kilometers, everyone content to conserve energy, and had only picked up a little by 15 kilometers. Suddenly, inexplicably, it lagged again, and Shorter knew he would have the lead if he didn't purposely slow down. "Okay, you've got this momentum. Let it carry you," he told himself—and soon opened a 5-second gap.

Shorter's advantage grew to 31 seconds at 20 kilometers, then a full minute by the time he reached 30 kilometers and the winding gravel

paths of the Englischem Garten. Heading back to the stadium, Shorter had 90 seconds on his closest pursuer. He was still running easily and said to himself, "If I don't die badly, I'm going to win." His legs didn't die, and there loomed the tunnel, leading down to the field and what Shorter expected to be the greatest glory moment for any Olympic athlete: 80,000 voices swelling in tribute to the conqueror of the marathon.

Arms held high, Frank Shorter emerged from the tunnel—and into a cacophony of boos, hisses, and whistles. He crossed the finish line and jogged a victory lap in amazed disbelief, wondering at the abuse. He remembered thinking, "I

Saddened by the massacre at Munich, Frank Shorter, shown leading in the marathon, nonetheless felt strongly that the Games should continue. His dedication helped make him the first American Olympic marathon champion since Johnny Hayes at London 1908.

know I'm an American, but give me a break." Someone waved a small U.S. flag and shouted, "Don't worry, Frank, we love you." That made him feel a little better as he watched young Karel Lismont come through the tunnel for second place. Next was the magnificent Mamo Wolde, still going strong to capture the bronze.

Shorter soon learned what had happened to irritate the crowd, and it had nothing to do with him or his country. For a nonsensical caper, a young student named Norbert Studhaus had joined the race half a mile from the finish and had sprinted from the tunnel as if he were the winner. The cheers burst forth, then became a din of disapproval as fans quickly spotted the

hoax and officials sent police to remove the prankster—just as Shorter ran onto the field.

Frank Shorter just shook his head. "An impostor," he said slowly. "A perfectly absurd ending to an absurdly imperfect Olympics."

How sad. The Games of Joy perceived as Theater of the Absurd. Munich 1972 was not that; the Games of the XX Olympiad were magnificent: Spitz, Gould, Matthes, Belote, Borzov, Wottle, Peters, Stecher, Rosendahl, Meyfarth, Akii-Bua, Keino. Milburn, Williams, Vasala, Viren, Shorter. Superb, every last one of them. Still, it remained bizarre how disarray in one form or another would stalk sport after sport.

Boxing, always vulnerable to poor officiating, suffered some bad moments. Under international amateur rules, the referee had no vote: He could stop a bout to prevent serious injury, but if the contest went the three-round distance, the man who knew most about what had happened in the ring had no voice in the decision. Calls were made by the judges—five of them, chosen by participating nations, more often for their connections and bias, some thought, than for their knowledge of the sweet science. Throughout the fights, these judges circled the ring as if engaged in some sort of musical chairs—the purpose of which, suggested *New York Herald Tribune* sports columnist Red Smith, was to keep their incompetence from stagnating.

So many decisions appeared tainted that boos and whistles rocked the Boxing Hall time and again. One well-qualified observer—Italy's Nino Benvenuti, ex-middleweight professional champion—grew so irritated that he publicly charged the judges with racial prejudice. The accusation had some force, since the beneficiaries of three highly controversial decisions were Communist bloc whites, while the losers were a Mongolian, a Ugandan, and an African-American. The decision that eliminated U.S. light middleweight

PACESETTER

West Germany's Liselott Linsenhoff puts the Swedish-bred stallion Piaff through his paces to become the first woman to win the individual dressage title. The landmark started a trend: Since Linsenhoff's victory, only one man has won the event.

Reggie Jones, 60-57 and 59-57. A Yugoslav voted for Comrade Tregubov, 59-58. The Dutch and Nigerian officials rated the fight even, 58 points each. But since there must be an Olympic winner, they picked Tregubov, reportedly for his "aggressiveness." On points, Jones still was ahead 293-289, but the fight went to the Russian, three judges to two.

That sort of folly led the International Amateur Boxing Association to dismiss the Dutch judge and give 16 of his colleagues stiff warnings. Even so, the charges of racially and politically motivated decisions kept flying until the end, sullying a medal count that saw the East European bloc pick up six of the 11 gold medals, five silvers, and five bronzes. The United States barely avoided a shutout when Ray Seales, a slick light welterweight, earned the gold in his 138-pound class and three of his teammates won bronzes.

What nobody begrudged was the prominent role suddenly assumed by fighters from a feisty Caribbean island just 90 miles from Miami. Cuba hadn't won an Olympic gold medal since 1904, when a couple of fencing masters captured the foil, épée, and saber. Then, in the mid-1960s, dictator Fidel Castro, casting about for something to take Cuba's mind off its wretched economy, imported a handful of East European coaches to set up a boxing program. Munich saw the payoff: A 10-man team of Cuban fighters jabbed, hooked, and generally walloped their way to three golds, a silver, and a bronze. The professional fight promoters who haunt every Olympics were impressed with one Cuban in particular.

The Games have been the cradle of heavyweight champions. Ingemar Johanssen, Floyd Patterson, Cassius Clay, Joe Frazier, and George Foreman all came to notice at the Olympics. In

Reggie Jones in favor of the Soviet Union's Valery Tregubov made no sense at all. The first round might have been judged even, as the more experienced Russian backpedaled out of reach. Jones rocked Tregubov several times in the second round, opening a nasty cut over his eye—and almost put him away three times in the final round, the Russian unable to punch back and clinching for dear life. Awaiting the decision, Jones danced for joy while Tregubov stood glumly, certain of defeat.

Then the referee raised Tregubov's right arm. The crowd of 6,000 exploded in outrage, screaming *"Schieber! Schieber! Schande! Schande! Schande!"*—"Crook! Crook! Shame! Shame! Shame!"—booing, whistling, and firing trash into the ring. The demonstration went on for 15 minutes. It turned out that judges from Liberia and Maylasia had scored the fight in favor of

1972, the hot prospect from Cuba was enough to make a promoter swallow his cigar: Teófilo Stevenson, just 20 years old, 6 feet 5 inches and 214 pounds, with Clay's good looks and a thundering right hand that evoked memories of Joe Louis. Those who watched Stevenson demolish his opponents judged him considerably more advanced than Clay and the others at the Olympic stage of their careers.

The first victim was a Pole whom Stevenson dismantled before the first round was half over. Next came Duane Bobick, a 22-year-old U.S. Navy quartermaster with 56 straight wins, including a split decision over Stevenson at the 1971 Pan-American Games. Stevenson had added a dozen pounds and sharpened his right since then—and Bobick, an eye tightly closed, was out of it by the start of round three. Stevenson met West Germany's veteran Peter Hussing in the semifinals, spent perhaps a minute sizing him up, then started crashing rights through a gap between the West German's hands. By the second round, Hussing was so bloodied and bemused that the referee stopped the fight. "You just don't see his right hand," said Hussing. "All of a sudden it is there—on your chin."

The final didn't take place. The Romanian slated to meet Stevenson fractured a thumb in his semifinal bout. That was probably just as well, since the big Cuban had knocked him out on the occasion of their only previous meeting, a bout in Bucharest.

Offers came pouring in. Angelo Dundee, the manager who had started Clay on the road to riches, figured that Stevenson was worth two million dollars right then; others put the figure at three to four million. The Cuban hero wanted

Duane Bobick covers up against the coming onslaught of Cuba's Teófilo Stevenson. America's Bobick, a fifth-place finisher, would lose to world champions Ken Norton and Frank Tate late in his journeyman pro career. Stevenson, the Olympic champion, would never fight a professional bout.

Leaping high in the air, Yugoslavia's Zoran Živković tries to block the coming shot of Romania's Adrian Cosma in final-round action of team handball. The Munich tournament started with a 16-team field and ended with Yugoslavia triumphant.

HANDBALL WITH NO WALL

The sport of team handball claims antecedents as ancient as Greek and Roman times. The modern game, however, was created in 1926. Europeans had played varied forms of it up until then, but an international conference that year brought conformity. A hybrid of soccer and basketball, handball fields teams of seven players who dribble or pass a cantaloupe-size ball on a 40-by-20-meter court. A player can take three steps without dribbling but can only hold the ball for 3 seconds. The object is to throw more balls through a soccer-type goal than the opposing team does.

Team handball was on the Olympic program at Berlin 1936, but that one time exception was an outdoor game with 11 players on a side. The indoor version that gained popularity in later years won permanent Olympic approval at the 1965 IOC Session. The Munich tournament was for men only; women would have their own matches at Montreal 1976.

none of it. "I don't believe in professionalism. I believe in the revolution," he said, and besides, "What is a million dollars against eight million Cubans who love me?"

Stout fellow, and properly rewarded when a delighted Castro gave Stevenson a town house in Havana, a five-bedroom beachside villa, two cars, and most anything else his young heart might desire. The gifts would turn out to be an excellent long-term investment, for Stevenson would bring Cuba glory in two more Olympics.

Socialist athletes scored yet another notable triumph in basketball, next to baseball the most American of all sports. The United States had gone to Munich owning the event, victorious in every Games since basketball was introduced to the Olympics at St. Louis 1904, winner of 62 matches without a single loss. The streak had to end sometime, and end it did in the small hours of Sunday morning, September 10. The new Olympic champion was an excellent Soviet team, but its victory provoked one of the bitterest controversies in the annals of international sport.

The American squad was the youngest ever, and as always, its members were unused to playing together. Still, they were tall and individually gifted enough to sweep through their first seven games, averaging 77 points while giving up only 44. The Soviets, for their part, were the meticulously drilled product of an all-court press to defeat the U.S. at its own game. They could not compare with the lowliest of American professional teams, but they could give most college aggregations a good battle, and certainly they were a match for the untried outfit representing America at Munich.

Going into the final undefeated, the smoothly maneuvering Soviets immediately established a lead and held it. Twice in the 40-minute game they opened a gap of 10 points, and with 6:07

left to play they still had 8 points on the struggling Americans. At last the Yanks got it together, but they still trailed by 1 point, 48-49, with 6 seconds left on the clock. Three seconds: Doug Collins of Illinois State got the ball. Bam! He was fouled so hard that he lay on the floor in a daze. Then he got to his feet and calmly sank two foul shots. The U.S. had its first lead of the game, 50-49—and the donnybrook started.

The Soviets passed the ball inbounds. They got nowhere. One second to go, and the referee signaled time-out. The Soviet coach claimed he had called a time-out when Collins took his first foul shot. The claim was allowed; another

3 seconds went on the clock. Again, the Soviets failed to score. The buzzer sounded. The United States appeared to have won, 50-49. The crowd rushed onto the floor; the American players danced in jubilation. But at the timer's table, R. William Jones of Great Britain, the honorary secretary of the International Federation of Amateur Basketball, decreed that the clock had been improperly reset and ordered still another 3 seconds of play. This time the Soviets scored at the buzzer. The history-making game was theirs, 51-50.

The U.S. filed a furious protest, backed up by the Brazilian referee, who refused to sign the

It's a premature celebration for the American basketball players *(left)*, who cheer wildly at the finish of the game with the Soviet Union—or what they thought was the finish. A controversial resetting of the clock allowed the Soviets a last-second score, prompting their own celebration *(right)* after managing the first defeat of an American basketball team in Olympic history.

89

Munich's field hockey final between Pakistan and West Germany shows the physicality typical of the game. A penalty shot decided the outcome for the West Germans. The two countries would meet in an Olympic final 12 years later at Los Angeles, and Pakistan would avenge the loss at Munich.

scoresheet. He and the Americans argued that the gift of an extra 3 seconds was totally illegal and that Jones had no right to interfere. They were technically correct; he didn't. He did have the right, though, to appoint a jury of appeal to adjudicate the protest. He named a Hungarian, a Pole, a Cuban, an Italian, and a Puerto Rican. They voted 3-2 against the U.S. protest.

Outraged, the 12 American players refused to accept their silver medals, becoming the first Olympians ever to scorn the laurels accorded them. There was a further addendum, possibly instructive: In an account written some weeks later, FIBA's Jones acknowledged that "with a real American team, the Russians can be beaten by 20 points," but he went on to write with satisfaction, "The time when even a second-rate American team could win the gold medal is passed!" His responsibilities—or irresponsibilities—in the matter would be the subject of much debate.

It seemed that the fireworks would never cease when a second longtime reign ended in wrath. For the past 44 years, men's field hockey had belonged first to India, which captured six gold medals in a row, and later to neighboring Pakistan, winner in 1960 and 1968. The play of these two feuding cousins more closely resembled combat than sport, with hockey sticks subbing for sabers. But field hockey was the main claim to athletic fame for both countries, and they played it with awesome intensity.

Then, at Munich, a stunning new competitor entered the lists. West Germany, which had finished fourth at Mexico City 1968, now fielded a rugged, smoothly coordinated team that easily made the final. Because of their individual brilliance, the Pakistanis, who had edged the Indians in the semifinals, were favored for the gold. The contest was violent and bitterly fought. For 60 minutes, the score stood at 0-0, German teamwork confounding the Pakistani stars. Then came the defining moment: Awarded a penalty shot from 10 yards out, West Germany's

26-year-old Michael Kraus stepped up and whacked the ball crisply into the net.

The German defense held for the final 10 minutes of play. They had prevailed—and the Pakistanis could not contain themselves. In frustration and fury, players and fans stormed the judges' table, jostling officials, shrieking insults, charging that the tournament was fixed. One Pakistani dumped a pitcher of water over René Frank, president of the International Hockey Federation. At the medal ceremony, the Pakistani players swung their medals around derisively, refused to honor the German anthem, and generally behaved atrociously. The IOC and the hockey federation had no choice: All 11 players were banned from the Olympics for life, and Pakistan was barred from international competition for four years.

It remained for the cyclists to provide a final contretemps. At least this one had some slight

Defending champion Daniel Morelon *(left)* engages Australia's John Nicholson in the cycling sprint's final. Morelon's second consecutive sprint title gave him the third gold medal of his career. In three Games, the French champion claimed more medals than any other cyclist in Olympic history.

air of humor to it—and at Munich, alas, humor of any description had been in exceedingly short supply. A dozen nations shared the 21 medals in seven events, the Irish conspicuously not among them. Still, the boys from Erin managed a share of the limelight when four cyclists from the Irish Republican Army rushed out from a hiding place to join the 125-mile road race. Led by one Batty Flynn, they intended to protest the inclusion of an Ulsterman from Northern Ireland on the official Irish team.

First came a little fun as they rode merrily along, with Flynn at one point leading the race—to the bafflement of TV commentators who kept referring to him as "an unknown Dutchman." After a while it was time to collar the Ulsterman, Noel Taggart, ride him madly into a ditch, and start distributing fiery pamphlets about the political troubles in Northern Ireland. Police naturally arrested Batty and his mates—and then, over the protest of the Irish team manager, the grinning cops let the quartet go.

At last it was over. At 7:30 p.m. on Monday, September 11, spectators filled the Olympiastadion for a reformulated and abbreviated closing ceremony. Only about 3,000 athletes were on hand, and they inclined to be a little disorderly, hundreds of them swirling in circles and snaking conga lines. After about 10 minutes, Haydn's "Kaiser-hymne," the West German national anthem, brought them back to passable order. Avery Brundage made a short speech and left the field as the huge scoreboard flashed, "THANK YOU AVERY BRANDAGE"—getting it just a little wrong.

There was more marvelous music, and then the Olympic flame slowly dimmed and died away. The German farewell, "AUF WIEDERSE-HEN," flashed on the scoreboard. And in the departing crowd, a voice, a dozen voices, a hundred scattered voices, who knows how many voices, softly murmured another farewell: *Shalom*.

After the Olympic fire was extinguished, Bavarians in dirndls and lederhosen came onto the field at the Olympic stadium to escort the athletes out, giving the closing ceremony a personal touch. The celebration was subdued because of the terrorist attack, but a fluttering rainbow symbolized the promise that the Games would endure.

THE CHANGING
OF THE GUARD

THE XX OLYMPIAD

Avery Brundage entered the press conference haltingly, one hand on the shoulder of an aide. It was the evening of August 22, two days into the IOC's 73rd Session. The Munich Games were scheduled to start four days later, and the committee had just concluded a bitterly divided meeting. Brundage displayed the effects of the struggle. The ageless president of the IOC, now ashen-faced and haggard, suddenly showed his 85 years. When he managed to speak, he did so, oddly, in the third person. To a reporter's probing about the debate, he said, "Mr. Brundage ceases to officiate at this Session and he prefers not to answer that question." The content of the comment was as strange as the form: Although he was about to retire, Brundage would remain in full command until the conclusion of the upcoming Games. The newsmen let that go but persisted about the meeting. Someone asked: Did he not find the political pressures growing with every Games? Yes, Brundage slowly nodded,

"the political pressures are now intolerable." Then he left the room, again relying on the aide for support.

The meeting that so affected the Olympic movement's longtime leader had seen yet another bare-knuckle confrontation with black Africa over who was fit to be an Olympian and who was not. The specific issue involved white-ruled Rhodesia, which Brundage and the IOC had invited to Munich under certain conditions but which the black Africans were determined to reject. In the showdown, threatening a boycott, the Africans had marshaled the necessary political power: The IOC would withdraw its invitation. And that unalloyed defeat, coming on the eve of his departure, had undone the ancient warrior.

Were he an introspective man, Brundage might have pondered the irony that cast an emergent black Africa as the nemesis of his final IOC years. For he more than any other had championed a universal Olympics, reaching out to athletes the world over

Avery Brundage, Fifth IOC President, September 28, 1887 - May 8, 1975

IOC Executive Committee members Lord Killanin *(left)* of Ireland and the Marquess of Exeter of England discuss Rhodesia at the Munich Games with Finland's Johan Rangell *(second from right)* and Avery Brundage *(right).* The IOC excluded Rhodesian athletes from Mexico City 1968 on a passport technicality. Rhodesia's racial policy threatened to keep its teams out of the Games permanently.

without regard to country, creed, or color. But in Brundage's immovable view, this all-encompassing inclusion also meant fighting to retain white-dominated South Africa as a member of the Olympic family; politics, he insisted, had no place in the immaculate world of amateur sports, the evils of apartheid notwithstanding. Brundage had lost one bruising battle in the ongoing African war at Amsterdam in 1970, when the IOC bowed to the continent's aroused young nations by voting to banish South Africa until it amended its racist attitudes.

The next target of black wrath was South Africa's neighbor, Rhodesia. In 1965, the British colony previously known as Southern Rhodesia had unilaterally declared its independence and, like the Afrikaners, its intent to perpetuate white supremacy in a land of blacks. There was a difference, however. In Olympic sports at least, the Rhodesians played fair. They mandated no separate and unequal facilities and trials for the two races. Athletes who represented the Rhodesian national Olympic committee were chosen on the basis of skill not skin; they trained together and competed together. And since the Rhodesians had upheld the Olympic code in

this regard, they felt entitled to full and honorable membership.

Not so the leaders of the 32-nation Organization of African Unity. For them the issue involved a higher morality, with sports a weapon to be employed in their cause. It was a view not unlike that of the Palestinian spokesman who would excuse the Munich murders on the basis of a powerful need. "Sport is the modern religion of the West," advised the Palestinian. "So we decided to use the Olympics, the most sacred ceremony of this religion, to make the world pay attention to us." Chilling, but an idea not at all alien in Africa. How Rhodesia's whites had or had not treated black athletes was of no consequence; by using the Olympics, the OAU would make the world pay attention to it and its crusade against racism.

The strategy had succeeded at Mexico City in 1968, when the Mexicans invoked a passport technicality to defuse a boycott and prevent Rhodesia from competing. Then came Munich. This time, Brundage and his IOC supporters were determined to have Rhodesia present, and they offered what they hoped would be a suitable plan: Rhodesian athletes would be welcome if they disavowed their breakaway government and called themselves citizens of colonial Southern Rhodesia. Their Olympic travel and identity cards would describe them as British subjects, they would march under the old blue banner with the Union Jack in one corner, and they would consent to "God Save the Queen" as their national anthem. This was how the Rhodesians had competed at Tokyo 1964. And since neither Great Britain nor the United Nations had recognized Rhodesia's claim to independence, the territory remained a colony as far as the world was concerned.

Rhodesian authorities had shrugged their acquiescence. Why not? The political impact at home would be nil. Acceptance at the Games, after all, was the important thing. And there they were, 46 men and women, seven of them black, come to Munich expecting to be part of the Games—while the OAU searched for ways to send them home again.

The militants focused on the Olympic identity cards, which they called "spurious"; only bona fide British passports could prove nationality. Heavier ammunition came from the ill-chosen words of Rhodesian team manager Ossie Plaskitt, who on arrival scoffed to the press: "We are ready to participate under any flag, be it the flag of the Boy Scouts or the Red flag. But

Rhodesian track coach Peter Hodder scowls on hearing that his country cannot take part in the Munich Games despite having fielded a mixed-race team. Ironically, when Rhodesia returned to the Games—as Zimbabwe at Moscow 1980—its only athletes would be an all-white women's field hockey team.

97

The leadership of the Supreme Council for Sport in Africa (SCSA) celebrates victory after learning that Rhodesia has been voted out of the Munich Games. The ouster averted an SCSA boycott at Munich, but the group would instigate a 26-country walkout from Montreal 1976 in its effort to isolate racist African regimes.

everyone knows very well that we are Rhodesians and will always remain Rhodesians."

Aha! said the critics. The charade unmasked, the sham revealed. Out from the OAU went the call to boycott. On Sunday evening, August 20, six days before the Games' opening ceremonies, the representatives of 21 African national Olympic committees, or NOCs, drafted a resolution demanding "the exclusion of the Southern Rhodesian team from the Games of the 20th Olympiad." Otherwise, they themselves would withdraw. A reporter asked one of the members why the African NOCs had not protested earlier. "Because the Rhodesians did not open their mouths earlier," the official shot back.

In near panic over their $640 million Games—not to mention relations with black Africa—the West Germans pleaded with the

IOC to reconsider the Rhodesian invitation. IOC members convened on August 22 to discuss the matter. Led by Nigeria's brigadier H. E. O. Adefope, the black Africans spoke out hotly against Rhodesia; as might be expected, they received support from the Soviet Union's pot-stirring Konstantin Andrianov. Others sided with the Rhodesians. Australia's Hugh R. Weir and New Zealand's Lance S. Cross urged their fellow delegates not to turn the IOC into a "political whipping boy." In an emotional appeal, Avery Brundage placed his personal prestige squarely on the line: He spoke of his 60 years' service to the Olympics and pleaded that the movement not be destroyed before his eyes.

At last the secret ballots were distributed, marked, and counted. The motion, offered by Brundage, was to uphold the IOC's previous

Lord Killanin *(right)* receives a key to the Château de Vidy, the IOC's headquarters, from Lausanne mayor Georges-André Chevallaz in a ceremony ending the long era of Avery Brundage's leadership of the Olympic movement. Killanin, a 20-year veteran of the IOC, would serve one eight-year term as the organization's president.

decision to invite Rhodesia's participation in the Games. Yes or no. The vote was close but conclusive: 31 ayes, 36 nays, with 3 abstentions. Brundage had lost. Jubilation swept the African NOCs. Members flashed the Churchillian V-for-victory sign and chanted, "We're in! They're out!" Brundage was stunned, unbelieving, scarcely able to speak. Later, after that pathetic press conference, he recovered sufficiently to rage at the African boycott tactics as "a savage attack on basic principles." His fury still flared a fortnight later at the memorial service for the slain Israelis. To 80,000 people in the Olympiastadion, he announced: "The Games of the XX Olympiad have been subject to two savage attacks. We lost the Rhodesian battle to naked political blackmail." Most observers were shocked or embarrassed, or both, to hear the old man equate the carnage at Munich with a political setback. But in his own mind, perhaps

there was a sort of parity of horror: In both cases, Olympism had been attacked, and Olympism was his one sacred, inviolable passion.

He was unprepared for the new reality. The IOC had been forced to choose between Brundage's view from Olympus and Africa's Kip Keino, John Akii-Bua, and Mamo Wolde. The decision shouldn't have come as so great a surprise, considering what had happened at Mexico City and Amsterdam. Yet it seemed to, for in breaking the news by telephone to Rhodesia's premier Ian Smith, the old autocrat said in apparent puzzlement, "For the first time in 20 years, the committee failed to follow my recommendation."

Technically, Brundage may have been correct, in the ego-salving sense that no motion he had personally authored had ever been defeated. But that begged the question. In scores of big and little ways, the Olympic movement, the IOC, and Brundage himself had for years been slowly, grudgingly, but nonetheless surely ceding ground to an impure world. Unless he had lost all touch with actuality, Brundage surely knew that—just as he must have understood that his authoritarian presence and apostolic Olympism no longer commanded a majority of the IOC. Indeed, immediately after his failure on Rhodesia, he remarked to a colleague, "It is obviously time to leave the presidency."

The IOC chose Brundage's successor two days later, on August 24, at the conclusion of its 73rd Session. The president-elect was 58-year-old Michael Morris, Lord Killanin, an affable, consensus-seeking Irish peer and sportsman, who had been a committee member for 20 years, the last four as Brundage's first vice president.

The formal transfer of power took place a month after the Games, on October 12, at the IOC's Château de Vidy headquarters in Lausanne. According to protocol, Georges-André Chevallaz, Lausanne's mayor, presided at a brief ceremony that exactly duplicated the one in which Brundage had assumed command 20 years before. At that time he had been given a large symbolic key to the IOC's secretariat, signifying his guardianship of Olympism. He now handed the key to Chevallaz, saying simply, "My time expires today," and thanking Lausanne for its hospitality during his presidency. Chevallaz responded in kind and passed the key to Lord Killanin with the words, "Here is the key which is heavy. Very heavy. But we will assist you in your work by providing a haven of tranquillity, which represents the Château de Vidy."

They parted then, Killanin to commence an eight-year term at the helm of what Brundage had always regarded as his personal ship of state, Brundage to contemplate a succession of ever-emptier days.

Retirement did not sit well with the old man.

The IOC had made available a small office at the Château de Vidy; Brundage haunted the place, waiting vainly for Killanin to ask him for help. Some years before, Brundage had installed Monique Berlioux, a forceful and capable one-time swimming champion, as the IOC's director of day-to-day operations. They got along well, and now Brundage turned to the Frenchwoman for comfort. "He would ask me to keep him company," she recalled. "I would just wander through the streets with him, aimlessly, for hours on end. He would not speak much. He was totally lost. He was desperately lonely."

Brundage didn't return to the United States very often. Aside from a superb collection of Oriental art on which he had lavished a fortune, there was little to bring him back. Elizabeth, his wife of 44 years, had died in 1971 after a period of poor health and seclusion at their Santa Barbara mansion; the two were not particularly close in any event, and Brundage had long found companionship elsewhere, although the full extent of his wanderings was not well known until after his death.

So the retired chieftain remained in Europe, where he felt most comfortable, particularly among the Germans, whom he admired extravagantly. Once, in jest, he had told Willi Daume that his ambition was to marry a German princess. And in June 1973, the forlorn millionaire did precisely that. Tongues were awag at the match: the 85-year-old Brundage and 37-year-old Princess Mariann Charlotte Katharina Stefanie von Reuss, daughter of Heinrich XXXVII of Reuss, a toy-size (15 square kilometers) principality that had long since vanished into Communist East Germany.

The two had first met in 1955 when Mariann's godfather, the grand duke of Mecklenburg and an IOC member, introduced the 19-year-old girl to the famous Avery Brundage at a function in Munich. They had met again during preparations for the Munich Games, and romance blossomed at a ball in February 1973. The princess was not movie-star beautiful, but she fulfilled Brundage's vision of tall, blonde, blue-eyed, athletic, vivacious German womanhood. To the inevitable questions about age, the bridegroom twinkled: "She is very mature for her age. People say I am young for my age. I think instead of it being 85-37, it is more like 55-46."

All of which drew a derisive hoot from Frederick Ruegsegger, the Swiss investment whiz who for 23 years had served as Brundage's financial adviser and confidant. When Brundage first told Ruegsegger of his intentions, the younger man replied, "Mr. B, I have one message for you: There is no fool like an old fool." When Brundage nevertheless asked Ruegsegger to be his best man, the adviser snorted, "I will do no

such thing." Willi Daume did the honors—with Ruegsegger conspicuously absent. Missing as well was Monique Berlioux, who thought "the whole thing was a farce." With the ingrained suspicion of chamberlains everywhere, Ruegsegger was convinced that Princess Mariann had married Brundage merely for his money. She had signed a premarital agreement forswearing any claim to his estate. But that said nothing about lifestyles. The thrifty Ruegsegger declared the marriage a "disaster zone" when the princess's mother moved in with the newlyweds and the bills started piling up: $200,000 for a luxurious five-rooms-with-view in Garmisch-Partenkirchen, $500,000 each for two houses in California, $300,000 for jewelry, plus what Ruegsegger totted up as $1.27 million in travel and incidentals

Avery Brundage and his second wife, Princess Mariann von Reuss, enjoy a quiet moment after a dinner in 1973. Friends who thought the couple mismatched reported that such quiet times were rare.

Elizabeth Brundage, the first Mrs. Avery Brundage, smiles as she and her husband attend a Tokyo reception in 1964. She usually accompanied Brundage to the Games, but he often traveled to other Olympic functions without her, taking those opportunities to seek other companions.

during the first 15 months of marriage. At the peak of his wealth, before the Depression, Brundage had been worth on the order of $20 million—a fabulous sum in those days. But he had always spent lavishly, particularly on his 6,000-piece art collection, and now this new out-flow reduced his liquid worth to the point where Ruegsegger informed his boss in March 1975 that he was "bankrupt or near bankrupt."

There were other gossipy bits—among them stories of the princess as a foul-mouthed binge drinker. True or not, she seemed to make Brundage happy. Liselott Diem, widow of Brundage's old friend and Olympic adviser Carl Diem, was struck by Mariann's wifely devotion and constant attention to her husband's comfort. Other friends were surprised—and delighted— to see Brundage abandon the funereal black suits and stark white shirts that had been his garb for decades in favor of more cheerful attire. The

couple traveled frequently and in royal style—to London, the Far East, Chicago, California. "It's like someone had come to open the world to me," said Mariann happily. "He wanted to show me all the beautiful things in life."

In January 1974, Brundage underwent surgery in Garmisch for severe cataracts and the glauco-ma he had been too busy to worry about. He remained in the clinic for 46 days, his wife and her mother in the room next door. His vision returned sufficiently for them to embark on a final trip to Japan. But now his overall health began to fail. In April 1975, Brundage entered the small district hospital at Garmisch with the flu and a heavy cough. He seemed to improve and spoke of looking forward "to some peaceful years with my family." Then, at 9:40 p.m. on May 8, Avery Brundage's strong heart failed at last. The giant was dead at 87. Mariann took his body back to Chicago for burial.

Brundage willed his art collection, subsequently valued at $40 million, to the city and county of San Francisco. He bequeathed his Olympic papers and memorabilia to his alma mater, the University of Illinois; $100,000 went to the Chicago Art Institute, with the remaining $1.5 million of his estate in trust to provide $6,000 monthly for life each to Princess Mariann and Frederick Ruegsegger. But Brundage left not a penny to three others in his life, important people whom he had virtually ignored for at least a decade.

They were Lilian Wahamake Dresden, Brundage's beautiful Finnish mistress for many years, and her two sons, Avery and Gregory, whom she had borne him in California in 1951 and 1952. Though he had provided a house and a $500,000 trust fund, Brundage had never formally acknowledged his paternity; in fact, he had insisted that the father's name remain blank on the boys' birth certificates. "Showing my name," he calculated, "may cause undue and adverse publicity in view of my present marital status." The odds were good that Brundage's primary concern was less with his marriage than with his image as the sparkling Mr. Clean of Olympic sports. "In most things A. B. was a thoroughly honest and honorable man," said Ruegsegger. "But during those years in the 1950s, he was terrified that the truth might come out, that he would be forced from his IOC position." Brundage apparently worried less as time passed. "Power feeds on itself," said Ruegsegger, "and soon you believe that you can't do anything wrong."

That probably was fortunate for Brundage, considering his appetites. Lilian Dresden was not the first and far from the last of his affairs. Away from home, the president of the IOC was an indefatigable womanizer. "He would keep us at meetings at the Palace Hotel in Lausanne until midnight," said one IOC staffer. "Then he would slip out of the hotel to the Tabaris nightclub nearby to check out the merchandise."

Over the years, Brundage sent monthly checks of $500 or more to half a dozen women at a time, and he patronized a favorite parfumerie on Paris' Rue de Rivoli where he would buy the biggest bottles of the most expensive scents for members of his harem.

Even at 81, Brundage was juggling liaisons around the globe with a Bulgarian, an Austrian, a Finn, an American, a Mexican, a Swiss, and a German. Inevitably there were collisions; friends shook their heads over a screaming catfight at the Mexico City Games between the Swiss and the Mexican mistresses when a jeweler delivered a gift, presumably inscribed, to the wrong

Avery Brundage poses next to a favorite statue in his art collection, an expressionistic figure of Don Quixote. Brundage seemed to realize that fiction's famous tilter at windmills might have been his alter ego, a romantic who gave his all in the service of hopeless causes. Brundage was the last great champion of amateurism, striving with dogged futility to keep the Olympics a pure haven where sports could be practiced for love alone.

The two aspirants to the post-Brundage IOC throne, Ireland's Lord Killanin and France's Count Jean de Beaumont, enjoy a collegial moment in 1972 at the IOC Session in Munich. Beaumont, a 68-year-old millionaire industrialist, had been an IOC member since 1951 and a member of the Executive Committee since 1968—tenures similar to Killanin's. But the Irishman's more progressive attitudes made him the winning candidate.

woman. Brundage's wife, Elizabeth, learned of Lilian Dresden and her sons when a San Francisco newspaper columnist ran a juicy item about "a nat-lly known sports figure (married)" and "his beautiful blonde keptive, a recent import from a Scandinavian country." How much Elizabeth Brundage knew about the others is open to conjecture; she was a well-bred lady, and inherent wifeliness aside, she may have chosen not to suffer the public embarrassment of a separation or divorce.

Yet here was the heir to Pierre de Coubertin, the high priest of rectitude, the Calvinist saint and scourge, the towering Avery Brundage revealed as an adulterer of epic proportions. Worse, here was a man who denied his own fatherhood. "Even kings acknowledged their children born out of wedlock," said Ruegsegger, adding that Brundage apparently felt "no guilt at

all." Those who had experienced the sting of Brundage's acerbic manner and imperial one-man rule, who called him "Avery Bondage," "Mr. Misery," "Old Ironsides," were tempted to use his personal flaws as a means of discrediting the whole man. That would have perpetrated an equivalent wrong.

Whatever else he was or was not, Avery Brundage had devoted a lifetime of love and labor to the Olympic movement. He was the passionate guardian of Olympism, of the amateur ideal. He was as well the stouthearted, never-say-die fighting captain of no fewer than five Olympiads. At the leave-taking ceremony, Lausanne's mayor Chevallaz had addressed Brundage: "You have known how to steer the Olympic ship with a steady hand. During this difficult journey you have met hazards, dangers, and even pirate ships." Truly. While the pirates had shot some large

holes in Brundage's vessel, he had kept it not only afloat but sailing resolutely onward. Perhaps some other leader could have done as much in his time. But that is doubtful.

One thing I can tell you," said the IOC's sixth president shortly after his election, "I am not Avery Brundage." And Lord Killanin had suggested his future course by adding, "I try to deal with things as they are, not as we'd like them to be in a more perfect world." Killanin's admirers described him as a Renaissance man: scholar, soldier, journalist, filmmaker, author, administrator, athlete, and sportsman. Born to a noble family that traced its lineage back five centuries, the young lord had followed the usual upper-class path through Eton and Cambridge's Magdalene College to a master's degree in English and history, while boxing, rowing, and riding; presiding over the drama club; and editing the university's *Varsity* weekly newspaper. Fleet Street claimed him next—as a political columnist and Sino-Japanese war correspondent—then the British Army, in which Major Michael Morris fought through Europe from D-Day onward, winning a Member of the British Empire knighthood among other honors.

Settled in Dublin, married (his wife, Sheila, had won her own MBE in intelligence during the war), raising a family of four, Killanin produced a well-received movie, *The Rising of the Moon*, with director John Ford and assisted on a number of others, including *The Quiet Man*, a highly successful vehicle for actor John Wayne. He wrote an erudite biography of Sir Godfrey Kneller, the 17th-century portrait painter, and co-authored the authoritative *Shell Guide to Ireland*. All this from a large, self-deprecating man, genial as gin, who knew so well how to get along with people that no fewer than 15 corporations made a place for him on their managing boards.

"He's got this nice, fey, Celtic way of pleasing people," noted a colleague, "flattering them a little, saying 'That's an awfully good idea. I really think we should take that up.' People are left with the warm feeling that they've contributed something." Then there was his pipe. "He sits back in a cloud of blue smoke, waving the damn thing like a clarinet," said another colleague, "and you're too distracted to think straight."

In 1950, Killanin was named to head the All-Ireland Olympic Committee. With his softly-softly style, he dealt so deftly with the fierce political divisions in his homeland's sports establishment that within two years he was tapped for the IOC. Avery Brundage was just starting his first term as president and found a welcome foil in this diplomatic Irishman who shared his views in most matters. In the last years, however, relations cooled as Brundage grew increasingly tyrannical and Killanin parted company with him on a number of issues, particularly on the old chief's ever-rigid stand on amateurism.

At Mexico City in 1968, Brundage's longtime ally, Kenya's Sir Reginald Alexander, had urged his friend to step aside. "Avery, you're 80. You're on the top," said Alexander, "and when you're on the top there's only one way to go and that's down. Move now, and history will record you as one of the greatest." But Brundage had waved away the advice, and Alexander joined a number of other ranking IOC members in urging Killanin to seek the presidency. An initial count showed at least 30 members in favor. But the Dump Brundage movement collapsed when the Irish lord declined to run. Aside from an unwillingness to be the instrument of Brundage's downfall, Killanin said frankly that as a working man he could afford neither the time nor the $75,000 annually that Brundage spent on Olympic business. The IOC should consider granting its president an expense account. Meantime, Killanin accepted the vice presidency under Brundage and awaited developments.

By 1972 the pressures on both Killanin and

German police deliver Mohammed Abdullah, Ibrahim Badran, and Abd es Kadir el Dnawy—the surviving Arab terrorists involved in the Munich massacre—to a waiting plane at Munich's Riem airport in October 1972. A hostage exchange kept the terrorists from facing trial in Germany. They were flown to Libya. Their fate thereafter is unknown.

the IOC had reached the point where he could no longer refuse nomination. With Brundage retiring, his only competitor was France's Count Jean de Beaumont, a longtime power in the IOC who openly lobbied for the job. But many members regarded the opinionated Beaumont as too like the outgoing president in personality. "We felt," confessed one member, "that 20 years of Brundage had been ample." Killanin won election on the first ballot, 39-29, with heavy support from the Communist bloc and from the Africans.

Brundage's own ballot was blank. "We need a leader, and Michael isn't a leader," he remarked sourly to Willi Daume. A number of others tended to regard Killanin as something of an easygoing lightweight, his career perhaps more haphazard than Renaissance. The U.S. Olympic Committee's William E. Simon, a notable type A personality and future U.S. secretary of the treasury, was particularly biting in his appraisal. "Explaining something sensible to Lord Killanin is akin to explaining something to a cauliflower," he once snapped. "The advantage of the cauliflower is that if all else fails, you can always cover it with melted cheese and eat it."

Amusing, but an opinion not shared by most of Killanin's colleagues, who saw no lack of intelligence or purpose in the new president's slow, careful, smooth, and healing ways. Quite the contrary. The leadership they sought—and he offered—was to nudge, ever so gently, the Olympic movement into the final quarter of the 20th century, to let it, like water, gradually find its own level. The burdensome problems that Avery Brundage had grappled with—

drugs, amateurism, politics and national ambitions, money and giantism—would not change during Killanin's presidency; only the responses would.

The IOC's new chief had been in office scarcely a fortnight when the Palestinians staged a dramatic epilogue to the Munich massacre. This time there was nothing for the IOC to do or not do; it played no role in the developments. Like the rest of the world, Killanin and his colleagues could only look on in amazement—and emotional outrage.

The 11 Israeli martyrs had been laid to rest in Jerusalem, and the bodies of the five dead Black September terrorists had been released to the Libyans for the ritual heroes' funeral. But that didn't quite end matters. The three surviving terrorists remained in Bavarian jails, giving lengthy interviews and preparing to make a circus of German jurisprudence when they came to trial.

They never did. Their deliverance arrived at 7:30 a.m. on Sunday, October 29, when two gunmen skyjacked a Lufthansa 727 on its way from Damascus to Frankfurt. The air pirates said they were Black Septembrists. They would, they promised, blow the plane, themselves, and 18 other occupants out of the sky unless their comrades were released immediately. The Bavarian authorities swiftly agreed. Accompanied by Lufthansa chairman Herbert Culmann and a handful of cops, the three terrorists were loaded onto a second Lufthansa plane and flown to Zagreb, Yugoslavia. There the joyful reunion took place, after which the 727 flew on to Libya, where the plane, passengers, and crew were finally set free.

Suspicion instantly fell on the Bavarians for a put-up deal. Aside from the propaganda bonanza that a trial would have afforded the Palestinians,

the whole hideous Munich affair and bungled rescue would have been dragged out again, with accusing fingers pointing everywhere. Even had the Germans been willing to endure that, there was also the threat of further terrorism. Those in the know whispered that Israel's Mossad secret service had warned of a Black September operation against Lufthansa in the very near future. Nevertheless, airline security had not been increased. Why? Because, went the stories, Black September had advised the Germans that if the rescue failed, it would trigger a massive campaign of bombing, kidnapping, and murder against Lufthansa the world over. And so a consensus was quickly reached: best to accept the moral wrong of releasing the killers and wipe the slate clean.

Israel, which scorned terrorists as a matter of national honor, put enough stock in the scenario to recall its ambassador for "consultations." Relations with Bonn turned frigid but quickly warmed again, and the following June when

A Denver 1976 promotional poster invites fans to a winter festival that would never happen. Denver organizers hoped to parlay America's bicentennial enthusiasm into a successful Winter Games, but faulty planning undermined the effort. Denver remains the only city ever to return an Olympic bid during peacetime.

Chancellor Willy Brandt visited Israel he was greeted cordially. The Israelis couldn't believe that Brandt, whom they knew as a friend, could possibly have been a party to any such deal. Whatever happened—if anything had—must have been at the local level. That conclusion, the Israelis agreed, would have to be good enough.

It is not recorded how either Brundage or Killanin reacted to this ugly postscript. Brundage, of course, would have been livid with indignation, Killanin appalled, too. But the Irishman likely would have understood the practicalities involved. He himself was already moving delicately on a number of fronts to bring a new pragmatism to the Olympic movement.

Of immediate concern to the IOC's president was the secretariat, the permanent headquarters staff in Lausanne that kept the records and attended to the needs of the world's most complex sports establishment. In her four years with Brundage, Monique Berlioux had not only proved an efficient administrator but had managed to accumulate considerable decision-making power. Killanin balked at that, in no small measure because he found the lady somewhat authoritarian, distressingly in the Brundage mold. He thought at first of replacing Berlioux as director. Typically, he decided instead to work with her—and later counted himself fortunate.

In his gentlemanly fashion, Killanin made clear what their relationship was to be: that of a top civil servant to a minister—close, but no question about who was boss. By and large, Berlioux accepted the boundaries. Whatever her secret feelings, she managed the Château de Vidy operation smoothly and loyally, freeing Killanin and his colleagues to deal with the large issues.

The first of these was the calamitous state of preparations for the 12th Winter Games, scheduled for 1976. At Amsterdam in 1970, the IOC had awarded the festival to Denver over disappointed bidders from Tampere, Finland; Sion, Switzerland; and Vancouver, Canada. Killanin recalled "the confidence and panache with which the Denver delegation made their original bid for the Games." In their slick presentation—bolstered by junkets to Mexico, Yugoslavia, Spain, and Switzerland—the Denverites wowed the IOC with a two-volume book and a 30-minute movie, everything in color, describing the beauties and virtues of their Rocky Mountain city.

For starters, said the promoters, something like 80 percent of the facilities already existed within reach of athletes and visitors. The Denverites assured the IOC that there would be no problem building whatever else was necessary: bobsled and luge runs, ski-jump hills, a new 5,000-seat speed-skating rink, a 20,000-seat ice hockey and figure-skating arena. Athletes, officials, and press could easily be accommodated at the University of Denver. Funds would come pouring in from local, state, and federal sources, as well as from private donors. After all, the conclusion of the XX Olympiad would not only salute Colorado's first century of statehood but would help celebrate the nation's bicentennial as well.

The grand scheme started coming apart as soon as the organizing committee returned home. Planning for something so big and important had to affect large numbers of citizens. Yet the organizing committee was composed exclusively of members of Denver's white, male power elite, most of them wealthy businessmen who stood to profit in one way or another. Environmentalists, minorities, neighborhood and civic activist groups protested that no one had consulted them about anything. When the committee dismissed the complainers as the malcontent 2 percent that never likes anything, they formed a coalition to fight.

The antis soon found plenty to shoot at. The bountiful snow that made Colorado a winter sports paradise fell mostly on the western side of the Continental Divide, at places like Vail and Steamboat Springs. Denver, alas, lay on the eastern slope: not much snow, an average February high of 45 degrees, and folks picking wildflowers on 60-degree days.

Nevertheless, the organizers had sited the ski-jumping and Nordic events at Evergreen, an aptly named suburb 20 miles west of Denver. "How can you make and hold snow for a 50-kilometer cross-country course in our kind of climate?" marveled Vance Dittman, chairman of Evergreen's determinedly opposed POME—for Protect Our Mountain Environment. No problem, insisted the organizers: A mere 17 million gallons of snow-making water each day would cover the jumps and trails nicely—as long as all events ended before 10 a.m., when it got warm.

The Evergreen people were further amazed, and incensed, when they saw maps showing the Nordic courses winding through their backyards, even through an elementary-school playground. "Some people would have to let us put gaps in their fences," confessed committee vice president Norman Brown. And Evergreen would have to stand still for bulldozers

Election results insure that the party never gets started at headquarters for Coloradans for '76, a lobbying group supporting the ballot initiative to use state funds to help finance the Winter Games. On November 7, 1972, state voters resoundingly rejected the measure, effectively killing Denver's chance to be host.

carving out jump hills, rerouting a residential road, and laying a concrete outrun across their town's beautiful Bear Creek. No way.

Then there was Mt. Sniktau, which the organizers chose as the prime site for Alpine skiing. The place was 50 miles west of Denver but still on the wrong side of the Rockies. Sniktau featured a lack of snow, high winds, and craggy slopes that only a rock climber could love. "If you and I were going to build ourselves a ski

the nod on condition that all sites would be within 45 minutes of the Olympic Village at the University of Denver. Technology to the fore: Special aircraft would fly officials, press, and athletes to and from the events. Spectators would be on their own.

What eventually undid this silliness was money. In their initial presentation to the IOC, the Denverites had put a figure of $14 million on staging the Winter Games. By ear-

The brochures carried by Innsbruck mayor Alois Lugger and IOC president Lord Killanin (left) show that the IOC reached a decision on a replacement for Denver during the 1973 IOC Executive Committee meeting at Lausanne. Innsbruck won the troubled 1976 Winter Games over two other former host cities—Chamonix and Lake Placid—and a third bidder, Tammerfors, Finland.

area, we wouldn't put it at Sniktau," said Pete Wingle, a U.S. Forest Service officer, noting that Sniktau also lacked the base terrain for spectators and parking.

Understanding finally dawned. The promoters shifted the Alpine events to Vail, 110 miles away, and the Nordic competitions to Steamboat Springs, 165 miles from Denver. Now there was a different headache; the IOC had given Denver

ly 1972, the budget had ballooned to either $50 million or $100 million, depending on who was counting. One major expense for little long-term benefit would be the construction of a multimillion-dollar bobsled run. When the problem at last was identified, the Denver committee suggested shifting the bobsled events 2,000 miles away, to Lake Placid, New York, where a run already existed. The

IOC firmly said no, and the Denverites then argued successfully to have the bobs removed from the program.

The saving helped only a little. In its budget, the committee figured TV revenues of $10 million, forgetting that it would cost considerably more just to provide facilities for the networks. The federal government was down for $19 million, but the U.S. Congress put off any funding until Colorado had defined its own position. By November 1972, the committee had spent $1.1 million of Colorado public funds and had budgeted another $5 million as the state's share.

The anti-Olympic coalition drew a careful bead. Collecting nearly 90,000 signatures, it put a referendum question on the November election ballot: Did the citizens of Denver and Colorado want to spend any more of their tax dollars on these Olympics? Politicians, business leaders, and Denver's two daily newspapers mounted a massive pro-Olympics campaign. But the election left no room for doubt. By 59.4 percent to 40.6 percent, Coloradans rejected further public expenditure. The Denver Winter Games were dead.

"I didn't vote against the Olympic Games," a citizen told *Colorado* magazine. "I voted against the politicians and arrogant organizers; against their smugness, secrecy, and bungling and against the promoters and hucksters who were jumping in for a fast buck."

Shortly after the vote, a telegram arrived at the Château de Vidy. It was from the Denver Olympic Organizing Committee. Without public funds, the committee had no choice but to withdraw its bid. All things considered, the IOC's Killanin and his colleagues might have breathed a large sigh of relief. If so, they were too polite to make it public. Instead, they buckled down to the job of finding a substitute. Salt Lake City offered to step into the breach but soon withdrew in the face of funding uncertainties. Then Chamonix, site of the 1924 Winter

Games, and Lake Placid, which had hosted in 1932, issued bids, as did Tammerfors, Finland. Innsbruck, 1964's host, also volunteered for the rescue. Innsbruck, which had staged a successful festival despite atrocious weather, had better facilities and thus got the nod. As with Munich, these Games would go on.

At the close of Lord Killanin's first year in office, a British journalist named Doug Gardner delivered himself of the novel notion that the IOC's president had "reversed the usual procedure and begun his new job with a year's sabbatical." Gardner was not being snide; he explained approvingly that Killanin had spent much time visiting important areas of the future Olympic world, particularly South America, which had never held a Games, and the Soviet Union, which hoped for Moscow in 1980.

Now in November 1973, Killanin had another bit of travel on his agenda—to the Bulgarian Black Sea resort of Varna, where he would preside over the first Olympic Congress in 43 years (Brundage had never held them because he didn't like them). There, the IOC would seek to repair the strained relations with its partners in sport, the 127 national Olympic committees and the 23 rule-making international federations.

Under Brundage, the IOC had regarded these important organizations as a collection of unruly adolescent relatives, to be suffered but definitely kept in their place. Eventually, the NOCs and the IFs rebelled against their elders. They organized. In 1967, the IFs established a General Association of International Federations (GAIF) to speak with a single voice loud enough for the IOC to hear. A year later, the NOCs founded their own Permanent General Assembly (PGA) for the same reason. The time had surely come not only for fence mending but for what Killanin called "a tripartite relationship" in which the three Olympic bodies worked together in a spirit of cooperation. The IOC must remain paramount, insisted Killanin,

Visitors to Bulgaria's Sports Palace take part in the 10th Olympic Congress at Varna, the first IOC Congress in 43 years. Lord Killanin used the conclave to push for greater tolerance of quasi-professionalism among Olympic athletes—a complete departure from Avery Brundage's hard-line insistence on pure amateurism.

but he added delicately, that it should not "be the club which it might have been many years ago."

The Varna Congress was a first step in Killanin's new direction. More than 300 delegates from the IOC, the NOCs, and the IFs met for a week in the resort's spectacular, glass-walled Sports Palace. Some delegates worried that the IOC would come in for sharp criticism, especially from the Third World and Communist bloc, which resented the primacy of the Western Europeans and Americans. But that didn't happen: The Soviets were on their best behavior, amiably intent on using the

Congress to launch their campaign for the 1980 Games in Moscow.

The working sessions proceeded without acrimony—and without much give-and-take, either. Almost to a man, the speakers read from prepared texts; some of them tended to drone, leading a Canadian to sigh, "It's like going to church every day to hear 24 sermons." Even so, a number of touchy items were offered for collective thought. In his speech, Killanin discussed the possibility of regionalizing Games by spreading the venues over a wide area; of reducing the opening-day pomp and ceremony—and thus the

nationalism; of eliminating certain team sports that held world championships of their own; of enlisting women to serve on the IOC; of establishing a system of IOC aid to athletes, particularly from smaller, less affluent nations; and most important, of finally coming to grips with the ever-nettlesome question of amateurism.

At the heart of the matter stood Rule 26 of the Olympic Charter, in force without substantial change since 1925. Under this regulation, only pure amateurs who observed "both spiritually and ethically the traditional Olympic ideals" need aspire to the Games.

An athlete who had ever received pay for any sport whatsoever, as either a player or a coach, was barred from Olympic competition. In numerous sections and subsections, Rule 26 specifically forbade Olympians from converting prizes into cash, from lending their names to commercial enterprises, from capitalizing on their athletic fame to secure jobs or promotions. They couldn't train at special camps for more than four weeks in any given year, couldn't accept expense money for more than 30 days a year, couldn't accept scholarships based solely on athletic ability. While all this reflected a sort of ultimate Olympism, the rule was unenforceable in a modern world of increasingly blurred distinctions. It was also an ideal long and widely ignored.

Avery Brundage had railed to the end against any dilution of the ideal. But Killanin, the pragmatist, understood the real world very well. He argued that Rule 26 forced athletes to lie about

their status under pressure from their medal-hungry NOCs. Moreover, since both the NOCs and the IFs were involved in verifying an athlete's amateur status, they, too, were forced to lie. Nothing could be more destructive—to the individuals, to the organizations, to the Games, to sport. And while Killanin made it clear that he did not believe in a professional Olympics, the IOC had to promulgate rules that could be obeyed. "We obviously have to be more rational about eligibility," he said.

Brundage had forestalled any change during his reign. But in 1974, at the IOC's 75th Session in Vienna, Rule 26 was shortened, streamlined, and liberalized to a considerable degree. Instead of the lengthy and complex series of sections and subsections, the entire rule now consisted of two sentences: Athletes must adhere to the rules of the IOC as well as to those of the international federations. And they must not have received any financial or material benefits from sport except as permitted in the bylaws.

The sacred word "amateur" no longer appeared either in Rule 26 or in the accompanying bylaws that dealt with specifics. Interpretations differed so widely that the term had lost meaning except in the broadest sense. Was the Soviet shot-putter who trained month after month at a state-run camp any less of an amateur than the American high jumper with a college track scholarship? A majority of Killanin's IOC thought not, and it regularized both practices.

A poster for the 1975 IOC Session at Lausanne, Switzerland

Out-and-out professionals still were ineligible. However, athletes could accept prizes at the discretion of their NOCs and federations, and they could lend themselves to commercial promotions favored by the NOCs and national federations so long as they didn't profit directly; the money would go to the parent organizations, which then would defray their transport, food and lodging, equipment, insurance, medical care, and such, and provide reasonable pocket money. ("Reasonable" was, of course, a most elastic concept.)

Among the absurdities of the old rule was the 30- to 60-day limit imposed on "broken time" compensation—money paid to make up for an athlete's time away from a regular job while training for the Olympics. Everyone knew that a world-class athlete had to spend at least 25 hours a week for months on end preparing for the Games. Killanin had long felt that competitors should be totally reimbursed for whatever income they lost in training. But Brundage, the millionaire, was aghast and wrote his vice presidents disapprovingly that an athlete receiving such aid "may be better off than when he is working." Charter changes in 1974 removed the time limit on the compensatory payments. An athlete couldn't wind up with more money than the job paid. But now at least men and women could train properly without fear of pauperizing themselves for the honor of the Olympics.

Killanin hadn't won all the concessions he felt necessary and desirable. He argued unsuccessfully that a professional in one sport shouldn't be barred from competing as an amateur in a different sport. "I can't see any objection for a stable boy or someone who rides horses for a living being an Olympic boxer," he said. The IOC wasn't quite ready for that. Nevertheless, the man who had promised "changes but no sweeping reforms" had started the Olympic movement down the road to the greatest reform in its existence.

There remained the issue of Rhodesia. Though the Rhodesians had been sent home from Munich 1972, the country still remained a member of the Olympic family. That ended in 1975 at the IOC's 76th Session in Lausanne. By then, black Africa's campaign to eject Rhodesia altogether had reached such intensity that the IOC had sent over a three-man Commission of Enquiry. The investigators had found that racial discrimination did exist in private clubs and in government-run lower schools. However, the bias ended at university level, and in any case, Rhodesia's NOC was not a party to prejudice. Rather, it had insisted on racial equality in all dealings with the national sports federations.

In selecting athletes for the Games, the committee had upheld the Olympic Charter.

The black Africans were not impressed. At Lausanne, their nations, including all the newly arrived powers in track, formally petitioned the IOC to banish Rhodesia's NOC from the Olympic movement. Their spokesmen repeated the charges of racial inequity at all levels of Rhodesian sports; the Rhodesians denied their NOC's involvement point by point, citing the Commission of Enquiry.

At the close of debate, Killanin called for a secret ballot. Unspoken but on everyone's mind was the threat of a boycott of Montreal 1976. The risk translated into votes. When the ballots were counted, Rhodesia's Olympic committee had been dismissed, 41-26, from the IOC. It wouldn't return until 1980, when majority rule swept a black government to power in the land now called Zimbabwe.

Black Africa's triumph was complete. But the politics of boycott would not end there. The genie, so powerful, so simple to summon, was to become a part of the Olympic experience—breathing blight on the Games of Montreal, of Moscow, of Los Angeles.

SCSA president Abraham Ordia *(center)*, **flanked by vice president John Kasonka** *(left)* **and Jean-Claude Ganga, announces the IOC's decision to expel Rhodesia from the Olympic movement.**

TYROLEAN SIMPLICITY

In keeping with their theme "the Simple Games," the organizers of the Olympic Winter Games at Innsbruck in 1976 began their festival with a minimum of fuss. There was no special stadium for the opening ceremony, as the French had built for Grenoble 1968, no expensive pageantry, as the Japanese had staged for Sapporo 1972. Rather, the Austrians held the opening rites in an open amphitheater beneath the Bergisel ski hill, the site for the large hill jumping competition. About 30,000 spectators gathered for the low-key celebration.

It was a mild Tyrolean morning on February 4 that greeted some 1,500 athletes and officials from 37 countries marching in the Parade of Nations. Instead of walking onto a stadium floor, athletes descended stairs into the amphitheater. Once they were settled, Lord Killanin made his first welcoming speech at a Games as IOC president. Then Killanin handed the microphone to Austrian president Rudolf Kirchschläger, who was ready to declare the Games open. But the microphone didn't work. An amused Kirchschläger handled the foul-up gracefully, remarking—once he could be heard—that Simple Games was more than just a slogan.

Christl Haas and Josef Feistmantl, Austrian gold medalists from 1964, ignited the Olympic flame in two cauldrons, one for the 1964 Innsbruck Games and one for 1976.

The ceremony came to a close with groups of Tyrolean dancers whirling into the stadium doing a routine with hoops. Then the athletes quietly filed out.

Simple and charming, just as the hosts had wanted.

INTO THE LIGHT

INNSBRUCK 1976

Being such a thoroughly nice young man, Franz Klammer always tried to oblige the press and his legion of fans. When they asked, as they always did, what made him such a sensational skier, he would explain that he was an Austrian farm boy, therefore blessed with strength and stamina, also that he wanted badly to excel in the downhill, that crown jewel of Alpine events. Entirely honest and true. Yet the slopes were aswarm with well-muscled young men ardent for victory. What set Klammer apart from the world was his style. And that was something no one—least of all the 22-year-old champion himself—could truly explain.

Klammer's approach to the downhill defied rationality. To some it seemed suicidal, like a man launching himself into the void and expecting to fly. On each run he faced a precipitous, winding, often icy track designed to drop perhaps 1,000 meters along its 3,000-meter length. It allowed speeds that topped 80 miles an hour; one slip

could mean catastrophe—or at least defeat in a sport where split seconds separate victor from vanquished. The thing demanded respect, a modicum of caution.

Klammer was not unaware of that. "You know what a car looks like if it hits a wall at that speed," he said soberly. Yet on the course he surrendered to passion. Down the slopes he hurtled, flat out and wonderfully wild, screaming into the schusses, careering around the bends, barreling over the bumps, forever on the brink of disaster, making one miraculous recovery after another. It was raw, not very elegant, frightfully dangerous. But it was swift, and when Klammer remained upright, which was almost always, scarcely anybody could touch him.

It went without saying that Franz had been on skis since childhood, testing the slopes around Mooswald, a dot of a village near the Yugoslavian border. Yet he had not competed seriously until his teens—and then showed such stunning promise that he was whisked

Austria's Franz Klammer, Olympic Gold Medalist, Innsbruck 1976

THE GAMES AT A GLANCE

	FEBRUARY 4	FEBRUARY 5	FEBRUARY 6	FEBRUARY 7	FEBRUARY 8	FEBRUARY 9	FEBRUARY 10	FEBRUARY 11	FEBRUARY 12	FEBRUARY 13	FEBRUARY 14	FEBRUARY 15
OPENING CEREMONY	■											
ALPINE SKIING		■			■	■	■	■		■	■	
BIATHLON			■							■		
BOBSLED				■	■						■	■
FIGURE SKATING		■	■		■	■	■	■	■	■		■
HOCKEY				■	■	■	■	■	■	■	■	
LUGE		■	■	■	■			■				
NORDIC SKIING			■		■	■	■	■		■		
SKI JUMPING								■				■
SPEED SKATING		■	■	■	■		■	■	■	■	■	
CLOSING CEREMONY												■

off to a special school where the mornings were spent in study and the afternoons in training. Alpine skiing, after all, put the oompah-pah in the Austrian economy—millions of winter visitors; 1,900,000 pairs of skis exported annually—and a youngster with speed found no lack of support.

Klammer's coaches soon realized that he would never be a technician: To watch the kid in headlong descent was to flirt with cardiac arrest. Yet he won so often that in 1972, at the age of 18, he was named to the Austrian national team. It took Klammer barely a year to win his first big-time downhill in competition for the World Cup, Alpine skiing's holy grail. That victory lit off the rocket. Within another two years he had established a record unparalleled in the annals of the event.

Klammer couldn't bring home the cup itself; that laurel belonged to the perfectly rounded skiers who excelled in the slalom and giant slalom as well as the downhill. No matter: The young Austrian cared little for the twisty-turny events. But in the downhill during the winter of 1974-75, the daredevil from Mooswald won eight of the nine World Cup races, every one of them in course-record time, by far surpassing the five 1967 triumphs of France's famed Jean-Claude Killy.

All Austria worshiped its new national hero. On some days the postman delivered close to 500 adoring letters and postcards. When the 1975-76 season rolled around, Klammer had his fans hoarse-throated all over again. By the end of January, he had whooshed to victory in four of the seven World Cup downhills held thus far. Now, at the beginning of February, it was time for him to do his countrymen proud in the supreme competition of them all—the 12th Olympic Winter Games at Innsbruck.

Austrians did not just expect Klammer to carry off the honors in the Olympic downhill, they demanded it. No one had forgotten how IOC president Avery Brundage had made a scapegoat of Austria's Karl Schranz at the 1972 Sapporo Winter Games. Charging professionalism in a sport of professionals, Brundage's IOC had banned the great Schranz from Alpine competition, depriving him—and Austria—of virtually certain glory. A year later, Lord Killanin, an inveterate peacemaker and the IOC's new president, may have favored Innsbruck's bid for the 1976 Winter Games partly as recompense for the Schranz debacle. Yet the wrong still rankled, and it was up to Franz Klammer to put it right.

The pressures on Innsbruck were no less fierce. Though the small Tyrolean resort city had staged highly successful Winter Games in 1964, numerous woes had afflicted the Olympic movement in the dozen years since. The peaceable Elysian Fields of Pierre de Coubertin were now a battleground for politicians, as the massacre at Munich had shown. The specter of an encore lurked in every mind. Added to that ghastly prospect was a history of runaway costs that threatened to destroy the Winter Games. The Japanese had spent nearly $700 million on Sapporo 1972. Pocket money for them, maybe. Yet hardly anybody else was wealthy enough to throw the national debt at 12 days of winter sport, only to demolish many of the venues immediately after.

At Innsbruck, though, a tough-minded organizing committee met the threat of terrorism head-on—and pulled an equally firm rein on expenses. Unlike the Munich organizers, Dr. Fred Sinowatz and his Innsbruck colleagues worried little about the effect of heavy security on the gemütlich joviality so desirable for the Olympics.

Instead, they turned the problem over to professionals with instructions to do it right. No fewer than 5,000 federal, provincial, and local police patrolled the town and its Olympic sites. The Olympic Village, so wide open at Munich, was surrounded by a 10-foot-high chain-link fence, topped with barbed wire and electrified throughout; the slightest touch by an intruder would set off jangling alarms at the guard posts. Inside the compound itself, more than 200 well-armed officers, plus nine attack dogs, watched over the athletes, coaches, and officials. No one entered without scrutiny. Journalists seeking stories were made to surrender their credentials for a special admittance badge, and even then they

Snow-topped Alps and rustic chalets accentuate the Tyrolean flavor of the Innsbruck Games. Below the picturesque Wetterstein and Karwendel Mountains is the town of Seefeld, the locale for the Nordic skiing events.

Uzi-toting guards and wire fences *(right)* were unfortunate innovations at the Innsbruck Olympic Village, where the athletes' security was top priority in the first Games following the Munich massacre. The police presence kept problems to a minimum, but it didn't inhibit the fun of crowds *(below)* flooding the narrow medieval Innsbruck streets for the 12 days of the Winter Games.

couldn't visit the living quarters; all interviews had to be conducted in the cafeterias.

Some athletes were shocked. "It looks like a POW camp," groaned Italian figure skater Susan Driano. Still, it took more than a guard demanding "Show me your pass" to repress so many happy, healthy, young people, and their normal ebullience rocked the Village beyond the gates. All in all, everyone lived through the security. The police protecting the 700-year-old town and its visitors did their best to remain inconspicuous; they succeeded well enough to earn an accolade from the Associated Press's Will Grimsley, who had expected a "Gestapo Olympics." "Your police were all magnificent, a part of the scenery, never exaggerating, never discourteous, but reliable and ever-present," he wrote the enormously pleased organizing committee.

Sinowatz, who would become Austria's chancellor in 1983, also merited a salute for the way he and his people managed the citizens' schillings. The finale of the XX Olympiad, the organizers declared, would see a return to "simple Games." Everybody had heard that before—about Grenoble, where the tab reached $250 million, about Munich, which wound up costing $640 million. The Innsbruckers meant it, and they did it.

Having hosted the Ninth Winter Games in 1964, Innsbruck benefited from having much of the necessary infrastructure still in place. Moreover, quite a few of the people who already knew how to stage a sports spectacular were willing to serve again and deal with the expected crush of 1.5 million visitors.

Nevertheless, much remained to be done. The Alpine runs at Patscherkofel and Axamer Lizum and the Nordic cross-country courses at Seefeld had lain derelict for 12 years; a force of 3,000 Austrian Army troopers turned to and contributed half a million man-hours clearing away trees and other debris, improving gradients, putting up safety nets, blasting out better areas for spectators and parking. The 60,000-seat U-shaped Olympic

WHERE THE GAMES WERE PLAYED

Olympic Ice Stadium

Bergisel Ski Jump

Igls Bobsled and Luge Run

SCHAUFELSPITZE
3333m

STUBAIER WILDSPITZE
3340m

DOWNHILL
Women's

GLUNGEZER 2677m

NOCKSPITZ
2406m

GIANT SLALOM
Men's

HOADL
2343m

PATSHERKOFEL
2247m

BIRGITZKOPFL
2098m

GIANT SLALOM
Women's

DOWNHILL
Men's

IGLS ICE RUN
Bobsled
Luge

Alternate
Course

AXAMER LIZUM

METTERER ALM

SLALOM
Men's
Women's

GLUNGEZER

IGLS

BERGISEL STADIUM
Opening Ceremony
Ski Jumping (Large Hill)
Closing Ceremony

SEEFELD
Ski Jumping (Small Hill)

OLYMPIC ICE STADIUM
Figure Skating
Hockey

SEEFELD
Biathlon

REITH

SOLSTIN

OLYMPIC VILLAGE

INNSBRUCK

SEEFELD

SEEFELD
Biathlon
Nordic Skiing

SPEED SKATING OVAL
Speed Skating

LEUTASCH

SEEGRUBE
1905m

HAFLEKAR
2334m

SEEGRUBE

stadium was still suitable for the opening ceremony. Also serviceable were the two skating venues—an indoor rink where 13,000 spectators could watch figure skating and ice hockey, and a 10,000-seat outdoor area for speed skating—although the speed-skating facility needed a new 400-meter oval. The 70-meter ski jump required attention, and because of a rules change, a brand new 90-meter hill had to be built. The old luge and bobsled runs were demolished and a new, dual-purpose facility was built, complete with equipment to make artificial ice—a hedge against the vagaries of weather.

Finally, since 1964's Olympic Village was now occupied by apartment dwellers, a new Village with quarters and other amenities for 2,500 athletes and coaches went up a short distance away from the old one. It cost around $23 million and with other expenditures brought the total tab for Innsbruck to $85.6 million, including such municipal improvements as new roads and another bridge over the river Inn. That was modest enough, actually a triumph of shrewd planning and thrifty execution. Moreover, everything at Innsbruck would find continuing use after the Winter Games, even the increasingly popular luge run. There would be, as committee spokesman Bertl Neumann put it, "no Olympic ruins at Innsbruck."

As 1976 arrived, the great worry was weather.

Ordinarily, Innsbruck could count on 20 inches of February snow, but in 1964 so little had fallen that the army had had to rush an emergency supply from the nearby Brenner Pass. This year an extraordinarily warm, dry early January rekindled the fears—and the ever-helpful army again trucked in uncounted tons of snow for the runs at Patscherkofel, Axamer Lizum, and Seefeld. Then the heavens opened wide; glorious snow came blanketing down, temperatures dropped, and all was well.

At 2:30 on the crisp, sunny afternoon of February 4, trumpets sounded a fanfare. Drums rolled. Helicopters aloft unfurled the Austrian, Tyrolean, and Olympic flags. Then came the athletes, filing into the ski-jump amphitheater at Bergisel. Marching last as always, the host country's contingent passed in review, the Austrians glittering in golden ski suits as they followed their flagbearer, Franz Klammer. At the end of the usual welcome ceremonies, bobsledder Werner Deller-Karth stepped forward to take the Olympic oath on behalf of the contestants. There was music and folk dancing, and as the athletes departed, a soft pealing of bells floated up from Innsbruck.

The next day, in midafternoon, Franz Klammer stood waiting his turn near the start of the Patscherkofel downhill, 3,145 meters of high-speed bends and dives falling 870 meters to the finish. The scenery was transfixing: velvety evergreens rolling across the valley of the Inn to the ancient town with its onion-domed churches and the snowy crags of the Limestone

SECOND TIME AROUND

The two cauldrons awaiting torch relay runners at Innsbruck 1976 were a reminder that this was the second Winter Games at Austria's Tyrolean capital. The first celebration had come 12 years earlier and was noteworthy as the first Winter Games to start its torch relay at Olympia, Greece. Relays for previous Winter Games had originated at Telemark, Norway, the presumptive birthplace of skiing, or in the case of Cortina d'Ampezzo 1956, at Rome, for its association with the ancient world. Innsbruck 1976 continued the Olympia tradition with a lighting ceremony that took place on January 30, 1976. The fire then went by plane from Greece to the Austrian capital of Vienna. A day later it was separated into two relays to Innsbruck. One covered a northern route of 537.5 miles, the other a southern trek of 450.5 miles.

The divergent routes converged at Innsbruck on February 1. A ceremony reunited the two flames, which burned at an Innsbruck promenade for three days before being carried into the opening ceremony. There, at the Bergisel ski-jump stadium (*left*), Josef Feistmantl, a luge champion from 1964, ignited the 1976 cauldron; Christl Haas, the 1964 downhill champion, lighted the one from 1964.

Alps in the distance. The young man averted his eyes. "You can't let yourself look at what is below," he said. "It might soften you with its beauty. Instead you must think only of the course—and the darkness of the challenge." Poetic. And somber. The Alpine downhill was among the first events of the Winter Games, and the challenge for Austria's ace loomed large.

Klammer had been skiing superbly. Yet so had his competition, in particular Switzerland's defending Olympic champion Bernhard Russi. The two men could not have been more dissimilar;

where Klammer was all fire and instinct, the 27-year-old Russi projected intellect—cool, scholarly, technical, charting every move with coaches, his form a textbook study. The year before, Klammer had defeated Russi by 0.49 of a second in a World Cup downhill at Innsbruck; his time was a course record 1:55.78. But in the pre-Olympic warm-ups, Russi had matched Klammer run for run. Now in the actual competition, before a thunderstruck crowd of 60,000 and half a billion television viewers worldwide—Russi had skied the perfect race. He looked unbeatable.

Under the rules, skiers drew lots for starting position and went down the Patscherkofel at one-minute intervals. Russi had drawn the third slot, while Klammer would be 15th—and fighting an icy, rutted course. Down the fresh run flashed Russi, every line exactly right, schussing between the red finish flags in an astonishing 1:46.06. True, the course had been doctored a little for added speed, but this run was almost 10 seconds faster than Klammer's 1975 record.

One after another, 13 skiers failed even to come close. Then it was time for No. 15. The figure in the old yellow ski suit pushed off with a mighty thrust of poles and within a few meters was streaking recklessly downhill, speed passing 60 miles per hour. Too fast. A course marker came rushing up. Klammer nearly missed it, wrenching himself back on track, losing precious time. Toni Sailer, the renowned Austrian Olympian turned coach, closed his eyes. "This is the end of the gold," he groaned to himself.

At the first 1,000-meter checkpoint, Klammer was 0.02 of a second behind Russi's time. On he came, skis chattering over the ice, bouncing into the air so often it seemed that he must crash. He wasn't gaining; he was falling further behind—by 0.19 of a second at the next 1,000-meter checkpoint.

The crowd's urging grew almost physical in its dimension, an avalanche of sound roaring down the mountain with his passing. At the notorious

Poised at the starting gate, Franz Klammer constitutes Austria's last hope for the downhill championship. Despite Klammer's efforts, Toni Sailer, coach of the Austrian ski team and a former triple gold medalist, resigned his post at the end of the Innsbruck Games because of the poor performance of the Austrian skiers.

Bear's Neck turn, spectators clinging to the snow fence had pulled it backward 45 degrees. Klammer laid his outside ski within a millimeter of the fence edge and leaned in over the slats, almost brushing the crowd and shooting through the curve virtually on a straight line. "I heard a shout or a scream from a lady. I thought I was hitting her with a pole," he later recalled. One of the spectators had a radar gun: Russi had gone into the Bear's Neck at 73 miles an hour and exited at 69; Klammer hit it at 70 and came out at 75. He had the momentum now—and 12 seconds later ripped across the finish at something like 90 miles per hour.

The crowd was shrieking "Franzi! Franzi!" when the scoreboard lit up: 1:45.73. He had done it, achieved the near impossible, by 0.33 of a second.

Franz Klammer's victory that February afternoon was the fastest downhill in Olympic history. The experts gave it more than that. Some declared it one of the defining moments of Olympic sport, what the Games were all about.

The Austrians didn't need to be told how great their hero's exploit had been. The entire country came aflutter in white and red flags. "KLAMMER!" screamed the headlines, and Chancellor Bruno Kreisky emotionally told the champion: "You have saved the Games for us." As for Klammer himself, as nice and uncomplicated as always, he quietly confessed: "A big stone has dropped from my heart. The whole nation trusted me and I won." And now? "My father has the pitchfork waiting," he grinned. "We have to spread the dung for the spring planting."

Inevitably, the remaining men's Alpine events seemed anticlimactic, even though the results were as staggering in their way as Klammer's victory. The world's No. 1 overall was Gustavo Thöni, at 24 the winner of no fewer than four World Cups, Olympic victor at Sapporo in the giant slalom, silver medalist in the slalom. Everybody expected the Italian star

to become the first skier ever to win an Alpine gold in two separate Winter Games; some experts figured him for a sweep of all three events at Innsbruck.

But Thöni faltered in the downhill and finished an ignominious 26th. That left the two slaloms on the tough, steep courses laid out at Axamer Lizum southeast of Innsbruck. Only two men were rated to have much chance against the confident Thöni: Sweden's Ingemar Stenmark, a 19-year-old whiz who had lost the 1975 World Cup to his older rival by a single gate in the last slalom of the season; and Italy's aggressive Piero Gros, 22, who hero-worshiped his countryman but had nonetheless defeated him for the 1974 World Cup.

As it turned out, form took a holiday in the giant slalom, when a pair of Swiss bricklayers walled off both Thöni and Stenmark. Neither Heini Hemmi, 27, nor Ernst Good, 26, had won a major race in years of campaigning. At Innsbruck, Hemmi somehow found the line through two runs on different courses in a combined time of 3:26.97, followed 0.20 of a second later by Good. Relegated to fourth after Stenmark, Thöni stormed angrily off the course, his only chance for a gold now resting on the slalom. That was not in the cards either. Standing fifth

Happy Swiss champions Heini Hemmi (*left*) and Ernst Good smile for the camera after hearing confirmation of results in the giant slalom. The Swiss ski team claimed Alpine bragging rights on the strength of their one-two finish. Hemmi took the gold, Good the silver.

A wide turn around a gate slows Italy's Piero Gros during the slalom. Nevertheless, Gros made a remarkable move from fifth place after his first run through the course to the top position in his next, finishing it a second faster than anyone else in the field.

after the first run, Piero Gros summoned a brilliant second effort to edge Thöni by 0.44 of a second. "Everything is all right as long as an Italian skier wins," gritted Thöni. Still, the silver would look nice with all the other trophies in the big restaurant-hotel complex the Thönis were building on the proceeds from Gustavo's skiing.

The Austrians, Swiss, and Italians had their heroes. But leave it to the West Germans to put up a heroine everybody could love. Rosi Mittermaier was only 21, yet she had been around so long that some of her teammates and admirers fondly called her "Granny." Cheerfully pursuing World Cup and Olympic laurels since she was 15, she had never won any, but she was usually somewhere near the top. Bizarre injuries had been part of the problem: getting clobbered

by a surfboard in Hawaii in 1973, being blindsided by a recreational skier while practicing at Innsbruck two years later. She was healthy for the 1976 Winter Games but dreamed only "in one corner of my head" of a bronze. Then Granny Mittermaier went out and put on a show that left everybody gasping.

In fairness, it must be acknowledged that Switzerland's Marie-Theres Nadig, defending Olympic champion in both the downhill and giant slalom, was bedridden with the flu. Yet who was to say that anybody—even Austria's just-retired Annemarie Pröll, winner of five consecutive World Cups—could have topped Rosi Mittermaier on this occasion?

At the pinnacle of her always elegant form, happiest on an icy piste, the most popular person in town demolished the downhill to win by a full

| Innsbruck logo pin | Soviet team pin | Soviet luge pin |

half second; had she and the second-place finisher, Austria's favored Brigitte Totschnigg, been racing together, Mittermaier's lead would have translated into an enormous 15 meters. It was her first major downhill victory in 100 tries, and the fans—Germans and Austrians alike—erupted in joy. Three hours after the event, thousands of them still besieged the hotel where she and her mother were dining, chanting Rosi's name and pleading for her to come out on a balcony and say hello.

"With one gold medal in your pocket," she was quoted as saying, "things go even easier." If that sounded a little casual, something must have been lost in translation. Rosi was anything but blasé. Hugging her mother—who had fearfully watched the downhill for the first time—Mittermaier cried, "When will I believe it, Mother? When?" Yet it really was beginning to look easy.

Three days later, the slalom courses at Axamer Lizum were so icy that only 19 of 42 contestants completed both runs without missing a gate. Beautiful, smiled Mittermaier, and swoop-swooped through the two runs to capture her second gold by 0.33 of a second. Now it took a flying wedge of 20 cops to escort her through the worshipful crowds.

Everyone at Innsbruck, everyone everywhere tuned to TV, started thinking about a historic Olympic triple. Toni Sailer had won all three Alpine events at Cortina 1956; Jean-Claude Killy had done the same at Grenoble in 1968. But no woman had ever achieved the zenith. Maybe Rosi Mittermaier could do it.

The tension mounted for two days, until February 13 and the giant slalom at Axamer Lizum. First down the bumpy, 1,225-meter course was Canada's 18-year-old Kathy Kreiner, surprise winner of a

Germany's Rosi Mittermaier skis to her first major-event victory in the Innsbruck downhill. Mittermaier had the best year of her 12-year racing career in 1976. In addition to her Olympic success, she won the World Cup slalom and overall titles.

129

World Cup giant slalom in 1974 but so lightly regarded that her team manager didn't bother to show up for the race; he thought she would be lucky to finish among the first 15. Yet the giant slalom favored technique over attack, and Kreiner was technically very exact. With the advantage of going first, before the course got rutted, she finessed the 49 gates perfectly and sped through the single run in an excellent 1:29.13.

Rosi Mittermaier came off the mark fourth, and the developing ruts didn't bother her in the slightest. Halfway down she was a comfortable 0.50 of a second ahead of Kreiner's time—until she made one small error. Approaching a gate, she took a too direct line and had to veer out and back, losing precious fractions of a second. Her time: 1:29.25, an eye-blink 0.12 of a second slower than Kreiner's.

The triple gold would not be hers, but Granny's army of fans thought she had done magnificently anyway. A man rushed up with a bouquet of flowers. Rosi Mittermaier immediately turned and presented them to Kreiner. Then, with an incandescent smile, she and French bronze medalist Danièlle Debernard lifted Kreiner aloft in triumph. It was a moment of pure and shining Olympism. Pierre de Coubertin would have wept.

That visionary father of the modern Games might have wished, however, for greater attention to ideals on the part of some judges. Except for gymnastics and diving, only figure skating among Olympic sports remained so utterly at the mercy of subjective officiating.

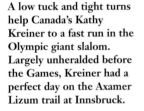

A low tuck and tight turns help Canada's Kathy Kreiner to a fast run in the Olympic giant slalom. Largely unheralded before the Games, Kreiner had a perfect day on the Axamer Lizum trail at Innsbruck.

Skaters had muttered for years about blatant political bias, particularly from the Soviets and their East European comrades. They often seemed to vote as a bloc, and while consultation was forbidden, they all seemed to know exactly what it took to push along their own people while putting down skaters from the West.

Most Westerners on the world circuit kept their protests to seething whispers. Not Great Britain's 26-year-old John Curry. After losing the 1975 European championships to the Soviet Union's Vladimir Kovalev, Curry was so outraged by the judging that he publicly charged prejudice on the part of the East Europeans. In fury, the Soviets tried to have Curry permanently disqualified—a sure tribute to his talents. They failed and were themselves warned by their governing international federation about unfair markings.

Even if he had been more tractable politically, Curry had a skating style sure to irritate the Soviets and their friends. He hadn't started out to be an athlete at all; his real love was dance. But his working-class family in Birmingham vetoed that idea, so figure skating it was—in a supremely graceful style that the Soviets ridiculed as "effeminate."

Curry's frustrating unacceptability to judges might have continued indefinitely had it not been for a wealthy American sponsor who staked the Englishman to training sessions in Denver with one of the best coaches in the business. That was Carlo Fassi, 46, a transplanted Italian who had skated to third in the 1953 world championships before finding his true métier helping others. In 1968, Fassi had guided Peggy Fleming to her Olympic gold. Now came Curry. Fassi worked on Curry's school figures—always a weakness. Next he replaced some of the more balletic moves with

enough high-flying jumps and other acrobatic maneuvers to blunt the charges of overartistry.

At Innsbruck, Curry was primed and peaking. New rules gave less weight to school figures and more to the free skating at which Westerners excelled. Moreover, Western judges outnumbered their Communist colleagues five to four. In the end, though, the results didn't play out along party lines. Curry placed a respectable second in the compulsory

A torch flickers across the front of the Innsbruck winners' medal *(top left)*, with the Austrian Alps and the Bergisel ski jump in the background. The reverse bears the Winter Games logo and a legend in German: 12th Olympic Winter Games. The logo set against jagged ice crystals and the legend appear again on the front of the commemorative medal *(above left)* given to every Winter Games athlete. The reverse has a stylized design of the Bergisel stadium with a panorama of Innsbruck and the Alps. At left is the diploma awarded to the top six finishers in each event.

figures—the judges getting down on all fours to examine the blade marks. Then he overwhelmed the field in the short and long free-skate programs, capping one of the greatest performances in skating to date with three towering triple jumps. The Soviet judge, as expected, put his countryman Kovalev first, but he still had to accord Curry second place. The Hungarian, Czech, and East German judges all followed their consciences and voted for Curry. That made it a runaway, with Curry collecting 105.9 of a possible 108 points for free skating, the highest score ever. He had his championship and Great Britain its first Winter Games medal since a pair of its bobsledders brought back the gold in 1964.

Someone else at Innsbruck owed a considerable debt to Carlo Fassi. She was America's 19-year-old Dorothy Hamill, who had been polishing her natural genius with the coach since she was 14. In many ways, she was the opposite of John Curry; while he yearned to do ballet on ice, Hamill brought a new athleticism to the dance-oriented routines of women's figure skating. Trim and strong at 5 feet 3 inches and 115 pounds, she soared aloft in daring leaps and spins—delayed axels, in which she seemed to hang suspended before completing one and a half revolutions and settling softly back onto the ice, and her own "Hamill Camel," which saw her twirl upright in a spiral, then slowly descend into a sitting spin. And all so delicately, fluidly done. Blessed with what the skaters call "total body control," Hamill never seemed to wind up for a jump; suddenly, somehow, she was airborne and gliding.

Combined with an innate musicality, Hamill's athletic talents would make her the greatest female free skater of her day. However, she was relatively weak in the compulsory figures. Fassi worked on that with a schedule that called for four hours of school figures and two hours of free skating six days a week, 11 months a year. "Before I got to Carlo," recalled Hamill, "I was tied up in a knot doing figures. I looked like a pretzel." In time, the compulsory routines got better. But there was a second, even bigger problem: the terrifying stage fright that consumed Hamill before every performance. "It's like going to an execution—your own," she grimaced. "I stand there in the dressing room thinking, 'Am I going to fall? Why am I doing this? I'll never do it again.'"

The agony usually vanished once she took the ice. "You're skating and doing the most difficult things," she said, "and the audience is with you. They're clapping, cheering. You're floating. It's like nothing else I've ever felt." But the assurance waned afterward. An ABC television crew once offered to rerun for her a tape of a spectacular free-skating performance. Hamill refused, saying, "I think I look lousy."

Nor was she the favorite at Innsbruck. In both the 1974 and 1975 world championships, she had been runner-up, first to East Germany's Christine Errath, then to the Netherlands' Dianne de Leeuw. Both were on hand for the 1976 Winter Games, Errath supreme at figures, de Leeuw solid all the way and as unflappable as Hamill was jittery.

Friday, the 13th. Dorothy Hamill awaited her turn, a four-leaf clover pinned to her pink costume as insurance against the ominous date. Then she saw the sign up in the crowd: "DOROTHY, WICKED WITCH OF THE

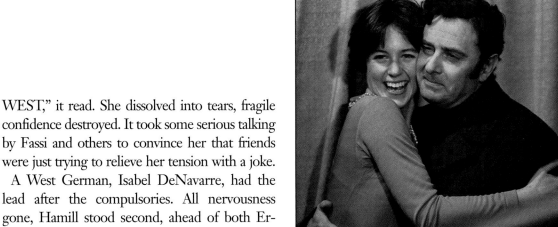

Carlo Fassi gets a hug from Dorothy Hamill, the third skater under his tutelage to win a gold medal. It was a mild upset when Hamill *(below)* edged the Netherlands' Dianne de Leeuw, but Fassi's first champion, Peggy Fleming, had won handily at Grenoble 1968. His second gold medalist, John Curry, won the men's event at Innsbruck two days before Hamill took her title.

WEST," it read. She dissolved into tears, fragile confidence destroyed. It took some serious talking by Fassi and others to convince her that friends were just trying to relieve her tension with a joke.

A West German, Isabel DeNavarre, had the lead after the compulsories. All nervousness gone, Hamill stood second, ahead of both Errath and de Leeuw, in perfect position for the free skating. "Now you can take it easy," said her father—causing near apoplexy in Fassi. "The best defense is to attack," he growled. "You can't hold back anything."

Hamill let it all out in the two-minute program. *New York Times* skating writer Fred Tupper reported glowingly how "Miss Hamill leaped into a delayed axel, then a double axel and in succession executed a flying sitspin, a double flip, then a double toe loop. The audience was all hers now, and she wound up with a dazzling stepwork and a layback spin." The judges held up 5.9s and 5.8s and one, the Italian judge, a perfect 6.0 for technical merit. She had the lead, and the next day she sewed up victory with a spellbinding four-minute performance climaxed by her Hamill Camel. Every judge, all nine of them, declared her the Olympic champion.

It took three ushers to gather up the daffodils, tulips, and roses her fans showered down on the rink. Back in the dressing room, she was Dorothy again. "I didn't really bomb out on anything," she said. "That's a first for me."

Though shut out of the singles, the East earned its full share of figure-skating glory in the pairs when Moscow's Irina Rodnina and her new partner-husband, Aleksandr Zaitsev, outclassed a strong field. Winner at Sapporo 1972, the diminutive (4 feet 11 inches, 90 pounds) Rodnina had lost her old partner to another woman shortly after the Olympics. So sports officials paraded a lot of big, strong young men past the 26-year-old ice queen until she settled on Zaitsev, 24, with whom she continued as

A beaming Lyudmila Pakhomova waltzes in the arms of ice-dancing partner Aleksandr Gorshkov. It was fitting that Gorshkov and Pakhomova won the first Olympic ice-dancing title, since they had dominated the discipline for most of a decade, winning six world championships in their career.

Returning champion Irina Rodnina skates with new partner Aleksandr Zaitsev in the pairs competition at Innsbruck. The couple was the unanimous choice for first place.

before—wowing the world with her artistry, though making few friends in the process. After the 1975 world championships in Colorado Springs, altitude 5,900 feet, a reporter asked Rodnina about their toughest rival. "The altitude," she snapped. Things like that led to such headlines as "Amazing Irina—But No Grace."

Still, no one could argue with what would eventually add up to 11 European championships, 10 world championships, and 3 Olympic golds.

The newest event at Innsbruck went to a second husband-and-wife Soviet team. Devotees of ice dancing had been campaigning for years to have their pastime accepted as an Olympic sport. Those who disparaged the activity thought the term "sport" quite a stretch, but the discipline unquestionably demanded a far greater level of athletic ability than ballroom dancing. Though rules deny ice dancers the dramatic lifts and throws that characterize pairs skating, the dancers must excel at synchrony and intricate footwork. The British had long been dominant in the discipline. More recently, however, the palm had gone east, with Lyudmila Pakhomova and Aleksandr Gorshkov world champions for five of the six years preceding Innsbruck. They easily took the Olympic gold, with another Soviet pair winning the silver and a third tripping along in fourth place. All that prevented a Soviet sweep was a couple of Colorado teenagers, Colleen O'Connor and Jim Millns, who took the bronze.

The Soviets and other East Europeans, in fact, were having a spectacular Olympics, their best Winter Games ever and a tribute to their state-run victory machines. The only sport on which Communist athletes had no impact was Alpine skiing. In everything else they reaped an unprecedented harvest of medals. Soviet and East German men and women won 20 of the 37 events, 46 of the 111 medals. The United States was closest behind with 10 medals, including three golds, followed by the Norwegians with three victories and the West Germans, Finns, and host Austrians, with two each.

No wonder the West Germans idolized Rosi Mittermaier; she was their lone champion. No wonder Franz Klammer had saved the Games for Austria; only jumpers Karl Schnabl and Anton Innauer, soaring 1-2 off the 90-meter hill,

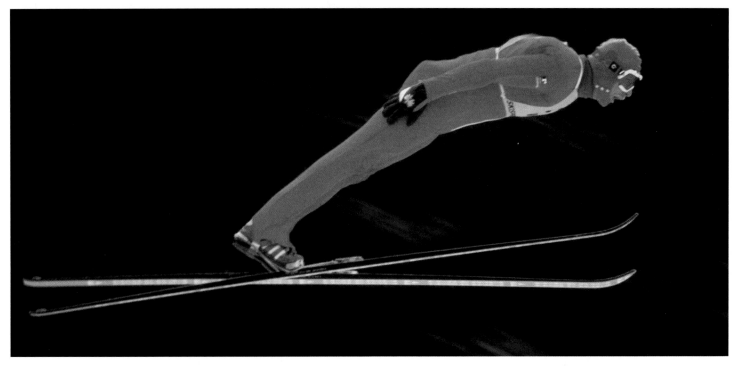

Consistency was Karl Schnabl's trademark at Innsbruck as he scored two near-identical jumps of almost 320 feet (97 meters and 97.50 meters) in his attempts off the large hill to win the gold medal. The Austrian finished third in the small-hill jump. The winner there was East Germany's Hans-Georg Aschenbach. Aschenbach, a physician, would flee to West Germany in 1988 and become a valuable source of information on doping in the G.D.R.

gave Austrians fresh reason to cheer. Yet an East German, Harry Glass, had taken the 90-meter bronze, and a pair of G.D.R. jumpers had captured the gold and silver on the 70-meter hill, with Schnabl salvaging a bronze.

The East German 70-meter showing was all the more remarkable because the victor, 25-year-old Hans-Georg Aschenbach, had suffered an apparent career-ending knee injury seven months before the Games. East German sports doctors had miraculously restored the knee to full strength. No one knew how; queries met with mumbo jumbo about a new form of electroshock therapy. Perhaps. But it turned out that another technique also was involved. Years later, Aschenbach confessed to East Germany's longtime use of illegal, muscle-enhancing anabolic steroids. He had been in a sweat of anxiety at Innsbruck. He had won, but then faced drug testing. "Will they catch you?" he remembered thinking. "Or was the timing correct once again? Was everything for nothing? Will you be the one they place the blame on, the idiot that is the butt of

laughter for everybody? Nobody can imagine what you go through. You even forget that you have won."

Doping was inexcusable, a mockery of Olympism. Yet there was much to respect, even admire, in the Soviet and East German dedication to supremacy. Steroids aside, few athletes had ever been brought along with such exquisite attention as Ulrich Wehling, East Germany's champion in the Nordic combined, an event that marries a 70-meter jump to a 15-kilometer cross-country, the idea being to produce an all-around Nordic champion.

Wehling came under the care of East Germany's coaches and doctors when he showed promise as a youngster. Everything about him went into the sports computers in Leipzig: blood counts, muscle mass, nutritional balances, training performances, personality, friends and family, long-range objectives and plans. By the Olympic year 1972, Wehling had developed into an excellent jumper but only a so-so skier. His mentors sought to correct the deficiency with 4,000 kilometers of trail work annually, plus 850 jumps from the 70-meter hill. That, they judged, was all

Wehling could absorb at his stage of development; a heavier load and he risked injury from what the doctors called "metabolic breakdown."

The regimen did the job. Wehling astounded the world by easily winning the Nordic combined at Sapporo. For the 1974 world championships in Sweden, Wehling's trainers upped the ante to 4,500 kilometers on the trail and 1,000 ski jumps. He was 21 then and could take it. He won again. Two years later came Innsbruck, by which time the 23-year-old Wehling was doing 5,000 kilometers and 1,300 jumps a year. In the competition, he managed only 13th in the cross-country but dominated the jump so thoroughly that a second Olympic gold was his by a good margin.

After Innsbruck the doctors and trainers didn't try to push him any higher. In world-class cross-country skiing, they knew, ability was almost totally dependent on lung volume and oxygen-uptake capacity, which can be developed only so far. Wehling had reached his plateau. Yet it was

NOT SO SURE SHOT

Innsbruck 1976 was the third Olympic Winter Games for the unlucky Aleksandr Tikhonov. The Soviet biathlete was a terrific cross-country skier, but not a steady shot—a serious handicap for an athlete whose event requires both skills. In his two previous Games he had skied the 20-kilometer circuit faster than any other athlete, but his aim had deserted him.

Two missed targets at Grenoble 1968 had saddled him with two penalty minutes and pushed him into second place. At Sapporo four years later, his skiing was still superb, but his shooting was worse: Four missed targets dropped him to fourth.

Marksmanship was again his bête noire at Innsbruck. He skied the course nearly 2 minutes faster than winner and teammate Nikolai Kruglov, but seven missed targets pushed him out of medal contention. For Tikhonov, satisfaction would come in the biathlon relay, where brilliant team skiing—and flawless marksmanship by all the Soviet shooters—won him a gold medal.

Cross-country skiers stop for a trial of marksmanship during the 20-kilometer biathlon at Innsbruck. Racers fire from standing and prone positions at targets 50 meters away.

East Germany's Ulrich Wehling displays classic form in the jumping portion of the Nordic combined. Innsbruck gave Wehling the second of his three consecutive titles in the event. The only other athlete to win the combined at consecutive Winter Games was Norway's Johan Gröttumsbråten, the victor in 1928 and 1932.

high enough, and he held it so well that at Lake Placid 1980, Ulrich Wehling, then 27, would become the first Olympian other than figure skater Sonja Henie to win three consecutive championships in the same winter event.

East Germany's approach to the bobsled illuminated a further facet of its sports philosophy:

Never sneer. Veteran competitors didn't much care for the $6 million combined run called Heiligwasserwiese (Holy Water Lawn) that the frugal Innsbruck organizers had constructed at Igls. They called it too short, too easy, too slow; one Italian sledder scoffed that the run was fit only for Disneyland. But the East Germans hadn't competed in bobsled before, and in 1975 test runs on Heiligwasserwiese, they were respectful enough to study speed through the chutes and curves with cameras and timing devices. Their captain, 35-year-old Meinhard Nehmer, was a onetime javelin thrower who had barely heard of the bobs a few years earlier. "When they came around to the track club and asked who was interested in trying bobsleigh, I was the one who put up my hand," he chuckled. Yet he and his compatriots learned fast enough for Nehmer to enter the pantheon as only the third driver in history to sweep both the two-man and four-man bobs in a single Olympics.

The luge events produced a second sweep for the G.D.R., though this one came as no surprise. German-speaking athletes held a near monopoly on the toboggans, with 23 of 27 medals and eight of the nine golds since the sport became a permanent part of the Winter Games in 1964. The women's victor, 23-year-old Margit Schumann, had finished third at Sapporo but had not lost since. When a reporter asked her for the secret of her success, she gravely replied: "I am a lieutenant in the People's Army." That probably was as good an answer as any, considering the manic nature of luge, in which contestants rocketed along clinging to a skeleton of steel, flat on their backs and struggling to steer with their feet.

If the luge struck some observers as slightly wacky, then the Nordic cross-country seemed more than a little cruel—men and women on narrow, sharply upturned skis rushing through the snow for 5, 10, 15, 30, even 50 punishing kilometers. In the car-happy United

States, only a handful of hardy souls partic- ipated in these grueling contests. Throughout much of Europe, too (the Alpine countries excepted), cross- country was a minor sport. But in the far reaches of the frozen north—Scandinavia and the Soviet Union—it was a way of life, a familiar mode of basic transportation.

That helped explain why only one comparative southerner—a Swedish- trained Italian mountaineer—had ever won an Olympic cross-country in 52 years of trying. It accounted, too, for the open-mouthed increduli- ty when an asthmatic 20-year-old American came within 28 seconds of winning the 30-kilo- meter at Innsbruck.

Growing up in Guilford, Vermont, Bill Koch had spent a good part of his childhood skiing 10 kilometers back and forth to school. He loved the serenity of swishing through the silent forests, and on reaching adoles- cence he decided to com- pete. "It's a lonely sport," he acknowledged, "but I'm a loner anyway, and it's a form of self-expression for me. It feels so good to train and be out there in the woods that if someone tried to stop me, I'd go bananas."

Koch skied more than 8,000 kilometers in the two years leading up to Innsbruck. The American coaches made sure to in- form Olympic authorities of his physical problem, an exertion-induced asthma

that made it hard for him to breathe during a race and entailed his using a decon- gestant called chromyl sodium. Officials eventually okayed the medication, and Koch boldly entered all three men's cross-countries: the 15-kilometer, his specialty, along with the 30- and 50-kilometer marathons.

The unknown Yank was unknown no longer when he finished third in a pre-Olympic 30- kilometer warm-up. And he earned everyone's ardent attention by opening up a 10-second lead over Finland's Juha Mieto, the heavy favorite, at the first checkpoint, about 10 kilometers into the race. He was running fifth at that point, Mieto sixth. Koch knew then that he could win a medal if he could block out fatigue and keep breathing. About 20 kilometers along, his lungs sounded to him "like a freight train," he report- ed later. But his time was still better than Mieto's, and the lungs kept chuff- ing to the finish line. The electronic timer read 1 hour 30 minutes 57.84 seconds—not quite fast enough to overcome the Red Army's experienced Sergei Saveliev, but more than 11 seconds better

Meinhard Nehmer pilots the East Germany II sled down a slow Igls bobsled run. Nehmer, a latecomer to bobsledding, would win three gold medals steering East German sleds at two Winter Games.

Bill Koch was the surprise of the Nordic events at Innsbruck. He finished sec- ond in the 30-kilometer race, becoming the first North American to earn a medal in cross-country. Later in his career, Koch would help popularize the side-to-side skating tech- nique of skiing that remains the prevailing style in most Nordic events.

than the next Soviet finisher. Saveliev won the gold, Koch the silver, the USSR's Ivan Garanin the bronze. Mieto finished fourth.

There was just a bit more to savor. Koch finished a respectable sixth to three Soviets, a Finn, and a Norwegian in the 15-kilometer. Then, skiing only the second 50-kilometer run of his life, he actually had the lead at the halfway mark before the asthma defeated him and he faded to 13th in a race won by Norway's great Ivar Formo.

In the women's cross-country, the only question was who among the dominant Soviets and Finns would triumph. The reigning queen was the USSR's 33-year-old Galina Kulakova, in her day the most decorated cross-country skier in Olympic history, with four gold medals, two silvers, and two bronzes in four Games, beginning with Grenoble 1968 and ending with a silver medal performance at Lake Placid 1980. Yet at

Innsbruck her only individual medals were two bronzes—and she lost one of those when, after finishing third in the 5-kilometer, she tested positive for the illegal drug ephedrine: Poor Galina had borrowed a roommate's nose drops on waking up the morning of the race with a stuffy nose. Though the IOC disqualified her in the 5-kilometer, it apparently deemed the ephedrine use an honest mistake and allowed Kulakova to continue racing. She collected a bronze in the 10-kilometer and the final gold in her career in the 4 x 5-kilometer relay.

The battle for Kulakova's cross-country crown matched a couple of deep-country young women: Helena Takalo, 26, who helped work a farm near Nivala in the heart of Finland, and Raisa Smetanina, 23, from Skyvkar in the Ural Mountains 1,000 miles from Moscow. They split it evenly— or almost. Takalo took the 5-kilometer from Smetanina by a mere second, while Smetanina

The Soviet Union's eight-time Olympic medalist Galina Kulakova, 33, anchors her team to victory in the 4 x 5-kilometer relay. Innsbruck 1976 was the first Winter Games where the women's relay races had four athletes per team instead of three.

found her revenge in the 10-kilometer by a similar margin. Smetanina, however, could claim precedence because of the relay victory against Takalo and her sister Finns. Indeed, Smetanina went on to an Olympic career that surpassed even that of the illustrious Kulakova, winning 10 medals over the course of four Winter Games.

Speed skating was another of those sports the Scandinavians and Soviets, along with the Dutch, put their hearts into. So focused were the Dutch that they had nine speed rinks in their small country, while the Soviets bragged about their $25 million "record factory" for speed-skater production at Medeo, high in the Pamir Mountains of Central Asia. Medeo's combination of altitude and perfect ice from glacier water were ideal for the sprints. Indeed,

eight of the world's top ten 500-meter racers in 1975 were Soviets who trained there.

The United States by rights should have been the most distant of also-rans. Skating round and round against the clock gave Americans the yawns—to the point where there was just one 400-meter racing oval in the whole country and maybe 3,000 racers. But numbers didn't tell the whole story: Those Americans who took to the sport were zealous enough and sharp enough to have won 19 medals over the years, including 10 golds. The total was skimpy compared with those of the Norwegians and Soviets, of course, but it outshined the output of the Swedes, Finns, and Dutch.

Now at Innsbruck, Yevgeny Kulikov and Valery Muratov, the ranking Soviets, zipped to a 1-2 finish in the 500—Kulikov's 39.17 on the slow, sleety track setting an Olympic record, while way off his 37-flat world mark at Medeo. But the bronze went to America's unheralded Dan Immerfall, just 0.29 of a second slower than Muratov, and fifth place fell to a teammate, 21-year-old Peter Mueller, only 0.03 of a second behind Immerfall. Two days later, Mueller went out and put a golden cap on 15 years of training. In the inaugural Olympic 1,000-meter, he swept to victory over Norway's Jorn Didriksen and Muratov by the enormous margin of 1.13 seconds.

That would be all for the American male speed skaters. A pair of superb Norwegians, Jan Egil Storholt and Sten Stensen, won the 1,500 and 5,000 meters respectively, while an indefatigable Hollander, Piet Kleine, glided off with the 10,000 meters. Meanwhile, there were the American women to consider.

America's Peter Mueller *(left)* drives hard toward the finish of the inaugural Olympic 1,000-meter speed-skating race. Mueller was the first American man to win a speed-skating gold medal since Lake Placid 1932.

In profile, America's Sheila Young shows her powerful form on the ice. Young was competitive at all four women's distances and, in the summer, could challenge the world's best cyclists. Three women, Young among them, have won Olympic speed-skating medals and cycling championships.

Sheila Young wasn't the greatest female speed skater at the 1976 Winter Games. That honor went to the Soviet Union's Tatyana Averina, who triumphed in both the 1,000 and 3,000 meters, while taking bronzes in the 500 and 1,500. But

Coasting after the finish of the 3,000-meter race, the Soviet Union's Tatyana Averina can reflect on an impressive Winter Games. Averina was the best female skater at Innsbruck, with two gold medals and top-three finishes in all four women's speed-skating events.

the gutsy, intensely competitive 25-year-old from Detroit was nevertheless one of the most interesting athletes at Innsbruck.

One of four children brought up by a widowed father, Sheila more or less was forced to learn about ice skating. "Going skating went with raising the kids," said father Clair. "I couldn't afford a baby-sitter, so everybody had to come along." Unenthusiastic at first, Sheila got to love the sensation of speed, and as she developed into a compact 5 feet 4 inches and 130 pounds, she started competing—and winning—as a sprinter. By 1972 she was swift enough to make the U.S. team at Sapporo, where she missed a bronze medal in the 500 meters by a mere 0.08 of a second. That disappointment energized her all the more. The next year she captured the world championship at 500 meters and set a world record in the bargain. When Innsbruck 1976 rolled around, Sheila Young was acknowledged as virtually unbeatable at her distance.

Skating without socks for "better rapport with my blades," she warmed up by winning an unexpected silver medal in the 1,500 meters. Next day, the 500 was hers hands down. An explosive start and she thought: "Here I go, 10.82 seconds at the 100 meters. That's pretty good." Round the turn she could hear her coach yelling, "Fight, fight, fight!" then a bunch of American fans howling, "Go, go, go!" Her legs were starting to tighten with the all-out effort. From somewhere she summoned a final surge and powered over the line in 42.76 seconds, almost 2 seconds off her world mark, but more than enough for the gold and for an Olympic record on slow ice. The maraschino on the sundae came a day later when she carried off a bronze medal in the 1,000 meters, while teammate Leah Poulos won the silver.

That gave Sheila Young a complete set—gold, silver, bronze—and made her the first American ever to win three medals in a single Winter

Olympics. But her abilities and aspirations didn't end there.

Almost all speed skaters bicycled in the off-season; it kept their thighs in shape. Sheila Young, however, took this "dry land training," as the skaters called it, to unprecedented heights: She became a world champion sprint cyclist and thus held titles in two different sports at the same time—not once, twice.

In Spain in 1973, the year of her first skating championship, she took on Europe's top sprint cyclists, including Galina Ermolasva, the Soviet Union's six-time titleholder. Jockeying for position in the preliminaries, Young suffered two bad crashes; her arms and legs were cut and bleeding, and there was a gash on her head so deep that a trackside doctor had to clamp it closed. No matter. She wiped out the competition in the final to become the first American, man or woman, in half a century to win a world cycling championship.

Again in 1976, after winning at Innsbruck, Sheila Young spent the summer on her bike, pedaling to both the U.S. and the world sprint championships. There were no women's cycling events at the Games of the XXI Olympiad in Montreal that year. Time would rectify the matter. But in those days, the Olympic authorities

Czechs sprawl on the ice, but they can't stop the Soviets from scoring during medal-round action in the Innsbruck hockey tournament. In the first Olympic century, the USSR won a hockey medal in every Winter Games it entered.

NOT AGAIN

Going into Innsbruck 1976, the Soviet Union had won the Olympic hockey tournament for three Winter Games in a row. During that streak, the teams from Czechoslovakia had been the Soviets' strongest opposition, but bad luck had always kept the Czechs from a championship. Even when they did manage to beat the Soviets, as at Grenoble 1968, an ensuing lackluster performance against a lesser foe deprived them of the gold medal.

The Innsbruck tournament shaped up as a chance for the Czechs to change their luck. But something worse than the Soviets got in the way. Czechoslovakia's František Pospíšil

tested positive for codeine, a banned drug, after a game with Poland. The infraction threatened to disqualify the entire team. Pospíšil had taken the codeine to combat a flu epidemic that had broken out in the Olympic Village. Rather than disqualify the Czechs, the IOC decided not to count their match with Poland. The ruling allowed the Czechs to face the Soviets in a winner-take-all final-round match. The Czechs led 3-2 in the last period but gave up two late goals to lose—again—to the USSR. The Soviets won another gold medal, while the Czechs finished a thoroughly frustrated second.

America's Terry Kubicka goes merrily head over heels during the anything-goes exhibition that followed the figure-skating events. The flips were outlawed in amateur competition in 1977.

held that the hurly-burly of world-class cycling, especially sprint cycling, was just too dangerous for the fair sex.

The final athletic event of the 12th Winter Games was not a competition. No points were scored, no medals awarded. It was termed an "exhibition," but celebration might have been a better word. For here was a radiant portrayal of youth and vitality, of the joyful spirit, indomitable character, and free-roving imagination that were supposed to be the essence of Olympism.

On the afternoon of Sunday, February 15, just prior to the closing ceremony, the figure skaters took the ice before an expectant crowd at the Olympic stadium. And then it happened: Gold medalist Dorothy Hamill, so tightly wound, so athletically aerial in competition, let the tensions ebb as she showed everybody a softer, gayer side of herself in a lyrical ice dance. The incomparable John Curry, whose lifelong yearning had been for the stage, not the rink, opened his soul with a magnificent interpretation of Rimsky-Korsakov's *Sheherazade*. California's bumptious young Terry Kubicka had been relegated to seventh place in the regular competition after scandalizing the judges with a back flip (banned immediately thereafter). So, with defiant verve, he won huzzahs from the crowd by back-flipping all over again.

Then came East Germany's bronze medalist, Christine Errath, world standard setter in the drab school figures and the poster model of a Young Communist. Errath appeared in heavy mascara and flapper garb to enchant spectators with an arm-swinging, leg-kicking, whoop-de-doo Charleston routine—most unsocialistic.

Later, when the whole company of athletes entered the stadium, when the bands played and the folk groups performed, when Lord Killanin declared the festivities ended, when the great five-ring flag was lowered and the sacred flames slowly extinguished, it could truly be said that these young people, these "Simple Games" of Innsbruck, had returned something of great value to the Olympic movement. The XX Olympiad, begun with such soaring hopes, shattered by such abysmal horror, had passed through the darkness and into the light again. The Games had gone on.

Couples in local costume perform a Tyrolean torch dance during the closing ceremony. The Innsbruck Games continued their thematic simplicity, offering little more than festive polka music to accompany athletes marching out of the stadium. But exuberant spectators livened up the Olympians' departure, showering them with tulips.

⬯⬯⬯ APPENDIX

CALENDAR OF THE XX OLYMPIAD

1972

AUGUST 2-10	4th Paralympic Games at Heidelburg
AUGUST 18-22, SEPTEMBER 1, 5-8, & 10-11	96th IOC Executive Board meeting at Munich
AUGUST 20	16th IOC Executive Board meeting with NOCs at Munich
AUGUST 21-24 & SEPTEMBER 5	**73rd Session of the IOC at Munich**
AUGUST 24	Michael Morris, the Lord Killanin, elected sixth IOC president
AUGUST 26-SEPTEMBER 11	**MUNICH 1972 17th Olympic Games**

1973

JANUARY 6-13	2nd African Games at Lagos
FEBRUARY 2-5	97th IOC Executive Board meeting at Lausanne
FEBRUARY 8-9	14th USOC Quadrennial meeting at the Broadmoor Hotel, Colorado Springs
JUNE 22-24	98th IOC Executive Board meeting at Lausanne
JULY 21-28	12th World Games for the Deaf at Malmö
AUGUST 15-25	7th University Games at Moscow
SEPTEMBER 1-8	7th South East Asian Games at Singapore
SEPTEMBER 29-30 & OCTOBER 2	99th IOC Executive Board meeting at Varna
SEPTEMBER 30-OCTOBER 4	24th IOC Executive Board meeting with IFs at Varna
SEPTEMBER 30-OCTOBER 4	17th IOC Executive Board meeting with NOCs at Varna

SEPTEMBER 30-OCTOBER 4	The 10th Olympic Congress at Varna
OCTOBER 5-7	**74th Session of the IOC at Varna**
NOVEMBER 24-DECEMBER 2	1st Central American Games at Guatemala City

1974

JANUARY 24-FEBRUARY 2	10th Commonwealth Games at Christchurch
FEBRUARY 9-11	100th IOC Executive Board meeting at Lausanne
FEBRUARY 27-MARCH 13	12th Central American and Caribbean Games at Santo Domingo
April 15-16	3rd CARIFTA Games at Kingston
JUNE 1-3	101st IOC Executive Board meeting at Lausanne
SEPTEMBER 1-16	7th Asian Games at Tehran
OCTOBER 18, 21, & 24	102nd IOC Executive Board meeting at Vienna
OCTOBER 20	25th IOC Executive Board meeting with IFs at Vienna
OCTOBER 21-24	**75th Session of the IOC at Vienna**

1975

FEBRUARY 11-16	8th World Winter Games for the Deaf at Lake Placid
FEBRUARY 20-22	103rd IOC Executive Board meeting at Lausanne
APRIL 6-13	7th University Winter Games at Livigno
MAY 8	Avery Brundage, 87, dies at Garmisch

MAY 14-16	104th IOC Executive Board meeting at Rome
MAY 16	17th IOC Executive Board meeting with NOCs at Rome
MAY 19-23	105th IOC Executive Board meeting at Lausanne
MAY 21-23	**76th Session of the IOC at Lausanne**
AUGUST 1-10	5th South Pacific Games at Guam
AUGUST 7-11	4th International Special Olympics at Mount Pleasant
AUGUST 23-SEPTEMBER 6	7th Mediterranean Games at Algiers
SEPTEMBER 18-21	8th University Games at Rome
OCTOBER 4-6	106th IOC Executive Board meeting at Montreal
OCTOBER 6	26th IOC Executive Board with IFs at Montreal
OCTOBER 12-26	7th Pan-American Games at Mexico City

1976

JANUARY 30-31, FEBRUARY 5-12, 14, & 15	107th IOC Executive Board meeting at Innsbruck
FEBRUARY 2-3	**77th Session of the IOC at Innsbruck**
FEBRUARY 4-15	**INNSBRUCK 1976 12th Olympic Winter Games**
FEBRUARY 23-28	1st Paralympic Winter Games at Orrsholdvisk

Saturday, AUGUST 26

PM	EVENT	VENUE
3:00	OPENING CEREMONY	...Olympic Park

Sunday, AUGUST 27

AM	EVENT	VENUE
8:30	GYMNASTICS	...Olympic Park Sports Hall

women's team competition, compulsories

| 9:00 | SHOOTING | ...Hochbrück Shooting Range |

- free pistol
- trap

MODERN PENTATHLON......Riem Riding Facility
equestrian

ROWING......Oberschleissheim Regatta Course
- single sculls, preliminaries
- pair-oared shell without coxswain, preliminaries

BASKETBALL......Basketball Hall
preliminary round, group B

| 10:00 | WRESTLING | ...Fairgrounds Wrestling-Judo Hall |

freestyle, eliminations
- light flyweight
- flyweight
- bantamweight
- featherweight
- lightweight

VOLLEYBALL......Olympic Park Volleyball Hall
preliminary round

WATER POLO......Olympic Park Swimming Hall
preliminary round

| 10:30 | FIELD HOCKEY | ...Olympic Park Hockey Facility |

preliminary round

| 11:15 | GYMNASTICS | ...Olympic Park Sports Hall |

team competition, compulsories

PM	EVENT	VENUE
1:00	BOXING	...Olympic Park Boxing Hall

- flyweight, eliminations
- bantamweight, eliminations
- featherweight, eliminations

WEIGHT LIFTING......Fairgrounds Weight Lifting Hall
flyweight, press

DIVING......Olympic Park Swimming Hall
women's springboard, preliminaries

| 1:30 | FIELD HOCKEY | ...Olympic Park Hockey Facility |

preliminary round

| 2:00 | ROWING | ...Oberschleissheim Regatta Course |

- double sculls, preliminaries
- pair-oared shell with coxswain, preliminaries
- four-oared shell without coxswain, preliminaries
- four-oared shell with coxswain, preliminaries
- eight-oared shell with coxswain, preliminaries

VOLLEYBALL......Olympic Park Volleyball Hall
preliminary round

| 2:30 | EQUESTRIAN | ...Riem Riding Facility |

cross-country

| 3:00 | BASKETBALL | ...Basketball Hall |

preliminary round

GYMNASTICS......Olympic Park Sports Hall
women's team competition, compulsories

FOOTBALL......Olympic Stadium, Augsburg, Passau, & Nürnberg
preliminary round

FIELD HOCKEY......Olympic Park Hockey Facility
preliminary round

| 3:30 | VOLLEYBALL | ...Olympic Park Volleyball Hall |

women's preliminary round

| 4:00 | WATER POLO | ...Olympic Park Swimming Hall |

preliminary round

| 4:30 | FIELD HOCKEY | ...Olympic Park Hockey Facility |

preliminary round

| 6:30 | BASKETBALL | ...Basketball Hall |

preliminary round

| 7:00 | WRESTLING | ...Fairgrounds Wrestling-Judo Hall |

freestyle, eliminations
- welterweight
- middleweight
- light heavyweight
- heavyweight
- super heavyweight

WEIGHT LIFTING......Fairgrounds Weight Lifting Hall
flyweight, snatch & jerk

GYMNASTICS......Olympic Park Sports Hall
team competition, compulsories

| 7:30 | VOLLEYBALL | ...Olympic Park Volleyball Hall |

preliminary round

| 8:00 | DIVING | ...Olympic Park Swimming Hall |

women's springboard, preliminaries

| 9:00 | VOLLEYBALL | ...Olympic Park Volleyball Hall |

women's preliminary round

Monday, AUGUST 28

AM	EVENT	VENUE
8:00	EQUESTRIAN	...Nymphenburg Dressage Facility

three-day event, dressage

| 9:00 | SHOOTING | ...Hochbrück Shooting Range |

- small-bore rifle, prone position
- trap

MODERN PENTATHLON.....Fairgrounds Fencing Hall 2
fencing

BASKETBALL......Basketball Hall
preliminary round

| 10:00 | WRESTLING | ...Fairgrounds Wrestling-Judo Hall |

freestyle, eliminations
- welterweight
- middleweight
- light heavyweight
- heavyweight
- super heavyweight

GYMNASTICS......Olympic Park Sports Hall
women's team competition, optionals

FIELD HOCKEY......Olympic Park Hockey Facility
preliminary round

| | VOLLEYBALL | ...Olympic Park Volleyball Hall |

preliminary round

SWIMMING......Olympic Park Swimming Hall
200-meter butterfly, preliminary heats

WATER POLO Dante Swimming Pool
preliminary round

| 10:30 | SWIMMING | ...Olympic Park Swimming Hall |

women's 200-meter backstroke, preliminary heats

| 11:15 | SWIMMING | ...Olympic Park Swimming Hall |

100-meter backstroke, preliminary heats

| 11:30 | FIELD HOCKEY | ...Olympic Park Hockey Facility |

preliminary round

| 11:45 | SWIMMING | ...Olympic Park Swimming Hall |

women's 100-meter freestyle, eliminations

PM	EVENT	VENUE
12:15	SWIMMING	...Olympic Park Swimming Hall

4 x 100-meter freestyle relay, preliminary heats

| 1:00 | BOXING | ...Olympic Park Boxing Hall |

- lightweight, eliminations
- light middleweight, eliminations
- light heavyweight, eliminations

WEIGHT LIFTING......Fairgrounds Weight Lifting Hall
bantamweight, press

CANOEING......Augsburg Canoe Slalom Course
- kayak slalom singles
- women's kayak slalom singles

| 2:00 | EQUESTRIAN | ...Nymphenburg Dressage Facility |

three-day event, dressage

VOLLEYBALL......Olympic Park Volleyball Hall
preliminary round

WATER POLO......Dante Swimming Pool
preliminary round

| 2:30 | BASKETBALL | ...Basketball Hall |

preliminary round

| 3:00 | FIELD HOCKEY | ...Olympic Park Hockey Facility |

preliminary round

| 3:30 | VOLLEYBALL | ...Olympic Park Volleyball Hall |

women's preliminary round

| 4:00 | WATER POLO Dante Swimming Pool | |

preliminary round

| 4:30 | FOOTBALL | ...Nürnberg, Ingolstadt, & Regensburg |

preliminary round

FIELD HOCKEY......Olympic Park Hockey Facility
preliminary round

| 5:30 | FOOTBALL | ...Olympic Stadium |

preliminary round

SWIMMING......Olympic Park Swimming Hall
100-meter backstroke, semifinals

| 5:45 | SWIMMING | ...Olympic Park Swimming Hall |

women's 100-meter freestyle, semifinal

| 6:00 | GYMNASTICS | ...Olympic Park Sports Hall |

women's team competition, optionals

| | VOLLEYBALL | ...Olympic Park Volleyball Hall |

preliminary round

SWIMMING......Olympic Park Swimming Hall
100-meter butterfly, final

| 6:20 | SWIMMING | ...Olympic Park Swimming Hall |

women's 200-meter backstroke, final

| 6:40 | SWIMMING | ...Olympic Park Swimming Hall |

4 x 100-meter freestyle, final

| 7:00 | WRESTLING | ...Fairgrounds Wrestling-Judo Hall |

freestyle, eliminations
- welterweight
- middleweight
- light heavyweight
- heavyweight
- super heavyweight

BOXING..Olympic Park Boxing Hall
- lightweight, eliminations
- welterweight, eliminations
- light heavyweight, eliminations

WEIGHT LIFTING......Fairgrounds Weight Lifting Hall
bantamweight, snatch & jerk

WATER POLO......Olympic Park Swimming Hall
preliminary round

| 7:30 | VOLLEYBALL | ...Olympic Park Volleyball Hall |

preliminary round

| 8:00 | DIVING | ...Olympic Park Swimming Hall |

women's springboard, finals

| 9:00 | VOLLEYBALL | ...Olympic Park Volleyball Hall |

women's preliminary round

Tuesday, AUGUST 29

AM	EVENT	VENUE
8:00	EQUESTRIAN	...Olympic Stadium

three-day event, jumping

FENCING......Fairgrounds Fencing Hall 1
individual foil, eliminations

| 9:00 | SHOOTING | ...Hochbrück Shooting Range |

trap

MODERN PENTATHLON.....Hochbrück Shooting Range
shooting

ROWING......Oberschleissheim Regatta Course
- single sculls, repechage heats
- pair-oared shell without coxswain, repechage heats
- four-oared shell with coxswain, repechage heats

BASKETBALL......Basketball Hall
preliminary round

| 10:00 | WRESTLING | ...Fairgrounds Wrestling-Judo Hall |

freestyle, quarterfinals
- light flyweight
- flyweight
- bantamweight
- featherweight
- lightweight

GYMNASTICS......Olympic Park Sports Hall
team competition, optionals

CYCLING......Autobahn Cycling Race Course
100-kilometer road race, final

VOLLEYBALL......Olympic Park Volleyball Hall
preliminary round

SWIMMING..................Olympic Park
Swimming Hall
200-meter freestyle
WATER POLO Dante Swimming Pool
preliminary round
SWIMMING..................Olympic Park
Swimming Hall
200-meter freestyle,
preliminary heats

10:50 SWIMMING..................Olympic Park
Swimming Hall
women's 200-meter breaststroke,
preliminary heats

11:30 YACHTING ....Olympic Yachting
Center at Kiel Schilksee
• Finn monotype
• Flying Dutchman
• Soling class

11:35 SWIMMING..................Olympic Park
Swimming Hall
100-meter breaststroke,
preliminary heats

11:40 YACHTING ....Olympic Yachting
Center at Kiel Schilksee
Tempest

11:50 YACHTING ....Olympic Yachting
Center at Kiel Schilksee
Star class

11:55 YACHTING ....Olympic Yachting
Center at Kiel Schilksee
Dragon class

PM	EVENT	VENUE

1:00 BOXING......................Olympic Park
Boxing Hall
• featherweight, eliminations
• light middleweight,
eliminations
WEIGHT LIFTING.............Fairgrounds
Weight Lifting Hall
featherweight, press
DIVING ....Olympic Park
Swimming Hall
springboard, preliminaries

1:30 FIELD HOCKEY.............Olympic Park
Hockey Facility
preliminary round

2:00 EQUESTRIAN ....Olympic Stadium
three-day event, jumping
ROWING ....Oberschleissheim
Regatta Course
• double sculls, repechage heats
• pair-oared shell without
coxswain, repechage heats
• four-oared shell without
coxswain, repechage heats
• eight-oared shell with
coxswain, repechage heats
VOLLEYBALL..................Olympic Park
Volleyball Hall
preliminary round
FENCING ....Fairgrounds
Fencing Hall 1
individual foil, eliminations
WATER POLO Dante Swimming Pool
preliminary round

3:00 FIELD HOCKEY.............Olympic Park
Hockey Facility
preliminary round

3:30 VOLLEYBALL..................Olympic Park
Volleyball Hall
women's preliminary round

4:30 FOOTBALL.............Augsburg, Passau,
& Ingolstadt
preliminary round
FIELD HOCKEY.............Olympic Park
Hockey Facility
preliminary round
BASKETBALL ....Basketball Hall
preliminary round

5:30 FOOTBALL.............Olympic Stadium
preliminary round
SWIMMING..................Olympic Park
Swimming Hall
100-meter breaststroke, semifinal

5:40 SWIMMING..................Olympic Park
Swimming Hall
women's 100-meter freestyle,
final

6:00 GYMNASTICS ....Olympic Park
Sports Hall
team competition, optionals
SWIMMING..................Olympic Park
Swimming Hall
100-meter backstroke, final

6:20 SWIMMING..................Olympic Park
Swimming Hall
women's 200-meter
breaststroke, final

6:40 SWIMMING..................Olympic Park
Swimming Hall
200-meter freestyle, final

7:00 WEIGHT LIFTING............Fairgrounds,
Weight Lifter's Hall
featherweight, snatch & jerk
WRESTLING ...Fairgrounds Wrestling-
Judo Hall
freestyle, quarterfinals
• welterweight
• middleweight
• light heavyweight
• heavyweight
• super heavyweight
BOXING..Olympic Park Boxing Hall
• featherweight, eliminations
• middleweight, eliminations
• light middleweight,
eliminations
WATER POLO ....Olympic Park
Swimming Hall
preliminary round

7:30 VOLLEYBALL..................Olympic Park
Volleyball Hall
preliminary round

8:00 DIVING ....Olympic Park
Swimming Hall
springboard, preliminaries

9:00 VOLLEYBALL..................Olympic Park
Volleyball Hall
women's preliminary round

Wednesday, AUGUST 30

AM	EVENT	VENUE

7:00 EQUESTRIAN ......Riem Riding Facility
three-day event, cross-country

8:00 FENCING ....Fairgrounds
Fencing Hall 1
individual saber, eliminations

9:00 SHOOTING ....Hochbrück Shooting
Range
small-bore rifle, 3 positions
BASKETBALL................Basketball Hall
preliminary round

10:00 WRESTLING ...Fairgrounds Wrestling-
Judo Hall
freestyle, all weights, quarterfinals
VOLLEYBALL..................Olympic Park
Volleyball Hall
preliminary round
SWIMMING..................Olympic Park
Swimming Hall
women's 4 x 100-meter
freestyle relay, preliminary heats
WATER POLO ....Dante
Swimming Pool
preliminary round

10:20 SWIMMING..................Olympic Park
Swimming Hall
400-meter individual medley,
preliminary heats

11:10 SWIMMING..................Olympic Park
Swimming Hall
100-meter butterfly, preliminary
heats

11:30 YACHTING ....Olympic Yachting
Center at Kiel Schilksee
Finn monotype

11:35 SWIMMING..................Olympic Park
Swimming Hall
women's 400-meter freestyle,
preliminary heats

PM	EVENT	VENUE

12:15 YACHTING ....Olympic Yachting
Center at Kiel Schilksee
Soling class

12:25 YACHTING ....Olympic Yachting
Center at Kiel Schilksee
Dragon class

12:30 YACHTING ....Olympic Yachting
Center at Kiel Schilksee
Flying Dutchman

12:40 YACHTING ....Olympic Yachting
Center at Kiel Schilksee
Star class

12:50 YACHTING ....Olympic Yachting
Center at Kiel Schilksee
Tempest

1:00 BOXING..Olympic Park Boxing Hall
• bantamweight, eliminations
• welterweight, eliminations
WEIGHT LIFTING.............Fairgrounds
Weight Lifting Hall
lightweight, press
CANOEING ....Augsburg Canoe
Slalom Course
• kayak slalom singles
• women's kayak slalom singles
• Canadian slalom pairs

1:30 FIELD HOCKEY.............Olympic Park
Hockey Facility
preliminary round

2:00 MODERN PENTATHLON Olympic Park
Swimming Hall
swimming
VOLLEYBALL..................Olympic Park
Volleyball Hall
preliminary round
FENCING ....Fairgrounds
Fencing Hall 1
individual saber, quarterfinals
WATER POLO ....Dante
Swimming Pool
preliminary round

3:00 FIELD HOCKEY.............Olympic Park
Hockey Facility
preliminary round

3:30 VOLLEYBALL..................Olympic Park
Volleyball Hall
women's preliminary round
FENCING ....Fairgrounds
Fencing Hall 1
individual foil, semifinals

4:00 GYMNASTICS ....Olympic Park
Sports Hall
women's all-around, individual
competition

4:30 FOOTBALL ....Regensburg
Nürnberg, & Passau
preliminary round
FIELD HOCKEY.............Olympic Park
Hockey Facility
preliminary round

5:30 FOOTBALL.............Olympic Stadium
preliminary round
SWIMMING..................Olympic Park
Swimming Hall
100-meter butterfly, semifinals

5:40 SWIMMING..................Olympic Park
Swimming Hall
women's 4 x 100-meter
freestyle relay, final

6:00 SWIMMING..................Olympic Park
Swimming Hall
400-meter individual medley,
final

6:20 SWIMMING..................Olympic Park
Swimming Hall
100-meter breaststroke, final

6:30 BASKETBALL................Basketball Hall
preliminary round

6:40 SWIMMING..................Olympic Park
Swimming Hall
women's 400-meter freestyle,
final

7:00 BOXING..Olympic Park Boxing Hall
• bantamweight, eliminations
• welterweight, eliminations
WEIGHT LIFTING.............Fairgrounds
Weight Lifting Hall
lightweight, snatch & jerk
WRESTLING ...Fairgrounds Wrestling-
Judo Hall
freestyle, all weights,
quarterfinals
TEAM HANDBALL
main round, four games
WATER POLO ....Olympic Park
Swimming Hall
preliminary round

7:30 VOLLEYBALL..................Olympic Park
Volleyball Hall
preliminary round
FENCING ....Fairgrounds
Fencing Hall 1
individual foil, finals

8:00 GYMNASTICS ....Olympic Park
Sports Hall
all-around, individual
competition
DIVING ....Olympic Park
Swimming Hall
springboard, finals

8:15 TEAM HANDBALL
main round, four games

9:00 VOLLEYBALL..................Olympic Park
Volleyball Hall
women's preliminary round

Thursday, AUGUST 31

AM	EVENT	VENUE

9:00 SHOOTING ....Hochbrück Shooting
Range
• rapid-fire pistol
• running game target
• skeet

10:00 WRESTLING ...Fairgrounds Wrestling-
Judo Hall
freestyle, all weights, semifinals
FIELD HOCKEY.............Olympic Park
Hockey Facility
preliminary round
VOLLEYBALL..................Olympic Park
Volleyball Hall
preliminary round
SWIMMING..................Olympic Park
Swimming Hall
4 x 200-meter freestyle relay,
preliminary heats
WATER POLO Dante Swimming Pool
preliminary round
ATHLETICS.............Olympic Stadium
• 400-meter hurdles, heats
• women's long jump,
qualifying round

10:30 SWIMMING..................Olympic Park
Swimming Hall
women's 100-meter butterfly,
preliminary heats
ATHLETICS.............Olympic Stadium
women's javelin throw,
qualifying round

10:50 SWIMMING..................Olympic Park
Swimming Hall
women's 400-meter individual
medley, preliminary heats

11:00 ATHLETICS.............Olympic Stadium
100 meters, heats

11:30 ROWING ....Oberschleissheim
Regatta Course
• single sculls, semifinal
• double sculls, semifinal
• pair-oared shell without
coxswain, semifinal

- pair-oared shell with coxswain, semifinal
- four-oared shell without coxswain, semifinal
- four-oared shell with coxswain, semifinal
- eight-oared shell with coxswain, semifinal

FIELD HOCKEY............*Olympic Park Hockey Facility*
preliminary round

YACHTING ....*Olympic Yachting Center at Kiel Schilksee*
- Finn monotype
- Flying Dutchman
- Soling class

11:40 **YACHTING** ....*Olympic Yachting Center at Kiel Schilksee*
- Tempest
- Dragon class

11:50 **YACHTING** ....*Olympic Yachting Center at Kiel Schilksee*
Star class

PM	EVENT	VENUE

12:00 **MODERN PENTATHLON**.....*Fairgrounds*
cross-country running

12:30 **WATER POLO** ....*Olympic Park Swimming Hall*
preliminary round

1:00 **BOXING** ....*Olympic Park Boxing Hall*
- flyweight, eliminations
- light welterweight, eliminations

WEIGHT LIFTING............*Fairgrounds Weight Lifting Hall*
middleweight, press

2:00 **FIELD HOCKEY**............*Olympic Park Hockey Facility*
preliminary round

JUDO............................*Fairgrounds*
heavyweight, eliminations

VOLLEYBALL.................*Olympic Park Volleyball Hall*
preliminary round

WATER POLO *Dante Swimming Pool*
preliminary round

WEIGHT LIFTING............*Fairgrounds Weight Lifting Hall*
heavyweight, press

3:00 **CYCLING**....................*Olympic Park Cycling Stadium*
4,000-meter individual pursuit, heats

ATHLETICS............*Olympic Stadium*
800 meters, heats

3:30 **FIELD HOCKEY**............*Olympic Park Hockey Facility*
preliminary round

VOLLEYBALL.................*Olympic Park Volleyball Hall*
women's preliminary round

FENCING ....*Fairgrounds Fencing Hall 1*
individual saber, semifinals

ATHLETICS............*Olympic Stadium*
women's long jump, final

3:45 **ATHLETICS**............*Olympic Stadium*
20,000-meter walk, final

4:15 **ATHLETICS**............*Olympic Stadium*
100 meters, 2nd round

4:30 **FOOTBALL** ....*Augsburg, Ingolstadt, & Regensburg*
preliminary round

4:45 **ATHLETICS**............*Olympic Stadium*
women's 800 meters, heats

5:30 **SWIMMING**.................*Olympic Park Swimming Hall*
women's 100-meter butterfly, semifinals

ATHLETICS............*Olympic Stadium*
10,000 meters, heats

5:40 **SWIMMING**.................*Olympic Park Swimming Hall*
100-meter butterfly, final

6:00 **SWIMMING**.................*Olympic Park Swimming Hall*
women's 400-meter individual medley, final

6:20 **SWIMMING**.................*Olympic Park Swimming Hall*
4 x 200-meter freestyle relay, final

7:00 **WRESTLING** ...*Fairgrounds Wrestling-Judo Hall*
freestyle, all weights, finals

WEIGHT LIFTING............*Fairgrounds Weight Lifting Hall*
middleweight, snatch & jerk

WATER POLO ....*Olympic Park Swimming Hall*
preliminary round

7:30 **VOLLEYBALL**.................*Olympic Park Volleyball Hall*
preliminary round

FENCING ....*Fairgrounds Fencing Hall 1*
individual saber, finals

8:00 **GYMNASTICS** ....*Olympic Park Sports Hall*
women's individual apparatus, finals

CYCLING....................*Olympic Park Cycling Stadium*
- 1,000-meter time trial, final
- 4,000-meter individual pursuit, quarterfinals

JUDO............................*Fairgrounds*
heavyweight, eliminations & finals

WEIGHT LIFTING............*Fairgrounds Weight Lifting Hall*
heavyweight, snatch & jerk

9:00 **FOOTBALL** ....*Olympic Stadium*
preliminary round

VOLLEYBALL.................*Olympic Park Volleyball Hall*
women's preliminary round

Friday, SEPTEMBER 1

AM	EVENT	VENUE

8:00 **FENCING** ....*Fairgrounds Fencing Hall 1*
team foil, eliminations

9:00 **SHOOTING** ....*Hochbrück Shooting Range*
- rapid-fire pistol
- running game target
- skeet

BASKETBALL...............*Basketball Hall*
preliminary round

10:00 **ROWING** ....*Oberschleissheim Regatta Course*
- single sculls, final
- double sculls, final
- pair-oared shell without coxswain, final
- pair-oared shell with coxswain, final
- four-oared shell without coxswain, final
- four-oared shell with coxswain, final
- eight-oared shell with coxswain, final

CYCLING....................*Olympic Park Cycling Stadium*
1,000-meter sprint, heats

FIELD HOCKEY............*Olympic Park Hockey Facility*
preliminary round

VOLLEYBALL.................*Olympic Park Volleyball Hall*
preliminary round

SWIMMING.................*Olympic Park Swimming Hall*
women's 100-meter backstroke, preliminary heats

WATER POLO ....*Dante Swimming Pool*
final round

ATHLETICS............*Olympic Stadium*
- pole vault, qualifying round
- discus throw, qualifying round

10:25 **SWIMMING**.................*Olympic Park Swimming Hall*
women's 100-meter breaststroke, preliminary heats

10:50 **SWIMMING**.................*Olympic Park Swimming Hall*
400-meter freestyle, preliminary heats

11:00 **ATHLETICS**............*Olympic Stadium*
women's 100 meters, heats

11:30 **FIELD HOCKEY**............*Olympic Park Hockey Facility*
preliminary round

YACHTING ....*Olympic Yachting Center at Kiel Schilksee*
- Finn monotype
- Flying Dutchman

11:40 **YACHTING** ....*Olympic Yachting Center at Kiel Schilksee*
Tempest

11:50 **YACHTING** ....*Olympic Yachting Center at Kiel Schilksee*
Star class

SWIMMING.................*Olympic Park Swimming Hall*
women's 200-meter freestyle, preliminary heats

PM	EVENT	VENUE

12:15 **YACHTING** ....*Olympic Yachting Center at Kiel Schilksee*
Soling class

12:55 **YACHTING** ....*Olympic Yachting Center at Kiel Schilksee*
Dragon class

1:00 **BOXING** ....*Olympic Park Boxing Hall*
- lightweight, eliminations
- welterweight, eliminations

DIVING ....*Olympic Park Swimming Hall*
women's platform, preliminaries

2:00 **JUDO**............................*Fairgrounds*
light heavyweight, eliminations

VOLLEYBALL.................*Olympic Park Volleyball Hall*
preliminary round

WATER POLO *Dante Swimming Pool*
final round

2:30 **BASKETBALL**...............*Basketball Hall*
preliminary round

ATHLETICS............*Olympic Stadium*
400-meter hurdles, 2nd round

3:00 **ATHLETICS**............*Olympic Stadium*
women's 100 meters, 2nd round

CYCLING....................*Olympic Park Cycling Stadium*
- 1,000-meter sprint, heats
- 4,000-meter individual pursuit, semifinals

3:30 **VOLLEYBALL**.................*Olympic Park Volleyball Hall*
women's preliminary round

ATHLETICS............*Olympic Stadium*
- 100 meters, semifinal
- women's javelin throw, final

4:00 **ATHLETICS**............*Olympic Stadium*
800 meters, 2nd round

4:30 **ATHLETICS**............*Olympic Stadium*
3,000-meter steeplechase, heats

FOOTBALL........................*Nürnberg, Regensburg, & Passau*
preliminary round

5:00 **FENCING** ....*Fairgrounds Fencing Hall 1*
team foil, quarterfinals

5:30 **ATHLETICS**............*Olympic Stadium*
100 meters, final

5:40 **ATHLETICS**............*Olympic Stadium*
women's 800 meters, 2nd round

6:00 **SWIMMING**.................*Olympic Park Swimming Hall*
women's 100-meter backstroke, semifinals

6:10 **SWIMMING**.................*Olympic Park Swimming Hall*
women's 100-meter breaststroke, semifinals

6:20 **SWIMMING**.................*Olympic Park Swimming Hall*
400-meter freestyle, final

6:30 **BASKETBALL**...............*Basketball Hall*
preliminary round

6:40 **SWIMMING**.................*Olympic Park Swimming Hall*
women's 100-meter butterfly, final

7:00 **BOXING**..*Olympic Park Boxing Hall*
- lightweight, eliminations
- welterweight, eliminations

TEAM HANDBALL
main round, four games

SWIMMING.................*Olympic Park Swimming Hall*
women's 200-meter freestyle, final

7:30 **GYMNASTICS** ....*Olympic Park Sports Hall*
individual apparatus, finals

WATER POLO ....*Olympic Park Swimming Hall*
final round

8:00 **JUDO**............................*Fairgrounds*
light heavyweight, eliminations & finals

CYCLING....................*Olympic Park Cycling Stadium*
- 1,000-meter sprint, heats
- 4,000-meter individual pursuit, final

8:15 **TEAM HANDBALL**
main round, four games

8:30 **DIVING** ....*Olympic Park Swimming Hall*
women's platform, preliminaries

9:00 **FOOTBALL**............*Olympic Stadium*
preliminary round

VOLLEYBALL.................*Olympic Park Volleyball Hall*
women's preliminary round

Saturday, SEPTEMBER 2

AM	EVENT	VENUE

8:00 **FENCING** ....*Fairgrounds Fencing Hall 1*
team foil, eliminations & semifinals

9:00 **SHOOTING** ....*Hochbrück Shooting Range*
- free rifle
- skeet

9:30 **ATHLETICS**............*Olympic Stadium*
women's pentathlon

10:00 **EQUESTRIAN** ....*Olympic Stadium*
jumping, individual

ROWING ....*Oberschleissheim Regatta Course*
four-oared shell with coxswain, final

FIELD HOCKEY............*Olympic Park Hockey Facility*
preliminary round

VOLLEYBALL.................*Olympic Park Volleyball Hall*
preliminary round

FENCING ....*Fairgrounds Fencing Hall 1*
women's individual foil, eliminations

SWIMMING.................*Olympic Park Swimming Hall*
100-meter freestyle, preliminary heats
ATHLETICS............*Olympic Stadium*
javelin throw, qualifying round
WATER POLO ....*Dante Swimming Pool*
final round

10:30 ROWING ....*Oberschleissheim Regatta Course*
pair-oared shell without coxswain, final

10:35 SWIMMING.................*Olympic Park Swimming Hall*
200-meter backstroke, preliminary heats

11:00 ROWING ....*Oberschleissheim Regatta Course*
single sculls, final

11:10 SWIMMING.................*Olympic Park Swimming Hall*
200-meter breaststroke, preliminary heats

11:30 ROWING ....*Oberschleissheim Regatta Course*
pair-oared shell with coxswain, final
FIELD HOCKEY............*Olympic Park Hockey Facility*
preliminary round

11:55 SWIMMING ....*Olympic Park Swimming Hall*
women's 800-meter freestyle, preliminary heats

PM	EVENT	VENUE

12:00 ROWING ....*Oberschleissheim Regatta Course*
four-oared shell without coxswain, final

12:30 ROWING ....*Oberschleissheim Regatta Course*
double sculls, final

1:00 BOXING..*Olympic Park Boxing Hall*
• bantamweight, eliminations
• light middleweight, eliminations
• light heavyweight, eliminations
WEIGHT LIFTING.............*Fairgrounds Weight Lifting Hall*
light heavyweight, press
ROWING ....*Oberschleissheim Regatta Course*
eight-oared shell with coxswain, final
ATHLETICS............*Olympic Stadium*
pole vault, final

2:00 JUDO............................*Fairgrounds*
middleweight, eliminations
WATER POLO ....*Dante Swimming Pool*
final round
VOLLEYBALL.................*Olympic Park Volleyball Hall*
preliminary round
FENCING ....*Fairgrounds Fencing Hall 1*
women's individual foil, eliminations & quarterfinals
WEIGHT LIFTING.............*Fairgrounds Weight Lifting Hall*
middleweight, press
CYCLING....................*Olympic Park Cycling Stadium*
• 1,000-meter sprint, quarterfinals
• 4,000-meter team pursuit, heats

3:00 ATHLETICS............*Olympic Stadium*
women's 100 meters

3:30 VOLLEYBALL.................*Olympic Park Volleyball Hall*
women's semifinal round

FENCING ....*Fairgrounds Fencing Hall 1*
team foil, finals
ATHLETICS............*Olympic Stadium*
women's 400 meters, heats

4:00 ATHLETICS............*Olympic Stadium*
discus throw, final

4:15 ATHLETICS............*Olympic Stadium*
400-meter hurdles, final

5:00 ATHLETICS............*Olympic Stadium*
800 meters, final

5:30 ATHLETICS............*Olympic Stadium*
women's 100 meters, final

6:00 SWIMMING.................*Olympic Park Swimming Hall*
100-meter freestyle, semifinals

6:10 SWIMMING.................*Olympic Park Swimming Hall*
200-meter backstroke, final

6:30 SWIMMING.................*Olympic Park Swimming Hall*
200-meter breaststroke, final

6:50 SWIMMING.................*Olympic Park Swimming Hall*
women's 100-meter backstroke, final

7:00 BOXING .*Olympic Park Boxing Hall*
• bantamweight, eliminations
• light middleweight, eliminations
• light heavyweight, eliminations
WEIGHT LIFTING.............*Fairgrounds Weight Lifting Hall*
light heavyweight, snatch & jerk

7:10 SWIMMING.................*Olympic Park Swimming Hall*
women's 100-meter breaststroke, final

7:30 VOLLEYBALL.................*Olympic Park Volleyball Hall*
preliminary round
FENCING ....*Fairgrounds Fencing Hall 1*
team foil, finals
WATER POLO ....*Olympic Park Swimming Hall*
final round

8:00 JUDO............................*Fairgrounds*
middleweight, eliminations & finals
WEIGHT LIFTING.............*Fairgrounds Weight Lifting Hall*
middleweight, snatch & jerk
CYCLING....................*Olympic Park Cycling Stadium*
• 1,000-meter sprint, semifinals & final
• 4,000-meter team pursuit, quarterfinals

8:30 DIVING ....*Olympic Park Swimming Hall*
women's platform, finals

9:00 VOLLEYBALL.................*Olympic Park Volleyball Hall*
women's semifinal round

Sunday, SEPTEMBER 3

AM	EVENT	VENUE

8:00 FENCING ....*Fairgrounds Fencing Hall 1*
team saber, eliminations

10:00 VOLLEYBALL.................*Olympic Park Volleyball Hall*
preliminary round
SWIMMING.................*Olympic Park Swimming Hall*
200-meter individual medley, preliminary heats
ATHLETICS............*Olympic Stadium*
• 110-meter hurdles, heats
• triple jump, qualifying round

• women's high jump, qualifying round
WATER POLO ....*Dante Swimming Pool*
final round

10:30 FIELD HOCKEY............*Olympic Park Hockey Facility*
preliminary round

10:45 SWIMMING.................*Olympic Park Swimming Hall*
women's 4 x 100-meter medley relay, preliminary heats

11:00 ATHLETICS............*Olympic Stadium*
• 200 meters, heats
• women's pentathlon

11:05 SWIMMING.................*Olympic Park Swimming Hall*
1,500-meter freestyle, preliminary heats

PM	EVENT	VENUE

1:00 BOXING..*Olympic Park Boxing Hall*
• flyweight, eliminations
• featherweight, eliminations
• lightweight, eliminations
• heavyweight, eliminations
WEIGHT LIFTING.............*Fairgrounds Weight Lifting Hall*
middle heavyweight, press
FIELD HOCKEY............*Olympic Park Hockey Facility*
preliminary round

2:00 JUDO............................*Fairgrounds*
welterweight, eliminations
VOLLEYBALL.................*Olympic Park Volleyball Hall*
preliminary round
DIVING ....*Olympic Park Swimming Hall*
platform, preliminaries
ATHLETICS............*Olympic Stadium*
50,000-meter walk
WEIGHT LIFTING.............*Fairgrounds Weight Lifting Hall*
welterweight, press
WATER POLO ....*Dante Swimming Pool*
final round

2:30 FIELD HOCKEY............*Olympic Park Hockey Facility*
preliminary round

3:00 FOOTBALL........................*Nürnberg, Regensburg, & Passau*
semifinal round
ATHLETICS............*Olympic Stadium*
women's 400 meters, 2nd round

3:30 VOLLEYBALL.................*Olympic Park Volleyball Hall*
women's semifinal round
FENCING ....*Fairgrounds Fencing Hall 1*
• team saber, quarterfinals
• women's individual foil, semifinals
ATHLETICS............*Olympic Stadium*
javelin throw, final

3:40 ATHLETICS............*Olympic Stadium*
200 meters, 2nd round

4:00 FIELD HOCKEY............*Olympic Park Hockey Facility*
preliminary round
ATHLETICS............*Olympic Stadium*
400 meters, heats

5:15 ATHLETICS............*Olympic Stadium*
10,000 meters, final

6:00 SWIMMING.................*Olympic Park Swimming Hall*
200-meter individual medley, final
ATHLETICS............*Olympic Stadium*
women's 800 meters, final

6:20 SWIMMING.................*Olympic Park Swimming Hall*
women's 800-meter freestyle, final

6:45 SWIMMING.................*Olympic Park Swimming Hall*
100-meter freestyle, final

7:00 BOXING..*Olympic Park Boxing Hall*
• flyweight, eliminations
• featherweight, eliminations
• lightweight, eliminations
• heavyweight, eliminations
WEIGHT LIFTING.............*Fairgrounds Weight Lifting Hall*
middle heavyweight, snatch & jerk

7:05 SWIMMING.................*Olympic Park Swimming Hall*
women's 4 x 100-meter medley relay, final

7:30 VOLLEYBALL.................*Olympic Park Volleyball Hall*
preliminary round
FENCING ....*Fairgrounds Fencing Hall 1*
women's individual foil, finals
WATER POLO ....*Olympic Park Swimming Hall*
final round

8:00 JUDO............................*Fairgrounds*
welterweight, eliminations & finals
TEAM HANDBALL
main round, four games
WEIGHT LIFTING.............*Fairgrounds Weight Lifting Hall*
welterweight, snatch & jerk
CYCLING....................*Olympic Park Cycling Stadium*
• 2,000-meter tandem, heats & quarterfinals
• 4,000-meter team pursuit, semifinals

8:30 DIVING ....*Olympic Park Swimming Hall*
platform, preliminaries

9:00 FOOTBALL.............*Olympic Stadium*
semifinal round
VOLLEYBALL.................*Olympic Park Volleyball Hall*
semifinal round

9:15 TEAM HANDBALL
main round, four games

Monday, SEPTEMBER 4

AM	EVENT	VENUE

8:00 EQUESTRIAN ....*Nymphenburg Dressage Facility*
dressage
FENCING ....*Fairgrounds Fencing Hall 1*
individual épée, eliminations

10:00 FIELD HOCKEY............*Olympic Park Hockey Facility*
preliminary round
SWIMMING.................*Olympic Park Swimming Hall*
women's 200-meter butterfly, preliminary heats
WATER POLO *Dante Swimming Pool*
final round
ATHLETICS.............*Olympic Stadium*
women's 100-meter hurdles, heats

10:30 FENCING ....*Fairgrounds Fencing Hall 1*
team saber, eliminations & semifinals
SWIMMING.................*Olympic Park Swimming Hall*
200-meter backstroke, preliminary heats
ATHLETICS.............*Olympic Stadium*
• women's shot put, qualifying round
• hammer throw, qualifying round

| 10:50 | ATHLETICS............*Olympic Stadium* |
women's 200 meters, heats
| 11:05 | SWIMMING.................*Olympic Park Swimming Hall* |
4 x 100-meter medley relay, preliminary heats
| 11:30 | FIELD HOCKEY.............*Olympic Park Hockey Facility* |
preliminary round
YACHTING ....*Olympic Yachting Center at Kiel Schilksee*
• Finn monotype
• Flying Dutchman
• Soling class
| 11:35 | ATHLETICS............*Olympic Stadium* |
400 meters, 2nd round
| 11:40 | YACHTING ....*Olympic Yachting Center at Kiel Schilksee* |
• Tempest
• Dragon class
| 11:50 | YACHTING ....*Olympic Yachting Center at Kiel Schilksee* |
Star class

PM	EVENT	VENUE
12:30	WATER POLO ....*Olympic Park Swimming Hall*	

final round
| 1:00 | BOXING..*Olympic Park Boxing Hall* |
• light flyweight, eliminations
• light welterweight, eliminations
• middleweight, eliminations
WEIGHT LIFTING............*Fairgrounds Weight Lifting Hall*
heavyweight, press
| 2:00 | JUDO............................*Fairgrounds* |
lightweight, eliminations
EQUESTRIAN ....*Nymphenburg Dressage Facility*
dressage
FIELD HOCKEY.............*Olympic Park Hockey Facility*
preliminary round
FENCING ....*Fairgrounds Fencing Hall 1*
individual épée, quarterfinals
WATER POLO *Dante Swimming Pool*
final round
WEIGHT LIFTING.............*Fairgrounds Weight Lifting Hall*
lightweight, press
| 2:30 | ATHLETICS.............*Olympic Stadium* |
110-meter hurdles, 2nd round
| 3:00 | ATHLETICS.............*Olympic Stadium* |
women's high jump, final
| 3:26 | ATHLETICS.............*Olympic Stadium* |
200 meters, semifinal
| 3:30 | FIELD HOCKEY.............*Olympic Park Hockey Facility* |
preliminary round
FENCING ....*Fairgrounds Fencing Hall 1*
team saber, finals
| 3:45 | ATHLETICS.............*Olympic Stadium* |
women's 1,500 meters, heats
| 4:00 | ATHLETICS.............*Olympic Stadium* |
triple jump, final
| 4:20 | ATHLETICS.............*Olympic Stadium* |
women's 200 meters, 2nd round
| 4:40 | ATHLETICS.............*Olympic Stadium* |
3,000-meter steeplechase, final
| 5:15 | ATHLETICS.............*Olympic Stadium* |
400 meters, semifinals
| 5:45 | ATHLETICS.............*Olympic Stadium* |
women's 400 meters, semifinals
| 6:00 | SWIMMING.................*Olympic Park Swimming Hall* |
women's 200-meter butterfly, final
| 6:10 | ATHLETICS.............*Olympic Stadium* |
200 meters, final
| 6:20 | SWIMMING.................*Olympic Park Swimming Hall* |
1,500-meter freestyle, final

| 6:50 | SWIMMING.................*Olympic Park Swimming Hall* |
200-meter backstroke, final
| 7:00 | BOXING..*Olympic Park Boxing Hall* |
• light flyweight, eliminations
• light welterweight, eliminations
• middleweight, eliminations
WEIGHT LIFTING............*Fairgrounds Weight Lifting Hall*
heavyweight, snatch & jerk
| 7:10 | SWIMMING.................*Olympic Park Swimming Hall* |
4 x 100-meter medley relay, final
| 7:30 | FENCING ....*Fairgrounds Fencing Hall 1* |
team saber, finals
WATER POLO ....*Olympic Park Swimming Hall*
final round
| 8:00 | JUDO............................*Fairgrounds* |
lightweight, eliminations & finals
CYCLING.....................*Olympic Park Cycling Stadium*
• 2,000-meter tandem, semifinals & final
• 4,000-meter team pursuit, final
TEAM HANDBALL
main round
WEIGHT LIFTING.............*Fairgrounds Weight Lifting Hall*
lightweight, snatch & jerk
| 8:30 | DIVING ....*Olympic Park Swimming Hall* |
platform, finals
| 9:15 | TEAM HANDBALL |
main round

Tuesday, SEPTEMBER 5

AM	EVENT	VENUE
9:00	VOLLEYBALL.................*Olympic Park Volleyball Hall*	

preliminary round
CANOEING............*Oberschleissheim Regatta Course*
• kayak singles, preliminaries
• women's kayak singles, preliminaries
• kayak pairs, preliminaries
• women's kayak pairs, preliminaries
• Canadian singles, preliminaries
• Canadian pairs, preliminaries
• kayak fours, preliminaries
| 10:00 | WRESTLING ...*Fairgrounds Wrestling-Judo Hall* |
Greco-Roman, eliminations
• light flyweight
• flyweight
• bantamweight
• featherweight
• lightweight
| 10:30 | VOLLEYBALL.................*Olympic Park Volleyball Hall* |
preliminary round
| 11:30 | YACHTING ....*Olympic Yachting Center at Kiel Schilksee* |
Finn monotype
| 11:45 | YACHTING ....*Olympic Yachting Center at Kiel Schilksee* |
Flying Dutchman

PM	EVENT	VENUE
12:00	YACHTING ....*Olympic Yachting Center at Kiel Schilksee*	

Tempest
| 12:20 | YACHTING ....*Olympic Yachting Center at Kiel Schilksee* |
Star class
| 1:00 | BOXING..*Olympic Park Boxing Hall* |

• flyweight, eliminations
• bantamweight, eliminations
• lightweight, eliminations
• welterweight, eliminations
• light middleweight, eliminations
• heavyweight, eliminations
WEIGHT LIFTING.............*Fairgrounds Weight Lifting Hall*
super heavyweight, press
| 2:00 | VOLLEYBALL.................*Olympic Park Volleyball Hall* |
preliminary round
| 3:00 | BASKETBALL...............*Basketball Hall* |
semifinal
| 3:30 | TEAM HANDBALL |
main round
VOLLEYBALL.................*Olympic Park Volleyball Hall*
preliminary round
FENCING ....*Fairgrounds Fencing Hall 1*
individual épée, semifinals
| 4:30 | FOOTBALL.............*Augsburg, Passau, & Ingolstadt* |
semifinal round
| 4:45 | BASKETBALL...............*Basketball Hall* |
semifinal
| 7:00 | WEIGHT LIFTING.............*Fairgrounds Weight Lifting Hall* |
super heavyweight, snatch & jerk

Wednesday, SEPTEMBER 6

PM	EVENT	VENUE
2:00	EQUESTRIAN ....*Nymphenburg Dressage Facility*	

dressage
| 5:00 | TEAM HANDBALL |
final round
| 7:00 | WEIGHT LIFTING.............*Fairgrounds Weight Lifting Hall* |
super heavyweight, snatch & jerk
WRESTLING ...*Fairgrounds Wrestling-Judo Hall*
Greco-Roman, eliminations
• welterweight
• middleweight
• light heavyweight
• heavyweight
• super heavyweight
BOXING..*Olympic Park Boxing Hall*
• flyweight, eliminations
• bantamweight, eliminations
• lightweight, eliminations
• welterweight, eliminations
• light middleweight, eliminations
• heavyweight, eliminations
| 7:30 | VOLLEYBALL.................*Olympic Park Volleyball Hall* |
preliminary round
FENCING ....*Fairgrounds Fencing Hall 1*
individual épée, finals
| 8:00 | TEAM HANDBALL |
main round
FOOTBALL ....*Olympic Stadium*
semifinal round
BASKETBALL...............*Basketball Hall*
semifinal
| 9:00 | VOLLEYBALL.................*Olympic Park Volleyball Hall* |
preliminary round

Thursday, SEPTEMBER 7

AM	EVENT	VENUE
8:00	FENCING ....*Fairgrounds Fencing Hall 1*	

women's team foil, eliminations

| 9:00 | CANOEING............*Oberschleissheim Regatta Course* |
• kayak singles, repechage heats
• women's kayak singles, repechage heats
• kayak pairs, repechage heats
• Canadian pairs, repechage heats
• kayak fours, repechage heats
| 10:00 | WRESTLING ...*Fairgrounds Wrestling-Judo Hall* |
Greco-Roman, eliminations
• welterweight
• middleweight
• light heavyweight
• heavyweight
• super heavyweight
ARCHERY...................*Archery Range*
• individual
• women's individual
FIELD HOCKEY.............*Olympic Park Hockey Facility*
semifinal round
ATHLETICS.............*Olympic Stadium*
decathlon
CYCLING ....*Grünwald Cycling Race Course*
road race, final
| 11:30 | FIELD HOCKEY.............*Olympic Park Hockey Facility* |
semifinal round

PM	EVENT	VENUE
1:00	BOXING ....*Olympic Park Boxing Hall*	

• lightweight, eliminations
• featherweight, eliminations
• light welterweight, eliminations
• middleweight, eliminations
• light heavyweight, eliminations
| 2:00 | ARCHERY...................*Archery Range* |
• individual
• women's individual
FIELD HOCKEY.............*Olympic Park Hockey Facility*
semifinal round
VOLLEYBALL.................*Olympic Park Volleyball Hall*
women's final round
ATHLETICS.............*Olympic Stadium*
women's 200 meters, semifinal
| 2:15 | ATHLETICS.............*Olympic Stadium* |
women's 1,500 meters, 2nd round
| 2:30 | ATHLETICS.............*Olympic Stadium* |
5,000 meters, heats
| 3:00 | BASKETBALL...............*Basketball Hall* |
semifinal
| 3:30 | TEAM HANDBALL |
final round
VOLLEYBALL.................*Olympic Park Volleyball Hall*
women's final round
| 4:00 | FIELD HOCKEY.............*Olympic Park Hockey Facility* |
semifinal round
FENCING ....*Fairgrounds Fencing Hall 1*
women's team foil, quarterfinals
ATHLETICS.............*Olympic Stadium*
110-meter hurdles, final
| 4:15 | ATHLETICS.............*Olympic Stadium* |
women's 100-meter hurdles, 2nd round
| 4:30 | ATHLETICS.............*Olympic Stadium* |
women's shot put, final
| 4:50 | ATHLETICS.............*Olympic Stadium* |
hammer throw, final
| 5:30 | ATHLETICS.............*Olympic Stadium* |
400 meters, final
| 5:45 | ATHLETICS.............*Olympic Stadium* |
women's 200 meters, final
| 6:00 | ATHLETICS.............*Olympic Stadium* |
women's 400 meters, final

7:00	WRESTLING ...Fairgrounds Wrestling-Judo Hall
	Greco-Roman, eliminations
	• light flyweight
	• bantamweight
	• featherweight
	• lightweight
	BOXING ..Olympic Park Boxing Hall
	• light flyweight, eliminations
	• featherweight, eliminations
	• light welterweight, eliminations
	• middleweight, eliminations
	• light heavyweight, eliminations
7:30	VOLLEYBALL ....Olympic Park Volleyball Hall
	women's final round
8:00	TEAM HANDBALL
	final round
	BASKETBALL ....Basketball Hall
	semifinal
9:00	VOLLEYBALL ....Olympic Park Volleyball Hall
	women's final round

Friday, SEPTEMBER 8

AM	EVENT	VENUE
8:00	FENCING ....Fairgrounds Fencing Hall 1	
	team épée, eliminations	
9:00	CANOEING ....Oberschleissheim Regatta Course	
	• kayak singles, semifinals	
	• women's kayak singles, semifinals	
	• women's kayak pairs, semifinals	
	• Canadian pairs, semifinals	
	• kayak fours, semifinals	
	ATHLETICS ....Olympic Stadium	
	decathlon	
10:00	WRESTLING ...Fairgrounds Wrestling-Judo Hall	
	Greco-Roman, quarterfinals	
	• light flyweight	
	• flyweight	
	• bantamweight	
	• featherweight	
	• lightweight	
	FIELD HOCKEY ....Olympic Park Hockey Facility	
	semifinal round	
	VOLLEYBALL ....Olympic Park Volleyball Hall	
	semifinal round	
	FENCING ....Fairgrounds Fencing Hall 1	
	women's team foil, semifinals	
	ATHLETICS ....Olympic Stadium	
	• long jump, qualifying round	
	• shot put, qualifying round	
	ARCHERY ....Archery Range	
	• individual	
	• women's individual	
11:30	FIELD HOCKEY ....Olympic Park Hockey Facility	
	semifinal round	
	YACHTING ....Olympic Yachting Center at Kiel Schilksee	
	• Flying Dutchman	
	• Star class	

PM	EVENT	VENUE
12:15	YACHTING ....Olympic Yachting Center at Kiel Schilksee	
	Soling class	
12:55	YACHTING ....Olympic Yachting Center at Kiel Schilksee	
	Tempest	
1:25	YACHTING ....Olympic Yachting Center at Kiel Schilksee	

Dragon class
2:00	ARCHERY ....Archery Range
	• individual
	• women's individual
	BOXING ..Olympic Park Boxing Hall
	all weights, semifinals
	EQUESTRIAN ....Nymphenburg Dressage Facility
	dressage
	FIELD HOCKEY ....Olympic Park Hockey Facility
	semifinal round
	VOLLEYBALL ....Olympic Park Volleyball Hall
	semifinal round
3:00	BASKETBALL ....Basketball Hall
	semifinal
3:30	TEAM HANDBALL
	final round
	VOLLEYBALL ....Olympic Park Volleyball Hall
	semifinal round
	FENCING ....Fairgrounds Fencing Hall 1
	women's team foil, finals
4:00	FIELD HOCKEY ....Olympic Park Hockey Facility
	semifinal round
	FENCING ....Fairgrounds Fencing Hall 1
	team épée, eliminations
	ATHLETICS ....Olympic Stadium
	women's 100-meter hurdles, final
4:30	FOOTBALL ....Olympic Stadium
	semifinal round
4:45	ATHLETICS ....Olympic Stadium
	1,500 meters, heats
7:00	WRESTLING ...Fairgrounds Wrestling-Judo Hall
	Greco-Roman, quarterfinals
	• welterweight
	• middleweight
	• light heavyweight
	• heavyweight
	• super heavyweight
	BOXING ..Olympic Park Boxing Hall
	all weights, semifinals
7:30	VOLLEYBALL ....Olympic Park Volleyball Hall
	semifinal round
	FENCING ....Fairgrounds Fencing Hall 1
	women's team foil, finals
8:00	TEAM HANDBALL
	final round
	BASKETBALL ....Basketball Hall
	semifinal
9:00	VOLLEYBALL ....Olympic Park Volleyball Hall
	semifinal round
9:30	FOOTBALL ....Nürnberg, Augsburg, & Regensburg
	semifinal round

Saturday, SEPTEMBER 9

AM	EVENT	VENUE
8:00	FENCING ....Fairgrounds Fencing Hall 1	
	team épée, quarterfinals & semifinals	
10:00	WRESTLING ...Fairgrounds Wrestling-Judo Hall	
	Greco-Roman, all weights, quarterfinals	
	FIELD HOCKEY ....Olympic Park Hockey Facility	
	final round	

	VOLLEYBALL ....Olympic Park Volleyball Hall
	final round
	CANOEING ....Oberschleissheim Regatta Course
	• kayak singles, final
	• women's kayak singles, final
	• kayak pairs, final
	• women's kayak pairs, final
	• Canadian singles, final
	• Canadian pairs, final
	• kayak fours, final
	ATHLETICS ....Olympic Stadium
	high jump, qualifying round
	ARCHERY ....Archery Range
	• individual
	• women's individual
10:30	ATHLETICS ....Olympic Stadium
	women's discus throw, qualifying round
11:30	FIELD HOCKEY ....Olympic Park Hockey Facility
	final round
	YACHTING ....Olympic Yachting Center at Kiel Schilksee
	• Flying Dutchman
	• Star class

PM	EVENT	VENUE
12:16	YACHTING ....Olympic Yachting Center at Kiel Schilksee	
	Soling class	
12:55	YACHTING ....Olympic Yachting Center at Kiel Schilksee	
	Tempest	
1:00	YACHTING ....Olympic Yachting Center at Kiel Schilksee	
	Finn monotype	
1:25	YACHTING ....Olympic Yachting Center at Kiel Schilksee	
	Dragon class	
2:00	JUDO ....Fairgrounds	
	open category, eliminations	
	WEIGHT LIFTING ....Fairgrounds Weight Lifting Hall	
	open category, press	
	ARCHERY ....Archery Range	
	• individual	
	• women's individual	
2:30	ATHLETICS ....Olympic Stadium	
	• 4 x 100-meter relay, heat 4 and semifinal	
	• shot put, final	
3:10	ATHLETICS ....Olympic Stadium	
	women's 4 x 400-meter relay, heats	
3:20	ATHLETICS ....Olympic Stadium	
	long jump, final	
3:30	TEAM HANDBALL	
	final round	
	VOLLEYBALL ....Olympic Park Volleyball Hall	
	final round	
	FENCING ....Fairgrounds Fencing Hall 1	
	team épée, finals	
3:45	ATHLETICS ....Olympic Stadium	
	4 x 400-meter relay, heats	
4:40	ATHLETICS ....Olympic Stadium	
	1,500 meters, 2nd round	
5:10	ATHLETICS ....Olympic Stadium	
	women's 4 x 100-meter relay, heats	
5:20	ATHLETICS ....Olympic Stadium	
	long jump, final	
5:40	ATHLETICS ....Olympic Stadium	
	4 x 100-meter relay, heats	
6:00	BASKETBALL ....Basketball Hall	
	semifinal	
	ATHLETICS ....Olympic Stadium	
	women's 1,500 meters, final	

7:30	VOLLEYBALL ....Olympic Park Volleyball Hall
	final round
	FENCING ....Fairgrounds Fencing Hall 1
	team épée, finals
8:00	JUDO ....Fairgrounds
	open category, eliminations & finals
	TEAM HANDBALL
	final round
	WEIGHT LIFTING ....Fairgrounds Weight Lifting Hall
	open category, snatch & jerk
9:00	VOLLEYBALL ....Olympic Park Volleyball Hall
	final round

Sunday, SEPTEMBER 10

AM	EVENT	VENUE
8:00	EQUESTRIAN ....Olympic Stadium	
	jumping, team	
10:00	WRESTLING ..Fairgrounds Wrestling-Judo Hall	
	Greco-Roman, all weights, semifinals	
	TEAM HANDBALL	
	final round	
	FOOTBALL ....Olympic Stadium	
	final round	
	FIELD HOCKEY ....Olympic Park Hockey Facility	
	final round	
	ARCHERY ....Archery Range	
	• individual	
	• women's individual	

PM	EVENT	VENUE
12:00	FIELD HOCKEY ....Olympic Park Hockey Facility	
	final round	
2:00	ARCHERY ....Archery Range	
	• individual	
	• women's individual	
2:30	ATHLETICS ....Olympic Stadium	
	high jump, final	
3:00	ATHLETICS ....Olympic Stadium	
	• marathon	
	• women's discus, final	
3:10	ATHLETICS ....Olympic Stadium	
	5,000 meters, final	
3:35	ATHLETICS ....Olympic Stadium	
	1,500 meters, final	
3:45	EQUESTRIAN ....Olympic Stadium	
	jumping, team	
3:55	ATHLETICS ....Olympic Stadium	
	women's 4 x 100-meter relay, final	
4:10	ATHLETICS ....Olympic Stadium	
	4 x 100-meter relay, final	
4:25	ATHLETICS ....Olympic Stadium	
	women's 4 x 400-meter relay, final	
4:45	ATHLETICS ....Olympic Stadium	
	4 x 400-meter relay, final	
7:00	WRESTLING	
	Greco-Roman, all weights, finals	
	BOXING ..Olympic Park Boxing Hall	
	all weights, finals	
8:15	FOOTBALL ....Olympic Stadium	
	final round	
9:00	TEAM HANDBALL	
	final round	

Monday, SEPTEMBER 11

PM	EVENT	VENUE
3:00	CLOSING CEREMONY ....Olympic Park	

LEGEND   MEN'S EVENT   WOMEN'S EVENT   MIXED EVENT  OLYMPIC RECORD   WORLD RECORD

DNF = Did Not Finish   DQ = Disqualified   est = estimated   NR = No Result   * refer to end maps for country codes

ATHLETICS (Track & Field)

Event	Gold	Silver	Bronze	4th–6th		
100 METERS	URS 10.14 VALERY BORZOV	USA 10.24 ROBERT TAYLOR	JAM 10.33 LENNOX MILLER	4. URS Aleksandr Kornelyuk 10.36 / 5. JAM Michael Fray 10.40 / 6. FRG Jobst Hirscht 10.40		
200 METERS	URS 20.00 VALERY BORZOV	USA 20.19 LAWRENCE BLACK	ITA 20.30 PIETRO MENNEA	4. USA Larry Burton 20.37 / 5. USA Charles Smith 20.55 / 6. GDR Siegfried Schenke 20.56		
400 METERS	USA 44.66 VINCE MATTHEWS	USA 44.80 WAYNE COLLETT	KEN 44.92 JULIUS SANG	4. KEN Charles Asati 45.13 / 5. FRG Horst-Rüdiger Schlöske 45.31 / 6. FIN Markku Kukkoaho 45.59		
800 METERS	USA 1:45.86 DAVID WOTTLE	URS 1:45.89 YEVGENY ARZHANOV	KEN 1:46.01 MIKE BOIT	4. FRG Franz-Josef Kemper 1:46.50 / 5. KEN Robert Ouko 1:46.53 / 6. GBR Andrew Carter 1:46.55		
1,500 METERS	FIN 3:36.33 PEKKA VASALA	KEN 3:36.81 H. KIPCHOGE KEINO	NZL 3:37.46 RODNEY DIXON	4. KEN Michael Boit 3:38.41 / 5. GBR Brendan Foster 3:39.02 / 6. BEL Herman Mignon 3:39.05		
5,000 METERS	FIN 13:26.42 LASSE VIREN	TUN 13:27.33 MOHAMED GAMMOUDI	GBR 13:27.61 IAN STEWART	4. USA Steve Prefontaine 13:28.25 / 5. BEL Emiel Puttemans 13:30.82 / 6. FRG Harald Norpoth 13:32.58		
10,000 METERS	FIN 27:38.35 LASSE VIREN	BEL 27:39.58 EMIEL PUTTEMANS	ETH 27:40.96 MIRUTS YIFTER	4. ESP M. Haro Cisneros 27:48.14 / 5. USA Frank Shorter 27:51.32 / 6. GBR David Bedford 28:05.44		
MARATHON	USA 2:12:19.8 FRANK SHORTER	BEL 2:14:31.8 KAREL LISMONT	ETH 2:15:08.4 MAMO WOLDE	4. USA Kenneth Moore 2:15:39.8 / 5. JPN Kenji Kimihara 2:16:27.0 / 6. GBR Ronald Hill 2:16:30.6		
110-METER HURDLES	USA 13.24 RODNEY MILBURN	FRA 13.34 GUY DRUT	USA 13.48 THOMAS HILL	4. USA Willie Davenport 13.50 / 5. GBR Frank Siebeck 13.71 / 6. POL Leszek Wodzyński 13.72		
400-METER HURDLES	UGA 47.82 JOHN AKII-BUA	USA 48.51 RALPH MANN	GBR 48.52 DAVID HEMERY	4. USA James Seymour 48.64 / 5. FRG Rainer Schubert 49.65 / 6. URS Yevgeny Gavrilenko 49.66		
3,000-METER STEEPLECHASE	KEN 8:23.6 H. KIPCHOGE KEINO	KEN 8:24.6 BENJAMIN JIPCHO	FIN 8:24.8 TAPIO KANTANEN	4. POL Bronislaw Malinowski 8:28.0 / 5. TCH Dušan Moravčik 8:29.2 / 6. KEN Amos Biwott 8:33.6		
4 x 100-METER RELAY	USA 38.19 LARRY BLACK ROBERT TAYLOR GERALD TINKER EDWARD HART	URS 38.50 ALEKSANDR KORNELYUK VLADIMIR LOVETSKI JURIS SILOVS VALERY BORZOV	FRG 38.79 JOBST HIRSCHT KARLHEINZ KLOTZ GERHARD WUCHERER KLAUS EHL	4. TCH Matoušek/Demeč/Kynos/Bohman 38.82 / 5. GDR Kokot/Borth/Bombach/Schenke 38.90 / 6. POL Wagner/Cuch/Czerbniak/Nowosz 39.03		
4 x 400-METER RELAY	KEN 2:59.83 CHARLES ASATI H. MUNYORO NYAMAU ROBERT OUKO JULIUS SANG	GBR 3:00.46 MARTIN REYNOLDS ALAN PASCOE DAVID HEMERY DAVID JENKINS	FRA 3:00.65 GILLES BERTOULD ROGER VÉLASQUEZ FRANCIS KERBIRIOU JACQUES CARETTE	4. FRG Herrmann/Honz/Köhler/Schlöske 3:00.88 / 5. POL Werner/Balachowski/Jaremski/Badeński 3:01.05 / 6. FIN Lönnqvist/Salin/Karttunen/Kukkoaho 3:01.12		
20,000-METER WALK	GDR 1:26:42.4 PETER FRENKEL	URS 1:26:55.2 VLADIMIR GOLUBNICHY	GDR 1:27:16.6 HANS REIMANN	4. GDR Gerhard Sperling 1:27:55.0 / 5. URS Nikolay Smaga 1:28:16.6 / 6. GBR Paul Nihill 1:28:44.4		
50,000-METER WALK	FRG 3:56:11.6 BERND KANNENBERG	URS 3:58:24.0 VENIAMIN SOLDATENKO	USA 4:00:46.0 LARRY YOUNG	4. URS Otto Barch 4:01:35.4 / 5. GDR Peter Selzer 4:04:05.4 / 6. FRG Gerhard Weidner 4:06:26.0		
HIGH JUMP	URS 2.23 JÜRI TARMAK	GDR 2.21 STEFAN JUNGE	USA 2.21 DWIGHT STONES	4. FRG Hermann Magerl 2.18 / 5. HUN Ádám Szepesi 2.18 / 6. two-way tie		
POLE VAULT	GDR 5.50 WOLFGANG NORDWIG	USA 5.40 ROBERT SEAGREN	USA 5.35 JAN JOHNSON	4. FRG Reinhard Kuretzky 5.30 / 5. CAN Bruce Simpson 5.20 / 6. FRG Volker Ohi 5.20		

LONG JUMP
	Country	Result	Athlete
1	USA	8.24	RANDY WILLIAMS
2	FRG	8.18	HANS BAUMGARTNER
3	USA	8.03	ARNIE ROBINSON
4	GHA	8.01	Joshua Owusu
5	USA	7.99	Preston Carrington
6	GDR	7.96	Max Klauss

TRIPLE JUMP
	Country	Result	Athlete
1	URS	17.35	VIKTOR SANEYEV
2	GDR	17.31	JÖRG DREHMEL
3	BRA	17.05	NELSON PRUDÊNCIO
4	ROM	16.85	Carol Corbu
5	USA	16.83	John Craft
6	SEN	16.83	Mamadou Mansour-Dia

SHOT PUT
	Country	Result	Athlete
1	POL	21.18	WLADYSLAW KOMAR
2	USA	21.17	GEORGE WOODS
3	GDR	21.14	HARTMUT BRIESENICK
4	GDR	21.14	Hans-Peter Gies
5	USA	21.01	Allan Feuerbach
6	USA	20.91	Brian Oldfield

DISCUS THROW
	Country	Result	Athlete
1	TCH	64.40	LUDVÍK DANĚK
2	USA	63.50	JAY SILVESTER
3	SWE	63.40	RICKARD BRUCH
4	USA	62.82	John Powell
5	HUN	62.62	Géza Fejér
6	GDR	62.42	Detlef Thorith

JAVELIN THROW
	Country	Result	Athlete
1	FRG	90.48	KLAUS WOLFERMANN
2	URS	90.46	JAŇIS LŪSIS
3	USA	84.42	WILLIAM SCHMIDT
4	FIN	84.32	Hannu Siitonen
5	NOR	83.08	Björn Grimnes
6	FIN	82.08	Jorma Kinnunen

HAMMER THROW
	Country	Result	Athlete
1	URS	75.50	ANATOLY BONDARCHUK
2	GDR	74.96	JOCHEN SACHSE
3	URS	74.04	VASILY KHMELEVSKY
4	FRG	71.52	Uwe Beyer
5	HUN	71.38	Gyula Zsivótzky
6	HUN	71.20	Sándor Eckschmidt

DECATHLON
	Country	Result	Athlete
1	URS	8,454	NIKOLAY AVILOV
2	URS	8,035	LEONID LITVINENKO
3	POL	7,984	RYSZARD KATUS
4	USA	7,974	Jeff Bennett
5	GDR	7,950	Stefan Schreyer
6	BEL	7,947	Freddy Hebrand

100 METERS
	Country	Result	Athlete
1	GDR	11.07	RENATE STECHER
2	AUS	11.23	RAELENE BOYLE
3	CUB	11.24	SILVIA CHIVÁS-BARO
4	USA	11.32	Iris Davis
5	FRG	11.38	Annegret Richter
6	GHA	11.41	Alice Annum

200 METERS
	Country	Result	Athlete
1	GDR	22.40	RENATE STECHER
2	AUS	22.45	RAELENE BOYLE
3	POL	22.74	I. SZEWIŃSKA-KIRSZENSTEIN
4	GDR	22.75	Ellen Stropahl
5	GDR	22.89	Christina Heinich
6	FRG	22.89	Annegret Kroniger

400 METERS
	Country	Result	Athlete
1	GDR	51.08	MONIKA ZEHRT
2	FRG	51.21	RITA WILDEN
3	USA	51.64	KATHY HAMMOND
4	CUB	51.86	Helga Seidler
5	USA	51.96	Mable Fergerson
6	AUS	51.99	Charlene Rendina

800 METERS
	Country	Result	Athlete
1	FRG	1:58.55	HILDEGARD FALCK
2	URS	1:58.65	NIJOLÉ SABAITÉ
3	GDR	1:59.19	GUNHILD HOFFMEISTER
4	BUL	1:59.72	Svetlana Zlateva
5	YUG	1:59.98	Vera Nikolić
6	ROM	2:00.04	Ileana Silai

1,500 METERS
	Country	Result	Athlete
1	URS	4:01.38	LYUDMILA BRAGINA
2	GDR	4:02.83	GUNHILD HOFFMEISTER
3	ITA	4:02.85	PAOLA CACCHI-PIGNI
4	GDR	4:04.11	Karin Burneleit
5	GBR	4:04.81	Sheila Carey
6	NED	4:05.13	Ilja Keizer

100-METER HURDLES
	Country	Result	Athlete
1	GDR	12.59	ANNELIESE EHRHARDT
2	ROM	12.84	VALERIA BUFANU
3	GDR	12.90	KARIN BALZER
4	AUS	12.98	Pamela Kilborn-Ryan
5	POL	13.17	Teresa Nowak
6	POL	13.18	Danuta Straszyńska

4 x 100-METER RELAY
	Country	Result	Athletes
1	FRG	42.81	CHRISTIANE KRAUSE, INGRID MICKLER, ANNEGRET RICHTER, HEIDEMARIE ROSENDAHL
2	GDR	42.95	EVELYN KAUFER, CHRISTINA HEINICH, BÄRBEL STRUPPERT, RENATE STECHER
3	CUB	43.36	MARLENE ELEJARDE, CARMEN VALDÉS, FULGENCIA ROMAY, SILVIA CHIVÁS-BARO
4	USA	43.39	Watson/Render/Netter/Davis
5	URS	43.59	Sidorova/Bukharina/Zharkova/Besfamilnaya
6	AUS	43.61	Caird/Boyle/Hoffman/Gillies

4 x 400-METER RELAY
	Country	Result	Athletes
1	GDR	3:22.95	DAGMAR KÄSLING, RITA KÜHNE, HELGA SEIDLER, MONIKA ZEHRT
2	USA	3:25.15	MABLE FERGERSON, MADELINE MANNING-JACKSON, CHERYL TOUSSAINT, KATHY HAMMOND
3	FRG	3:26.51	ANETTE RÜCKES, INGE BÖDDING, HILDEGARD FALCK, RITA WILDEN
4	FRA	3:27.52	Duvivier/Besson/Martin/Duclos
5	GBR	3:28.74	Bernard/Simpson/Roscoe/Stirling
6	AUS	3:28.84	Rose-Edwards/Boyle/Peasley/Rendina

HIGH JUMP
	Country	Result	Athlete
1	FRG	1.92	ULRIKE MEYFARTH
2	BUL	1.88	YORDANKA BLAGOEVA
3	AUT	1.88	ILONA GUSENBAUER
4	GBR	1.85	Barbara Inkpen
5	GDR	1.85	Rita Schmidt
6	ITA	1.85	Sara Simeoni

LONG JUMP
	Country	Result	Athlete
1	FRG	6.78	HEIDEMARIE ROSENDAHL
2	BUL	6.77	DIANA YORGOVA
3	TCH	6.67	EVA SURANOVÁ
4	CUB	6.52	Marcia Garbey
5	FRG	6.51	Heidi Schüller
6	SUI	6.49	Meta Antenen

SHOT PUT
	Country	Result	Athlete
1	URS	21.03	NADEZHDA CHIZHOVA
2	GDR	20.22	M. GUMMEL-HELMBOLDT
3	BUL	19.35	IVANKA KHRISTOVA
4	URS	19.24	Esfir Dolzhenko
5	GDR	18.94	Marianne Adam
6	GDR	18.85	Marita Lange

DISCUS THROW
	Country	Result	Athlete
1	URS	66.62	FAINA MELNIK
2	ROM	65.06	ARGENTINA MENIS
3	BUL	64.34	VASILKA STOEVA
4	URS	62.86	Tamara Danilova
5	FRG	62.18	Liesel Westermann
6	GDR	61.72	Gabrielle Hinzmann

JAVELIN THROW
	Country	Result	Athlete
1	GDR	63.88	RUTH FUCHS
2	GDR	62.54	JAQUELINE TODTEN
3	USA	59.94	KATHY SCHMIDT
4	BUL	59.36	Liutvian Mollova
5	YUG	59.06	Nataša Urbančič
6	AUT	58.56	Eva Janko

PENTATHLON
	Country	Result	Athlete
1	GBR	4,801	MARY PETERS
2	FRG	4,791	HEIDEMARIE ROSENDAHL
3	GDR	4,768	BURGLINDE POLLAK
4	GDR	4,671	Christine Bodner
5	URS	4,597	Valentina Tikhomirova
6	BUL	4,496	Nedialka Angelova

ARCHERY

INDIVIDUAL	🌐 **USA** 2528 JOHN WILLIAMS	○ **SWE** 2481 GUNNAR JARVIL	● **FIN** 2467 KYÖSTI LAASONEN	4. BEL Robert Cogniaux 2445 5. USA Edwin Eliason 2438 6. CAN Donald Jackson 2437
INDIVIDUAL	🌐 **USA** 2424 DOREEN WILBER	○ **POL** 2407 IRENA SZYDLOWSKA	● **URS** 2403 EMMA GAPTCHENKO	4. URS Keto Lossaberidze 2402 5. USA Linda Myers 2385 6. POL Maria Maczyńska 2371

BASKETBALL

FINAL STANDINGS	○ **URS**	○ **USA**	● **CUB**	4. ITA 5. YUG 6. PUR

BOXING

LIGHT FLYWEIGHT 106 lbs. (48 kg)	○ **HUN** GYÖRGY GEDÓ	○ **KOR** U-GIL KIM	● **GBR** RALPH EVANS **BRA** ENRIQUE RODRIGUEZ	5. four-way tie
FLYWEIGHT 112.5 lbs. (51 kg)	○ **BUL** GEORGI KOSTADINOV	○ **UGA** LEO RWABAWOGO	● **POL** LESZEK BLAZYŃSKI **CUB** DOUGLAS RODRIGUEZ	5. four-way tie
BANTAMWEIGHT 119.5 lbs. (54 kg)	○ **CUB** ORLANDO MARTINEZ	○ **MEX** ALFONSO ZAMORA	● **USA** RICARDO CARRERAS **GBR** GEORGE TURPIN	5. four-way tie
LIGHTWEIGHT 132 lbs. (60 kg)	○ **POL** JAN SZCZEPAŃSKI	○ **HUN** LÁSZLÓ ORBÁN	● **KEN** SAMUEL MBUGUA **COL** ALFONSO PÉREZ	5. four-way tie
LIGHT WELTERWEIGHT 140 lbs. (63.5 kg)	○ **USA** RAY SEALES	○ **BUL** ANGEL ANGELOV	● **NIG** ISSAKA DABORG **YUG** ZVONIMIR VUJIN	5. four-way tie
WELTERWEIGHT 148 lbs. (67 kg)	○ **CUB** EMILIO CORREA	○ **HUN** JÁNOS KAJDI	● **KEN** DICK TIGER MURUNGA **USA** JESSE VALDEZ	5. four-way tie
LIGHT MIDDLEWEIGHT 156 lbs. (71 kg)	○ **FRG** DIETER KOTTYSCH	○ **POL** WIESLAW RUDKOWSKI	● **GBR** ALAN MINTER **GDR** PETER TIEPOLD	5. four-way tie
MIDDLEWEIGHT 165.5 lbs.(75 kg)	○ **URS** VYACHESLAV LEMECHEV	○ **FIN** REIMA VIRTANEN	● **GHA** PRINCE AMARTEY **USA** MARVIN JOHNSON	5. four-way tie
LIGHT HEAVYWEIGHT 179 lbs. (81 kg)	○ **YUG** MATE PARLOV	○ **CUB** GILBERTO CARRILLO	● **POL** JANUSZ GORTAT **NGR** ISAAC IKHOURIA	5. four-way tie

SUPER HEAVYWEIGHT > 179 lbs. (> 81 kg)	**CUB** TEÓFILO STEVENSON	**ROM** ION ALEXE	**FRG** PETER HUSSING **SWE** HASSE THOMSÉN	5. four-way tie

CANOEING

KAYAK SINGLES 1,000 METERS	**URS** 3:48.06 ALEKSANDR SHAPARENKO	**SWE** 3:49.38 ROLF PETERSON	**HUN** 3:49.38 GÉZA CSAPÓ	4. BEL Jean-Pierre Burny 3:50.29 5. TCH Ladislav Souček 3:51.05 6. GDR Joachim Mattern 3:51.94
KAYAK PAIRS 1,000 METERS	**URS** 3:31.23 NIKOLAI GORBACHEV VIKTO KRATASSYUK	**HUN** 3:32.00 JÓZSEF DEME JÁNOS RÁTKAI	**POL** 3:33.83 WLADYSLAW SZUSZKIEWICZ RAFAL PISZCZ	4. GDR Kurth/Slatnow 3:34.16 5. ROM Coşnită Simiocenco 3:35.66 6. FRA Cordebois/Niquet 3:36.51

KAYAK FOURS
 1,000 METERS
	URS 3:14.02
	 YURI FILATOV
	 YURI STEZENKO
	 VLADIMIR MOROZOV
	 VALERY DIDENKO
		ROM 3:15.07
		 AUREL VERNESCU
		 MIHAI ZAFIU
		 ROMAN VARTOLOMEU
		 ATANASE SCIOTNIC
			NOR 3:15.27
			 EGIL SÖBY
			 STEINAR AMUNDSEN
			 TORE BERGER
			 JAN JOHANSEN
				4. ITA Ughi/Congiu/ 3:15.60
				      Pedretti/Perri
				 5. FRG Blass/Fischer/ 3:16.63
				      Hennes/Pasch
				 6. HUN Szabó/Várhelyi/ 3:16.88
				      Bakó/Vargha

CANADIAN SINGLES 1,000 METERS	**ROM** 4:08.94 IVAN PATZAICHIN	**HUN** 4:12.42 TAMÁS WICHMANN	**FRG** 4:13.63 DETLEF LEWE	4. GDR Dirk Weise 4:14.38 5. URS Vassili Yurchenko 4:14.43 6. BUL Boris Lyubenov 4:14.65
CANADIAN PAIRS 1,000 METERS	**URS** 3:52.60 VLADISLAVAS C̆ESIUNAS YURI LOBANOV	**ROM** 3:52.63 IVAN PATZAICHIN SERGHEI COVALIOV	**BUL** 3:58.24 FEDIA DAMIANOV IVAN BURCHIN	4. FRG Hoffmann/Glaser 3:59.24 5. HUN Dravas/Povázsay 4:00.42 6. USA Muhlen/Weigand 4:01.28
KAYAK SLALOM SINGLES	**GDR** 268.56 SIEGBERT HORN	**AUT** 270.76 NORBERT SATTLER	**GDR** 277.95 HARALD GIMPEL	4. FRG Ulrich Peters 282.82 5. FRG Alfred Baum 288.01 6. TCH Marian Havlíček 289.56
CANADIAN SLALOM SINGLES	**GDR** 315.84 REINHARD EIBEN	**FRG** 327.89 REINHOLD KAUDER	**USA** 335.95 JAMIE MCEWAN	4. GDR Jochen Förster 354.42 5. FRG Wolfgang Peters 356.25 6. GDR Jürgen Köhler 372.88
CANADIAN SLALOM PAIRS	**GDR** 310.68 WALTER HOFMANN ROLF-DIETER AMEND	**FRG** 311.90 H. OTTO SCHUMACHER WILHELM BAUES	**FRA** 315.10 JEAN-LOUIS OLRY JEAN-CLAUDE OLRY	4. GDR Kretschmer/Trummer 329.57 5. POL Fra̧czek/Seruga 366.21 6. YUG Andrijasić/Guzelj 368.01
KAYAK SINGLES 500 METERS	**URS** 2:03.17 YULIA RYABCHINSKAYA	**NED** 2:04.03 MIEKE JAAPIES	**HUN** 2:05.50 ANNA PFEFFER	4. FRG Irene Pepinghege 2:06.55 5. GDR Bettina Müller 2:06.85 6. ROM Maria Nichiforov 2:07.13
KAYAK PAIRS 500 METERS	**URS** 1:53.50 L. PINAYEVA-KHVEDOSYUK EKATERINA KURYSHKO	**GDR** 1:54.30 ILSE KASCHUBE PETRA GRABOWSKI	**ROM** 1:55.01 MARIA NICHIFOROV VICTORIA DUMITRU	4. HUN Pfeffer/Hollósy 1:55.12 5. FRG Esser/Breuer 1:55.64 6. POL Kazanecka/Kulczak 1:55.05
KAYAK SLALOM SINGLES	**GDR** 364.50 ANGELIKA BAHMANN	**FRG** 398.15 GISELA GROTHAUS	**FRG** 400.50 MAGDALENA WUNDERLICH	4. POL Maria Ćwiertniewicz 432.30 5. POL Kunegunda Godawska 441.05 6. GBR Victoria Brown 443.71

CYCLING

1,000-METER SPRINT	**FRA** 2-0 DANIEL MORELON	**AUS** JOHN NICHOLSON	**URS** OMARI PHAKADZE	4. NED Klaas Balk 5. four-way tie
2,000-METER TANDEM SPRINT	**URS** 3-0 VLADIMIR SEMENETS IGOR TSELOVALNIKOV	**GDR** JÜRGEN GESCHKE WERNER OTTO	**POL** ANDRZEJ BEK BENEDYKT KOCOT	4. FRA Morelon/Tentin 5. four-way tie
1,000-METER TIME TRIAL	**DEN** 1:06.44 NIELS FREDBORG	**AUS** 1:06.87 DANIEL CLARK	**GDR** 1:07.02 JÜRGEN SCHÜTZE	4. FRG Karl Köther 1:07.21 5. POL Janusz Kierzkowski 1:07.22 6. BUL Dimo Angelov 1:07.55
TEAM TIME TRIAL	**URS** 2:11:17.8 ROBERT HAYES	**POL** 2:11:47.5 E. FIGUEROLA CAMUE	**BEL** 2:12:36.7 HARRY JEROME	4. NOR 2:13:20.7 5. SWE 2:13:36.9 6. HUN 2:14:18.8

Event	Gold	Silver	Bronze	4–6 Place
4,000-METER INDIVIDUAL PURSUIT	NOR 4:45.74 KNUT KNUDSEN	SUI 4:51.96 ZAVER KURMANN	FRG 4:50.80 HANS LUTZ	4. AUS J. Christopher Bylsma 4:54.93 5. four-way tie
4,000-METER TEAM PURSUIT	FRG 4:22.14 JÜRGEN COLOMBO GÜNTER HARITZ UDO HEMPEL GÜNTHER SCHUMACHER	GDR 4:25.25 THOMAS HUSCHKE HEINZ RICHTER HERBERT RICHTER UWE UNTERWALDER	GBR 4:23.78 MICHAEL BENNETT IAN HALLAM RONALD KEEBLE WILLIAM MOORE	4. POL Kreczyński/Kaczorowski/4:26.06 Kierzkowski/Nowicki 5. four-way tie
ROAD RACE 182.4 KILOMETERS	NED 4:14.37 HENNIE KUIPER	AUS 4:15.04 KEVEN CLYDE SEFTON	NZL 4:15.04 BRUCE BIDDLE	4. GBR Philip Bayton 4:15.07 5. FRG Philip Edwards 4:15.13 6. FRG Wilfried Trott 4:15.13

DIVING

Event	Gold	Silver	Bronze	4–6 Place
PLATFORM	ITA 504.12 KLAUS DIBIASI	USA 480.75 RICHARD RYDZE	ITA 475.83 F. GIORGIO CAGNOTTO	4. GDR Lothar Matthes 465.75 5. URS David Ambarsumyan 463.56 6. USA Richard Early 462.45
SPRINGBOARD	URS 594.09 VLADIMIR VASIN	ITA 591.63 F. GIORGIO CAGNOTTO	USA 577.29 CRAIG LINCOLN	4. ITA Klaus Dibiasi 559.05 5. USA Michael Finneran 557.34 6. URS Vyacheslav Strahov 556.20
PLATFORM	SWE 390.00 ULRIKA KNAPE	TCH 370.92 MILENA DUCHKOVÁ	GDR 360.54 MARINA JANICKE	4. USA Janey Ely 352.68 5. USA Maxine King 346.38 6. GDR Sylvia Fiedler 341.67
SPRINGBOARD	USA 450.03 MAXINE KING	SWE 434.19 ULRIKA KNAPE	GDR 430.92 MARINA JANICKE	4. USA Janet Ely 420.99 5. CAN Beverly Boys 418.89 6. SWE Agneta Henriksson 417.48

EQUESTRIAN

Event	Gold	Silver	Bronze	4–6 Place
THREE-DAY EVENT, INDIVIDUAL	GBR -57.73 RICHARD MEADE	ITA -43.33 ALESSANDRO ARGENTON	SWE -39.67 JAN JÖNSSON	4. GBR Mary Gordon-Watson -30.27 5. USA Kevin Freeman -29.87 6. AUS J. William Roycroft -29.60
THREE-DAY EVENT, TEAM	GBR +95.53 RICHARD MEADE MARY GORDON-WATSON BRIDGET PARKER	USA +10.81 KEVIN FREEMAN BRUCE DAVIDSON J. MICHAEL PLUMB	FRG -18.00 HARRY KLUGMANN LUDWIG GOESSING KARL SCHULTZ	4. AUS Roycroft/Sands/ Schrapel - 27.86 5. GDR Beerbohm/Niehls/ Brohmann - 127.93 6. SUI Hürlimann/Bühler/ Schwarzenbach - 156.43
DRESSAGE, INDIVIDUAL	FRG 1,229 LISELOTT LINSENHOFF	URS 1,185 YELENA PETUSHKOVA	FRG 1,177 JOSEF NECKERMANN	4. URS Ivan Kizimov 1,159 5. SWE Ulla Håkansson 1,126 6. URS Ivan Kalita 1,130
DRESSAGE, TEAM	URS 5,095 YELENA PETUSHKOVA IVAN KIZIMOV IVAN KALITA	FRG 5,083 LISELOTT LINSENHOFF JOSEF NECKERMANN KARIN SCHLÜTER	SWE 4,849 ULLA HÅKANSSON NINNA SWAAB MAUD VON ROSEN	4. DEN Mikkelsen/Petersen Ingemann 4,606 5. GDR Brockmüller/Müller Köhler 4,552 6. CAN Hanson/Neal Stubbs 4,418
JUMPING, INDIVIDUAL	ITA GRAZIANO MANCINELLI	GBR ANN MOORE	USA NEAL SHAPIRO	4. CAN James Day 4. AUT Hugo Simon 4. FRG Hartwig Steenken
JUMPING, TEAM	FRG 32.00 FRITZ LIGGES GERHARD WILTFANG HARTWIG STEENKEN HANS-GÜNTER WINKLER	USA 32.25 WILLIAM STEINKRAUS NEAL SHAPIRO KATHRYN KUSNER FRANK CHAPOT	ITA 48.00 VITTORIO ORLANDI RAIMONDO D'INZEO GRAZIANO MANCINELLI PIERO D'INZEO	4. GBR Saywell/Smith/ Broome/Moore 51.00 5. SUI Weier/Weier/ Hauri/von Siebenthal 61.25 6. CAN Elder/Day/ Millar/Miller 64.00

FENCING

Event	Gold	Silver	Bronze	4–6 Place
ÉPÉE, INDIVIDUAL	HUN CSABA FENYVESI	FRA JACQUES LA DEGAILLERIE	HUN GYÖZÖ KULCSÁR	4. ROM Anton Alex Pongratz 5. SWE Rolf Edling 6. FRA Jacques Brodin
ÉPÉE, TEAM	HUN	SUI	URS	4. FRA 5. ROM 6. POL
FOIL, INDIVIDUAL	POL WITOLD WOYDA	HUN JENÖ KAMUTI	FRA CHRISTIAN NOËL	4. ROM Mihai Tiu 5. URS Vladimir Denissov 6. POL Marek Dabrowski

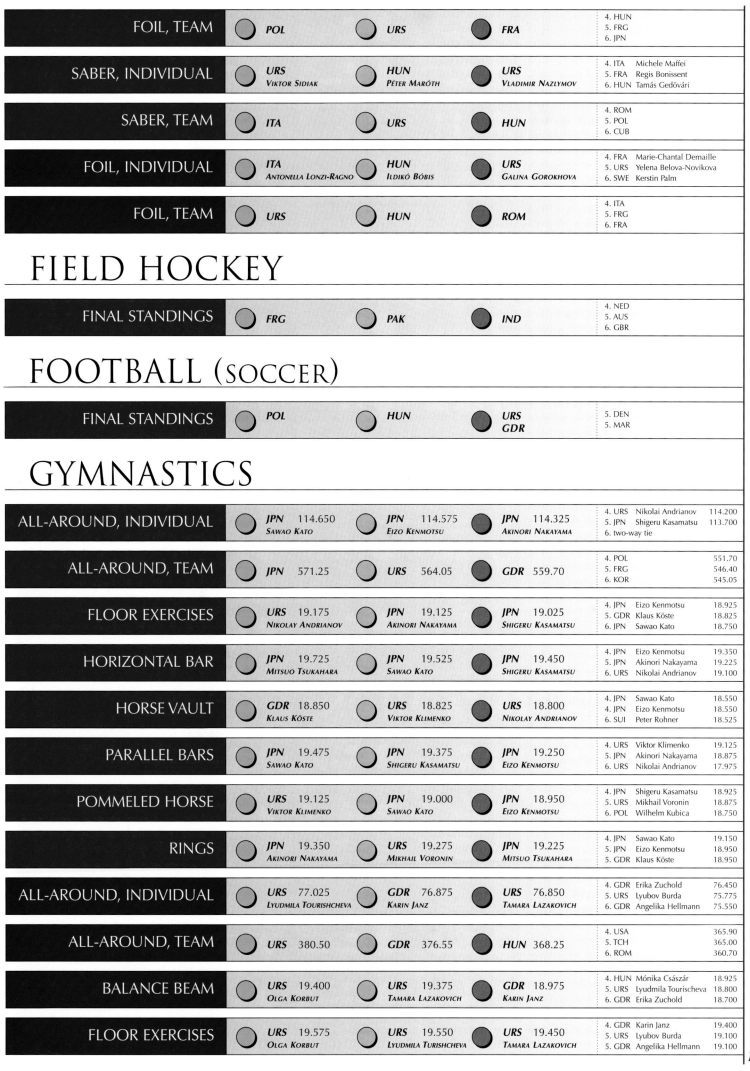

FOIL, TEAM	POL	URS	FRA	4. HUN 5. FRG 6. JPN
SABER, INDIVIDUAL	URS VIKTOR SIDIAK	HUN PÉTER MARÓTH	URS VLADIMIR NAZLYMOV	4. ITA Michele Maffei 5. FRA Regis Bonissent 6. HUN Tamás Gedöväri
SABER, TEAM	ITA	URS	HUN	4. ROM 5. POL 6. CUB
FOIL, INDIVIDUAL	ITA ANTONELLA LONZI-RAGNO	HUN ILDIKÓ BÓBIS	URS GALINA GOROKHOVA	4. FRA Marie-Chantal Demaille 5. URS Yelena Belova-Novikova 6. SWE Kerstin Palm
FOIL, TEAM	URS	HUN	ROM	4. ITA 5. FRG 6. FRA

FIELD HOCKEY

FINAL STANDINGS	FRG	PAK	IND	4. NED 5. AUS 6. GBR

FOOTBALL (SOCCER)

FINAL STANDINGS	POL	HUN	URS GDR	5. DEN 5. MAR

GYMNASTICS

ALL-AROUND, INDIVIDUAL	JPN 114.650 SAWAO KATO	JPN 114.575 EIZO KENMOTSU	JPN 114.325 AKINORI NAKAYAMA	4. URS Nikolai Andrianov 114.200 5. JPN Shigeru Kasamatsu 113.700 6. two-way tie
ALL-AROUND, TEAM	JPN 571.25	URS 564.05	GDR 559.70	4. POL 551.70 5. FRG 546.40 6. KOR 545.05
FLOOR EXERCISES	URS 19.175 NIKOLAY ANDRIANOV	JPN 19.125 AKINORI NAKAYAMA	JPN 19.025 SHIGERU KASAMATSU	4. JPN Eizo Kenmotsu 18.925 5. GDR Klaus Köste 18.825 6. JPN Sawao Kato 18.750
HORIZONTAL BAR	JPN 19.725 MITSUO TSUKAHARA	JPN 19.525 SAWAO KATO	JPN 19.450 SHIGERU KASAMATSU	4. JPN Eizo Kenmotsu 19.350 5. JPN Akinori Nakayama 19.225 6. URS Nikolai Andrianov 19.100
HORSE VAULT	GDR 18.850 KLAUS KÖSTE	URS 18.825 VIKTOR KLIMENKO	URS 18.800 NIKOLAY ANDRIANOV	4. JPN Sawao Kato 18.550 4. JPN Eizo Kenmotsu 18.550 6. SUI Peter Rohner 18.525
PARALLEL BARS	JPN 19.475 SAWAO KATO	JPN 19.375 SHIGERU KASAMATSU	JPN 19.250 EIZO KENMOTSU	4. URS Viktor Klimenko 19.125 5. JPN Akinori Nakayama 18.875 6. URS Nikolai Andrianov 17.975
POMMELED HORSE	URS 19.125 VIKTOR KLIMENKO	JPN 19.000 SAWAO KATO	JPN 18.950 EIZO KENMOTSU	4. JPN Shigeru Kasamatsu 18.925 5. URS Mikhail Voronin 18.875 6. POL Wilhelm Kubica 18.750
RINGS	JPN 19.350 AKINORI NAKAYAMA	URS 19.275 MIKHAIL VORONIN	JPN 19.225 MITSUO TSUKAHARA	4. JPN Sawao Kato 19.150 5. JPN Eizo Kenmotsu 18.950 5. GDR Klaus Köste 18.950
ALL-AROUND, INDIVIDUAL	URS 77.025 LYUDMILA TOURISHCHEVA	GDR 76.875 KARIN JANZ	URS 76.850 TAMARA LAZAKOVICH	4. GDR Erika Zuchold 76.450 5. URS Lyubov Burda 75.775 6. GDR Angelika Hellmann 75.550
ALL-AROUND, TEAM	URS 380.50	GDR 376.55	HUN 368.25	4. USA 365.90 5. TCH 365.00 6. ROM 360.70
BALANCE BEAM	URS 19.400 OLGA KORBUT	URS 19.375 TAMARA LAZAKOVICH	GDR 18.975 KARIN JANZ	4. HUN Mónika Császár 18.925 5. URS Lyudmila Tourischeva 18.800 6. GDR Erika Zuchold 18.700
FLOOR EXERCISES	URS 19.575 OLGA KORBUT	URS 19.550 LYUDMILA TURISHCHEVA	URS 19.450 TAMARA LAZAKOVICH	4. GDR Karin Janz 19.400 5. URS Lyubov Burda 19.100 5. GDR Angelika Hellmann 19.100

HORSE VAULT		GDR 19.525 Karin Janz		GDR 19.275 Erika Zuchold		URS 19.250 Lyudmila Turishcheva	4. URS Lyubov Burda 19.225 5. URS Olga Korbut 19.175 6. URS Tamara Lazakovitch 19.050
UNEVEN BARS		GDR 19.675 Karin Janz		URS 19.450 Olga Korbut		GDR 19.450 Erika Zuchold	4. URS Lyudmila Tourischeva 19.425 5. HUN Ilona Békési 19.275 6. GDR Angelika Hellmann 19.20

TEAM HANDBALL

FINAL STANDINGS		YUG		TCH		ROM	4. GDR 5. URS 6. FRG

JUDO

LIGHTWEIGHT 139 lbs. (63 kg)		JPN Takao Kawaguchi		KOR Yong-Ik Kim		FRA Jean-Jacques Mounier	5. FRG Wolfram Koppen 5. CUB Hector Rodriguez Torres
HALF-MIDDLEWEIGHT 154 lbs. (70 kg)		JPN Toyokazu Nomura		POL Antoni Zajkowski		GDR Dietmar Hötger URS Anatoly Novikov	5. FRG Englebert Doerbandt 5. HUN Antal Hetényi
MIDDLEWEIGHT 176 lbs. (80 kg)		JPN Shinobu Sekine		KOR Oh Seung-Lip		GBR Brian Jacks FRA Jean-Paul Coche	5. URS Guram Gogalauri 5. AUT Lutz Lischka
HALF-HEAVYWEIGHT 205 lbs. (93 kg)		URS Shota Chochishvili		GBR David Starbrook		FRG Paul Barth BRA Chiaki Ishii	5. GDR Helmut Howiller 5. USA James Wooley
HEAVYWEIGHT >205 lbs. (93 kg)		NED Willem Ruska		FRG Klaus Glahn		JPN Motoki Nishimura URS Givi Onashvili	5. FRA Jean-Claude Brondani 5. USA Douglas Nelson
OPEN		NED Willem Ruska		URS Vitaly Kuznetsov		FRA Jean-Claude Brondani GBR Angelo Parisi	5. FRG Klaus Glahn 5. CAN Alfred Douglas Rogers

MODERN PENTATHLON

INDIVIDUAL		HUN 5,412 András Balczó		URS 5,335 Boris Onishchenko		URS 5,328 Pavel Lednev	4. GBR Jeremy Fox 5,311 5. URS Vladimir Shmelev 5,302 6. SWE Björn Ferm 5,283
TEAM		URS 15,968 Boris Onischenko Pavel Lednev Vladimir Shmelev		HUN 15,348 András Balczó Zsigmond Villányi Pál Bakó		FIN 14,812 Risto Hurme Veikko Salminen Martti Ketelä	4. USA Richards/Fitzgerald/ Taylor 14,802 5. SWE Ferm/Jansson/ Lyljenvall 14,708 6. FRG Thade/Esser/ Rössler 14,682

ROWING

SINGLE SCULLS		URS 7:10.12 Yury Malyshev		ARG 7:11.53 Alberto Demiddi		GDR 7:14.45 W. Güldenpfennig	4. IRL Sean Drea 7:42.53 5. URS Nikolai Dovgan 7:57.39 6. ARG Ricardo Ibarra 8:03.05
DOUBLE SCULLS		URS 7:01.77 Aleksandr Timoshinin Gennady Korshikov		NOR 7:02.58 Frank Hansen Svein Thögersen		GDR 7:05.55 Joachim Böhmer Hans-Ulrich Schmied	4. DEN Secher/Engelbrecht 7:14.19 5. GBR Crooks/Delafield 7:16.29 6. TCH Straka/Lacina 7:17.60

Event	Gold	Silver	Bronze	4th / 5th / 6th
PAIR-OARED SHELL WITHOUT COXSWAIN	GDR 6:53.16 — SIEGFRIED BRIETZKE, WOLFGANG MAGER	SUI 6:57.06 — HEINRICH FISCHER, ALFRED BACHMANN	NED 6:58.70 — ROELOF LUYNENBURG, RUUD STOKVIS	4. TCH Zapletal/Lakomy 6:58.77 5. POL Ślusarski/Broniec 7:02.74 6. ROM Oantă Grumezescu 7:42.90
PAIR-OARED SHELL WITH COXSWAIN	GDR 7:17.25 — WOLFGANG GUNKEL, JÖRG LUCKE, KLAUS-DIETER NEUBERT	TCH 7:19.57 — OLDŘICH SVOJANOVSKÝ, PAVEL SVOJANOVSKÝ, VLADIMÍR PETŘÍČEK	ROM 7:21.36 — STEFAN TUDOR, PETRE CEAPURA, LADISLAU LOVRENSKI	4. FRG Mussmann/Krause/Kuhnke 7:21.52 5. URS Eshinov/Ivanov/Lorenson 7:24.44 6. POL Repsz/Dlugosz/Rylski 7:28.92
FOUR-OARED SHELL WITHOUT COXSWAIN	GDR 6:24.27 — FRANK FORBERGER, DIETER GRAHN, FRANK RÜHLE, DIETER SCHUBERT	NZL 6:25.64 — DICK TONKS, DUDLEY STOREY, ROSS COLLINGE, NOEL MILLS	FRG 6:28.41 — JOACHIM EHRIG, PETER FUNNEKÖTTER, FRANZ HELD, WOLFGANG PLOTTKE	4. URS Tkachuk/Kashurov/Motin/Sparonov 6:31.92 5. ROM Tusa/Agh/Naumencu/Papp 6:35.60 6. DEN Poulsen/Christiansen/Peterson/Andersen 6:37.28
FOUR-OARED SHELL WITH COXSWAIN	FRG 6:31.85	GDR 6:33.30	TCH 6:35.64	4. URS 6:37.71 5. USA 6:41.86 6. NZL 6:42.55
EIGHT-OARED SHELL WITH COXSWAIN	NZL 6:08.94	USA 6:11.61	GDR 6:11.67	4. URS 6:14.48 5. FRG 6:14.91 6. POL 6:29.35

SHOOTING

Event	Gold	Silver	Bronze	4th / 5th / 6th
RAPID-FIRE PISTOL	POL 595 — JÓZEF ZAPĘDZKI	TCH 594 — LADISLAV FALTA	URS 593 — VIKTOR TORSHIN	4. SUI Paul Buser 593 5. ESP Jaime Gonzalez 592 6. ITA Giovanni Liverzani 591
FREE PISTOL	SWE 567 — RAGNAR SKANÁKER	ROM 562 — DAN IUGA	AUT 560 — RUDOLF DOLLINGER	4. POL Rajmund Stachurski 559 5. GDR Harald Vollmar 558 6. TCH Hynek Hromada 556
SMALL-BORE RIFLE PRONE	KOR 599 — LI HO-JUN	USA 598 — VICTOR AUER	ROM 598 — NICOLAE ROTARU	4. ITA Giuseppe de Chirico 597 5. TCH Jiři Vogler 597 6. PUR Jaime Santiago 597
SMALL-BORE RIFLE THREE POSITIONS	USA 1,166 — JOHN WRITER	USA 1,157 — LANNY BASSHAM	GDR 1,153 — WERNER LIPPOLDT	4. TCH Petr Kovařik 1,153 5. URS Vladimir Agishev 1,152 6. POL Andrzej Sieledcow 1,151
FREE RIFLE THREE POSITIONS	USA 1,155 — LONES WIGGER	URS 1,155 — BORIS MELNIK	HUN 1,149 — LAJOS PAPP	4. GDR Uto Wunderlich 1,149 5. TCH Karl Bulan 1,146 6. FIN Jaakko Minkkinen 1,146
TRAP	ITA 199 — ANGELO SCALZONE	FRA 198 — MICHEL CARREGA	ITA 195 — SILVANO BASAGNI	4. GDR Burckhardt Hoppe 193 5. SWE Johnny Påhlsson 193 6. USA James Poindexter 192
SKEET	FRG 195/25 — KONRAD WIRNHIER	URS 195/24 — YEVGENY PETROV	GDR 195/23 — MICHAEL BUCHHEIM	4. GBR Joe Neville 194 5. CUB Roberto Castrillo Garcia 194 6. GDR Klaus Reschke 193
MOVING TARGET	URS/UKR 569 — YAKOV ZHELEZNYAK	COL 565 — HELMUT BELLINGRODT	GBR 562 — JOHN KYNOCH	4. URS Valery Postoianov 560 5. FRG Christoph-Michael Zeisner 554 6. SWE Göete Gåård 553

SWIMMING

Event	Gold	Silver	Bronze	4th / 5th / 6th
100-METER FREESTYLE	USA 51.22 — MARK SPITZ	USA 51.65 — JERRY HEIDENREICH	URS 51.77 — VLADIMIR BURE	4. USA John Murphy 52.08 5. AUS Michael Wenden 52.41 6. URS Igor Grivennikov 52.44
200-METER FREESTYLE	USA 1:52.78 — MARK SPITZ	USA 1:53.73 — STEVEN GENTER	FRG 1:53.99 — WERNER LAMPE	4. AUS Michael Wenden 1:54.40 5. USA Frederick Tyler 1:54.96 6. FRG Klaus Steinbach 1:55.65
400-METER FREESTYLE	AUS 4:00.27 — BRADFORD COOPER	USA 4:01.94 — STEVEN GENTER	USA 4:02.64 — THOMAS MCBREEN	4. AUS Graham Windeatt 4:02.93 5. GBR Brian Brinkley 4:06.69 6. SWE Bengt Gingsjö 4:06.75
1,500-METER FREESTYLE	USA 15:52.58 — MICHAEL BURTON	AUS 15:58.48 — GRAHAM WINDEATT	USA 16:09.25 — DOUGLAS NORTHWAY	4. SWE Bengt Gingsjö 16:16.01 5. AUS Graham White 16:17.22 6. NZL Mark Treffers 16:18.84
100-METER BACKSTROKE	GDR 56.58 — ROLAND MATTHES	USA 57.70 — MICHAEL STAMM	USA 58.35 — JOHN MURPHY	4. USA Mitchell Ivey 58.48 5. URS Igor Grivennikov 59.50 6. GDR Lutz Wanja 59.80

Event	Gold	Silver	Bronze	4th–6th
200-METER BACKSTROKE	GDR 2:02.82 ROLAND MATTHES	USA 2:04.09 MICHAEL STAMM	USA 2:04.33 MITCHELL IVEY	4. AUS Bradford Cooper 2:06.59 5. USA Alezander mcKee 2:07.29 6. GDR Lothar Noack 2:08.67
100-METER BREASTSTROKE	JPN 1:04.94 NOBUTAKA TAGUCHI	USA 1:05.43 THOMAS BRUCE	USA 1:05.61 JOHN HENCKEN	4. USA Mark Chatfield 1:06.01 5. FRG Walter Kusch 1:06.23 6. BRA José Sylvio Fiolo 1:06.36
200-METER BREASTSTROKE	USA 2:21.55 JOHN HENCKEN	GBR 2:23.67 DAVID WILKIE	JPN 2:23.88 NOBUTAKA TAGUCHI	4. USA Richard Colella 2:24.28 5. MEX Felipe Muñoz 2:26.44 6. FRG Walter Kusch 2:26.55
100-METER BUTTERFLY	USA 54.27 MARK SPITZ	CAN 55.56 BRUCE ROBERTSON	USA 55.74 JERRY HEIDENREICH	4. GDR Roland Matthes 55.87 5. USA David Edgar 56.11 6. CAN Byron MacDonald 57.27
200-METER BUTTERFLY	USA 2:00.70 MARK SPITZ	USA 2:02.86 GARY HALL	USA 2:03.23 ROBIN BACKHAUS	4. ECU Jorgé Delgado 2:04.60 5. FRG Hans Fassnacht 2:04.69 6. HUN András Hargitay 2:04.69
200-METER INDIVIDUAL MEDLEY	SWE 2:07.17 GUNNAR LARSSON	USA 2:08.37 ALEXANDER MCKEE	USA 2:08.45 STEVEN FURNISS	4. USA Gary Hall 2:08.49 5. HUN András Hargitay 2:09.66 6. URS Mikhail Suharev 2:11.78
400-METER INDIVIDUAL MEDLEY	SWE 4:31.981 GUNNAR LARSSON	USA 4:31.983 ALEXANDER MCKEE	HUN 4:32.700 ANDRÁS HARGITAY	4. USA Steven Furniss 4:35.440 5. USA Gary Hall 4:37.380 6. SWE Bengt Gingsjö 4:37.960
4 x 100-METER FREESTYLE RELAY	USA 3:26.42 DAVID EDGAR JOHN MURPHY JERRY HEIDENREICH MARK SPITZ	URS 3:29.72 VLADIMIR BURE VIKTOR MAZANOV VIKTOR ABOIMOV IGOR GRIVENNIKOV	GDR 3:32.42 ROLAND MATTHES WILFRIED HARTUNG PETER BRUCH LUTZ UNGER	4. BRA Oliveira/Zanetti/ Becskehazy/Diaz-Aranha 3:33.14 5. CAN Robertson/Phillips/ Bach/Kasting 3:33.20 6. FRG Steinbach/Lampe/ Hermitte/Rousseau 3:34.13
4 x 200-METER FREESTYLE RELAY	USA 7:35.78 JOHN KINSELLA FREDERICK TYLER STEVEN GENTER MARK SPITZ	FRG 7:41.69 KLAUS STEINBACH WERNER LAMPE HANS-GÜNTER VOSSELER HANS FAßNACHT	URS 7:45.76 IGOR GRIVENNIKOV VIKTOR MAZANOV GEORGI KULIKOV VLADIMIR BURE	4. SWE Gingsjö/Lungberg/ Bellbring/Larsson 7:47.37 5. AUS Wenden/Windeatt/ Nay/Cooper 7:48.66 6. GDR Hartung/Bruch/ Poser/Unger 7:49.11
4 x 100-METER MEDLEY RELAY	USA 3:48.16 MICHAEL STAMM THOMAS BRUCE MARK SPITZ JERRY HEIDENREICH	GDR 3:52.12 ROLAND MATTHES KLAUS KATZUR HARTMUT FLÖCKNER LUTZ UNGER	CAN 3:52.26 ERIC FISH WILLIAM MAHONY BRUCE ROBERTSON ROBERT KASTING	4. AUS Byrom/O'Brien/ Cusack/Wenden 4:00.80 5. JPN Tanaka/Taguchi/ Maruya/Iwasaki 4:01.80 6. FRG Biechert/Betz/ Stoklasa/Kremer 4:05.40
100-METER FREESTYLE	USA 58.59 SANDRA NEILSON	USA 59.02 SHIRLEY BABASHOFF	AUS 59.06 SHANE GOULD	4. GDR Gabriele Wetzko 59.73 5. FRG Heidemarie Reineck 59.73 6. GDR Andrea Eife 59.91
200-METER FREESTYLE	AUS 2:03.56 SHANE GOULD	USA 2:04.33 SHIRLEY BABASHOFF	USA 2:04.92 KEENA ROTHHAMMER	4. USA Ann Marshall 2:05.45 5. GDR Andrea Eife 2:06.27 6. NED Hansje Bunschoten 2:08.40
400-METER FREESTYLE	AUS 4:19.04 SHANE GOULD	ITA 4:22.44 NOVELLA CALLIGARIS	GDR 4:23.11 GUDRUN WEGNER	4. USA Shirley Babashoff 4:23.59 5. USA Jenny Wylie 4:24.07 6. USA Keena Rothhammer 4:24.22
800-METER FREESTYLE	USA 8:53.68 KEENA ROTHHAMMER	AUS 8:56.39 SHANE GOULD	ITA 8:57.46 NOVELLA CALLIGARIS	4. USA Ann SImmons 8:57.62 5. GDR Gudrun Wegner 8:58.89 6. USA Jo Harshberger 9:01.21
100-METER BACKSTROKE	USA 1:05.78 MELISSA BELOTE	HUN 1:06.26 ANDREA GYARMATI	USA 1:06.34 SUSAN ATWOOD	4. USA Karen Moe 1:06.69 5. CAN Wendy Cook 1:06.70 6. NED Enith Brigitha 1:06.82
200-METER BACKSTROKE	USA 2:19.19 MELISSA BELOTE	USA 2:20.38 SUSAN ATWOOD	CAN 2:23.22 DONNA MARIE GURR	4. FRG Annegret Kober 2:23.35 5. GDR Christine Herbst 2:23.44 6. NED Enith Brigitha 2:23.70
100-METER BREASTSTROKE	USA 1:13.58 CATHERINE CARR	URS 1:14.99 G. STEPANOVA-PROZUMENSHCHIKOVA	AUS 1:15.73 BEVERLY WHITFIELD	4. HUN Ágnes Kiss-Kaczander 1:16.26 5. USA Judy Melick 1:17.16 5. FRG Verena Eberle 1:17.16
200-METER BREASTSTROKE	AUS 2:41.71 BEVERLY WHITFIELD	USA 2:42.05 DANA SCHOENFIELD	URS 2:42.36 G. STEPANOVA-PROZUMENSHCHIKOVA	4. USA Claudia Clevenger 2:42.88 5. FRG Petra Nows 2:43.41 6. HUN Ágnes Kiss-Kaczander 2:43.41
100-METER BUTTERFLY	JPN 1:03.34 MAYUMI AOKI	GDR 1:03.61 ROSWITHA BEIER	HUN 1:03.73 ANDREA GYARMATI	4. USA Deena Deardurff 1:03.95 5. USA Dana Shrader 1:03.98 6. USA Ellie Daniel 1:04.08
200-METER BUTTERFLY	USA 2:15.57 KAREN MOE	USA 2:16.34 LYNN COLELLA	USA 2:16.74 ELLIE DANIEL	4. USA Karen Thornton-Moe 2:12.90 5. JPN Noriko Asano 2:19.50 6. GDR Helga Lindner 2:20.47

200-METER INDIVIDUAL MEDLEY	AUS 2:23.07 SHANE GOULD	GDR 2:23.59 KORNELIA ENDER	USA 2:24.06 LYNN VIDALI	4. AUS Lisa Curry 2:16.75 5. FRG Christiane Pielke 2:17.82 6. GDR Evelyn Stolze 2:25.90
400-METER INDIVIDUAL MEDLEY	AUS 5:02.97 GAIL NEALL	CAN 5:03.57 LESLIE CLIFF	ITA 5:03.99 NOVELLA CALLIGARIS	4. USA Jennifer Bartz 5:05.56 5. GDR Evelyn Stolze 5:06.80 6. USA Mary Montgomery 5:09.98

4 x 100-METER FREESTYLE RELAY	USA 3:55.19 SANDRA NEILSON JENNIFER KEMP JANE BARKMAN SHIRLEY BABASHOFF	GDR 3:55.55 KORNELIA ENDER GABRIELE WETZKO ANDREA EIFE ELKE SEHMISCH	FRG 3:57.93 JUTTA WEBER HEIDEMARIE REINECK GUDRUN BECKMANN ANGELA STEINBACH	4. HUN Gyarmati/Turóczy/ 4:00.39
				   Kovács/Patoh
				5. NED Brigitha/Rijnders/ 4:01.49
				   Bunschoten/Elzerman
				6. SWE Zarnowiecki/Andersson/4:02.69
				   Olsson/Johansson

4 x 100-METER MEDLEY RELAY	USA 4:20.75 MELISSA BELOTE CATHERINE CARR DEENA DEARDURFF SANDRA NEILSON	GDR 4:24.91 CHRISTINE HERBST RENATE VOGEL ROSWITHA BEIER KORNELIA ENDER	FRG 4:26.46 SILKE PIELEN VERENA EBERLE GUDRUN BECKMANN HEIDEMARIE REINECK	4. URS Lekveishvili/Ustimenko/4:27.81
				   Zolotnickaia/
				   Stepanova-Prozumenshikova
				5. NED Brigitha/Rijnders/ 4:29.99
				   Bunschoten/te Riet
				6. JPN Matsumura/Yamamoto/4:31.56
				   Aoki/Nishigawa

VOLLEYBALL

FINAL STANDINGS	JPN	GDR	URS	4. BUL 5. ROM 6. TCH
FINAL STANDINGS	URS	JPN	KOR	4. KOR 5. HUN 6. CUB

WATER POLO

FINAL STANDINGS	URS	HUN	USA	4. FRG 5. YUG 6. ITA

WEIGHT LIFTING

FLYWEIGHT 114.61 lbs. (52 kg)	POL 337.5 ZYGMUNT SMALCERZ	HUN 330.0 LAJOS SZÜCS	HUN 327.5 SÁNDOR HOLCZREITER	4. JPN Tetsuhide Sasaki 322.5 5. MYA Gyi Aung 320.0 6. KOR Pak Dong-geun 317.5
BANTAMWEIGHT 123 lbs. (56 kg)	HUN 377.5 IMRE FÖLDI	IRN 370.0 MOHAMMAD NASSIRI	URS 367.5 GENNADY CHETIN	4. POL Henryk Trebicki 365.0 5. BUL Atanas Kirov 362.5 6. AUS George Vasiliades 355.0
FEATHERWEIGHT 132 lbs. (60 kg)	BUL 402.5 NORAIR NURIKYAN	URS 400.0 DITO SHANIDZE	HUN 390.0 JÁNOS BENEDEK	4. JPN Yoshinobu Miyake 385.0 5. AUT Kurt Pittner 382.5 6.CUB Rolando Chang 377.5
LIGHTWEIGHT 148.75 lbs. (67.5 kg)	URS 460.0 MUKHARBY KIRZHINOV	BUL 450.0 MLADEN KUCHEV	POL 437.5 ZBIGNIEW KACZMAREK	4. POL Waldemar Baszanowski 435.0 5. IRN Nasrollah Dehnavi 435.0 6. HUN Jenö Ambrózi 427.5
MIDDLEWEIGHT 165 lbs. (75 kg)	BUL 485.0 YORDAN BIKOV	LIB 472.5 MOHAMED TRABOULSI	ITA 470.0 ANSELMO SILVINO	4. TCH Ondrej Hekel 462.5 5. GDR Franklin Zielecke 460.0 6. HUN Gábor Szarvas 460.0
LIGHT HEAVYWEIGHT 181.5 lbs. (82.5 kg)	NOR 507.5 LEIF JENSSEN	POL 497.5 NORBERT OZIMEK	HUN 495.0 GYÖRGY HORVÁTH	4. GDR Bernhard Radtke 492.5 5. GRE Christos Iakovou 490.0 6. FIN Kaarlo Kangasniemi 480.0
MIDDLE HEAVYWEIGHT 198.25 lbs. (90 kg)	BUL 525.0 ANDON NIKOLOV	BUL 517.5 ATANAS SHOPOV	SWE 512.5 HANS BETTEMBOURG	4. USA Philip Grippaldi 505.0 5. USA Patrick Holbrook 505.0 6. AUS Nicolo Ciancio 505.0
HEAVYWEIGHT 242.5 lbs. (110 kg)	URS 580.0 JAAN TALTS	BUL 562.5 ALEKSANDAR KRAYCHEV	GDR 555.0 STEFAN GRÜTZNER	4. GDR Helmut Losch 547.5 5. ITA Roberto Vezzani 545.0 6. HUN János Hanzlik 542.5
SUPER HEAVYWEIGHT (unlimited weight)	URS 640.0 VASILY ALEKSEYEV	FRG 610.0 RUDOLF MANG	GDR 572.5 GERD BONK	4. FIN Jouko Leppä 572.5 5. GDR Manfred Rieger 557.5 6. TCH Petr Pavlazek 557.5

WRESTLING, FREESTYLE

	Gold	Silver	Bronze	
LIGHT FLYWEIGHT 106 lbs. (48 kg)	URS ROMAN DMITRIYEV	BUL OGNYAN NIKOLOV	IRN EBRAHIM JAVADI	4. TUR Sefer Baygin 5. ROM Ion Arapu 6. JPN Masahiko Umeda
FLYWEIGHT 114.5 lbs. (52 kg)	JPN KIYOMI KATO	URS ARSEN ALAKHVERDIYEV	KOR KIM GWONG-HYONG	4. IND Sudesh Sudeshkumar 5. ROM Petru Ciarnău 6. CAN Gordon Bertie
BANTAMWEIGHT 125.5 lbs. (57 kg)	JPN HIDEAKI YANAGIDA	USA RICHARD SANDERS	HUN LÁSZLÓ KLINGA	4. IND Prem Premnath 5. BUL Ivan Shavov 6. GDR Horst Mayer
FEATHERWEIGHT 136.5 lbs. (62 kg)	URS ZAGALAV ABDULBEKOV	TUR VEHBI AKDAG	BUL IVAN KRASTEV	4. JPN Kiroshi Abe 5. IRN Shamseddin Seyyedabbasi 6. ROM Petre Coman
LIGHTWEIGHT 149.5 lbs. (68 kg)	USA DAN GABLE	JPN KIKUO WADA	URS RUSLAN ASHURALIYEV	4. MON Tsedendamba Natsagdorj 5. TUR Ali Sahin 6. GDR Udo Schröder
WELTERWEIGHT 163 lbs. (74 kg)	USA WAYNE WELLS	SWE JAN KARLSSON	FRG ADOLF SEGER	4. BUL Yandho Pavlov 5. three-way tie
MIDDLEWEIGHT 181 lbs. (82 kg)	URS LEVAN TEDIASHVILI	USA JOHN PETERSON	ROM VASILE IORGA	4. GDR Horst Stottmeister 5. JPN Tatsuo Sasaki 6. FRG Peter Neumair
LIGHT HEAVYWEIGHT 198.5 lbs. (90 kg)	USA BENJAMIN PETERSON	URS GENNADY STRAKHOV	HUN KÁROLY BAJKÓ	4. BUL Russi Petrov 5. IRN Reza Khorrami 5. CUB Barbaro Morgan
HEAVYWEIGHT 220 lbs. (100 kg)	URS IVAN YARYGIN	MGL KHORLOO BAIANMUNKH	HUN JÓZSEF CSATÁRI	4. BUL Vsil Todorov 5. ROM Enache Panait 6. POL Ryszard Dlugosz
SUPER HEAVYWEIGHT (unlimited weight)	URS ALEKSANDR MEDVED	BUL OSMAN DURALIEV	USA CHRIS TAYLOR	4. IRN Eskandar Filabi 5. FRG Wilfried Dietrich 6. GDR Peter Germer

WRESTLING, GRECO-ROMAN

	Gold	Silver	Bronze	
LIGHT FLYWEIGHT 106 lbs. (48 kg)	ROM GHEORGHE BERCEANU	IRN RAHIM ALIABADI	BUL STEFAN ANGELOV	4. FIN Raimo Hirvonen 5. JPN Kazuharu Ishida 6. ITA Lorenzo Calafiore
FLYWEIGHT 114.5 lbs. (52 kg)	BUL PETAR KIROV	JPN KOICHIRO HIRAYAMA	ITA GIUSEPPE BOGNANNI	4. HUN József Doncsecz 4. POL Jan Michalik 4. TCH Miroslav Zeman
BANTAMWEIGHT 125.5 lbs. (57 kg)	URS RUSTEM KAZAKOV	FRG HANS-JÜRGEN VEIL	FIN RISTO BJÖRLIN	4. HUN János Varga 5. BUL Hristo Traikov 6. ROM Ion Baciu
FEATHERWEIGHT 136.5 lbs. (62 kg)	BUL GEORGI MARKOV	GDR HEINZ-HELMUT WEHLING	POL KAZIMIERZ LIPIEŃ	4. JPN Hideo Fujimoto 5. URS Djemal Megreshvili 6. ROM Ion Păun
LIGHTWEIGHT 150 lbs. (68 kg)	URS SHAMIL KHISAMUTDINOV	BUL STOYAN APOSTOLOV	ITA GIAN-MATTEO RANZI	4. FRG Mangred Schöndorfer 5. JPN Takashi Tanoue 6. two-way tie
WELTERWEIGHT 163 lbs. (74 kg)	TCH VÍTĚZSLAV MÁCHA	GRE PETROS GALAKTOPOULOS	SWE JAN KARLSSON	4. BUL Ivan Kolev 5. YUG Momir Kecman 6. FRA Daniel Robin
MIDDLEWEIGHT 181 lbs. (82 kg)	HUN CSABA HEGEDÜS	URS ANATOLY NAZARENKO	YUG MILAN NENADIČ	4. TCH Miroslav Janota 5. ROM Ion Gabor 6. GDR Frank Hartmann
LIGHT HEAVYWEIGHT 198.5 lbs. (90 kg)	URS VALERY REZANTZEV	YUG JOSIP ČORAK	POL CZESLAW KWIECIŃSKI	4. HUN József Percsi 5. NOR Håkon Överbye 6. ROM Nicolae Neguț
HEAVYWEIGHT 220 lbs. (100 kg)	ROM NICOLAE MARTINESCU	URS NIKOLAY YAKOVENKO	HUN FERENC KISS	4. BUL Hristo Ignatov 5. GDR Fredi Albrecht 6. NOR Tore Hem
SUPER HEAVYWEIGHT (unlimited weight)	URS ANATOLY ROSHCHIN	BUL ALEKSANDAR TOMOV	ROM VICTOR DOLIPSCHI	4. HUN József Csatári 4. FRG Wilfried Dietrich 4. YUG Istvan Semeredi

YACHTING

Event	Gold	Silver	Bronze	4th / 5th / 6th
FINN MONOTYPE	**FRA** 58.0 *Serge Maury*	**GRE** 71.0 *Ilias Khatzipavlis*	**URS** 74.7 *Viktor Potapov*	4. AUS John Bertrand 76.7 5. SWE Thomas Lundqvist 81.0 6. FIN Kim Weber 85.7
DRAGON CLASS	**AUS** 13.7 *John Bruce Cuneo, Thomas Anderson, John Shaw*	**GDR** 41.7 *Paul Borowski, Konrad Weichert, Karl-Heinz Thun*	**USA** 47.7 *Donald Cohan, Charles Horter, John Marshall*	4. FRG Heilmeier/Kuchler/Glas 47.7 5. NZL Watson/Everett/Beer 51.0 6. SWE Sundelin/Sundelin/Sundelin 67.4
FLYING DUTCHMAN	**GBR** 22.7 *Rodney Pattisson, Christopher Davies*	**FRA** 40.7 *Yves Pajot, Marc Pajot*	**FRG** 51.1 *Ullrich Libor, Peter Naumann*	4. BRA Conrad/Cordes 62.4 5. YUG Grego/Nikolić 63.7 6. URS Leontiev/Zoubanov 67.7
STAR CLASS	**AUS** 28.1 *David Forbes, John Anderson*	**SWE** 44.0 *Pelle Pettersson, Stellan Westerdahl*	**FRG** 44.4 *Wilhelm Kuhweide, Karsten Meyer*	4. BRA Bruder/Aten 52.7 5. ITA Scala/Testa 58.4 6. POR Correia/Anjos 68.4
SOLING CLASS	**USA** 8.7 *Harry Melges, William Bentsen, William Allen*	**SWE** 31.7 *Stig Wennerström, Lennart Roslund, Bo Knape, Stefan Krook*	**CAN** 47.1 *David Miller, John Ekels, Paul Cote*	4. FRA le Guillou/Drubay/Pellerin 53.0 5. GBR Oakeley/Reynolds/Dunning 54.7 6. BRA Schmidt-Preben/Mascarenhas/Schmidt-Preben 64.7
TEMPEST CLASS	**URS** 28.1 *Valentin Mankin, Vitaly Dyrdyra*	**GBR** 34.4 *Alan Warren, David Hunt*	**USA** 47.7 *Glen Foster, Peter Dean*	4. SWE Albrechtson/Hansson 57.4 5. NED Staartjes/Kuppershoek 58.7 6. NOR Lunde/Gresvig 70.0

NATIONAL MEDAL COUNT

COMPETITORS   COUNTRIES: 122   ATHLETES: 7,123   MEN: 6,065   WOMEN: 1,058

	GOLD	SILVER	BRONZE	TOTAL
URS	50	27	22	99
USA	33	31	30	94
GDR	20	23	23	66
FRG	13	11	16	40
HUN	6	13	16	35
JPN	13	8	8	29
POL	7	5	9	21
BUL	6	10	5	21
ITA	5	3	10	18
GBR	4	5	9	18
AUS	8	7	2	17
SWE	4	6	6	16

	GOLD	SILVER	BRONZE	TOTAL
ROM	3	6	7	16
FRA	2	4	7	13
KEN	2	3	4	9
CUB	3	1	4	8
FIN	3	1	4	8
TCH	2	4	2	8
NED	3	1	1	5
YUG	2	1	2	5
KOR	1	1	3	5
CAN		2	3	5
NOR	2	1	1	4
NZL	1	1	1	3

	GOLD	SILVER	BRONZE	TOTAL
SUI		3		3
IRN		2	1	3
COL		1	2	3
AUT		1	2	3
UGA	1	1		2
BEL		2		2
GRE		2		2
BRA			2	2
ETH			2	2
DEN	1			1
MGL		1		1
ARG		1		1

	GOLD	SILVER	BRONZE	TOTAL
MEX		1		1
PAK		1		1
COR		1		1
LIB		1		1
TUN		1		1
TUR		1		1
NGR			1	1
NIG			1	1
JAM			1	1
IND			1	1
GHA			1	1
ESP		1		1

Wednesday, FEBRUARY 4

PM	EVENT	VENUE
2:30	OPENING CEREMONY	Bergisel Stadium
5:00	FIGURE SKATING	Olympic Ice Stadium
	ice dancing, compulsories	
7:00	LUGE	Igls Bobsled and Luge Run
	• single	
	• women's single	

Thursday, FEBRUARY 5

AM	EVENT	VENUE
9:00	NORDIC SKIING	Seefeld
	30 kilometers	
	LUGE	Igls Bobsled and Luge Run
	• single	
	• women's single	
10:00	SPEED SKATING	Speed-Skating Oval
	women's 1,500 meters	

PM	EVENT	VENUE
12:30	ALPINE SKIING	Patsherkofel
	downhill	
2:00	HOCKEY	Olympic Ice Stadium
	group A	
6:00	FIGURE SKATING	Olympic Ice Stadium
	ice dancing, compulsories	
8:00	FIGURE SKATING	Olympic Ice Stadium
	pairs, short program	

Friday, FEBRUARY 6

AM	EVENT	VENUE
8:30	BIATHLON	Seefeld
	20 kilometers	
9:00	LUGE	Igls Bobsled and Luge Run
	• single	
	• women's single	
10:30	SPEED SKATING	Speed-Skating Oval
	women's 500 meters	

PM	EVENT	VENUE
1:00	HOCKEY	Olympic Ice Stadium
	group A	
2:30	BOBSLED	Igls Bobsled and Luge Run
	two-man	

Saturday, FEBRUARY 7

AM	EVENT	VENUE
9:00	LUGE	Igls Bobsled and Luge Run
	• single	
	• women's single	
10:00	NORDIC SKIING	Seefeld
	women's 5 kilometers	
10:30	SPEED SKATING	Speed-Skating Oval
	women's 1,000 meters	

PM	EVENT	VENUE
1:00	SKI JUMPING	Seefeld
	small hill	
2:00	HOCKEY	Olympic Ice Stadium
	group B	
2:30	BOBSLED	Igls Bobsled and Luge Run
	two-man	
7:30	FIGURE SKATING	Olympic Ice Stadium
	free skating, pairs	

Sunday, FEBRUARY 8

AM	EVENT	VENUE
8:00	FIGURE SKATING	Olympic Ice Stadium
	compulsories	
9:00	NORDIC SKIING	Seefeld
	15 kilometers	
9:45	SPEED SKATING	Speed-Skating Oval
	women's 3,000 meters	

PM	EVENT	VENUE
12:30	ALPINE SKIING	Axamer Lizum
	women's downhill	
1:00	HOCKEY	Olympic Ice Stadium
	group A	
	NORDIC SKIING	Seefeld
	combined, small hill	

Monday, FEBRUARY 9

AM	EVENT	VENUE
9:00	NORDIC SKIING	Seefeld
	combined, 15 kilometers	

PM	EVENT	VENUE
12:30	ALPINE SKIING	Axamer Lizum
	giant slalom, 1st run	
2:00	HOCKEY	Olympic Ice Stadium
	group B	
2:30	FIGURE SKATING	Olympic Ice Stadium
	short program, individual	

7:30	FIGURE SKATING	Olympic Ice Stadium
	ice dancing, free skate	

Tuesday, FEBRUARY 10

AM	EVENT	VENUE
8:00	FIGURE SKATING	Olympic Ice Stadium
	women's compulsories	
9:00	LUGE	Igls Bobsled and Luge Run
	two-seater	
9:30	NORDIC SKIING	Seefeld
	women's 10 kilometers	
10:30	SPEED SKATING	Speed-Skating Oval
	500 meters	

PM	EVENT	VENUE
12:30	ALPINE SKIING	Axamer Lizum
	giant slalom, 2nd run	
1:00	HOCKEY	Olympic Ice Stadium
	group A	

Wednesday, FEBRUARY 11

AM	EVENT	VENUE
9:00	NORDIC SKIING	Seefeld
	4 x 10-kilometer relay	
9:30	SPEED SKATING	Speed-Skating Oval
	5,000 meters	
11:30	ALPINE SKIING	Axamer Lizum
	women's slalom, 1st and 2nd runs	

PM	EVENT	VENUE
2:00	HOCKEY	Olympic Ice Stadium
	group B	
2:30	FIGURE SKATING	Olympic Ice Stadium
	women's individual short program	
7:30	FIGURE SKATING	Olympic Ice Stadium
	free skate	

Thursday, FEBRUARY 12

AM	EVENT	VENUE
9:00	NORDIC SKIING	Seefeld
	women's 4 x 5-kilometer relay	
10:00	SPEED SKATING	Speed-Skating Oval
	1,000 meters	

1:00	HOCKEY	Olympic Ice Stadium
	group A	

Friday, FEBRUARY 13

AM	EVENT	VENUE
10:00	BIATHLON	Seefeld
	4 x 7.5-kilometer relay	
	SPEED SKATING	Speed-Skating Oval
	1,500-meters	

PM	EVENT	VENUE
12:30	ALPINE SKIING	Axamer Lizum
	women's giant slalom	
2:00	HOCKEY	Olympic Ice Stadium
	group B	
2:30	BOBSLED	Igls Bobsled and Luge Run
	four-man	
7:30	FIGURE SKATING	Olympic Ice Stadium
	women's free skate	

Saturday, FEBRUARY 14

AM	EVENT	VENUE
8:30	NORDIC SKIING	Seefeld
	50 kilometers	
9:00	SPEED SKATING	Speed-Skating Oval
	10,000 meters	
10:00	ALPINE SKIING	Axamer Lizum
	slalom, 1st and 2nd runs	

PM	EVENT	VENUE
1:00	HOCKEY	Olympic Ice Stadium
	group A	
2:30	BOBSLED	Igls Bobsled and Luge Run
	four-man	

Sunday, FEBRUARY 15

PM	EVENT	VENUE
1:00	SKI JUMPING	Bergisel Stadium
	large hill	
4:30	FIGURE SKATING	Olympic Ice Stadium
	exhibition	
8:00	CLOSING CEREMONY	Bergisel Stadium

INNSBRUCK 1976
12TH OLYMPIC GAMES

BIATHLON

	Gold	Silver	Bronze	4.	5.	6.
20 KILOMETERS	URS 1:14:12.26 *Nikolai Kruglov*	FIN 1:15:54.10 *Heikki Ikola*	URS 1:16:05.57 *Aleksandr Elizarov*	4. ITA Willy Bertin 1:16:50.36	5. URS Aleksandr Tikhonov 1:17:18.33	6. FIN Esko Saira 1:17:32:84
4 x 7.5-KILOMETER RELAY	URS 1:57:55.64 *Aleksandr Elizarov* *Ivan Biakov* *Nikolai Kruglov* *Aleksandr Tikhonov*	FIN 2:01:45.58 *Henrik Flöjt* *Esko Saira* *Juhani Suutarinen* *Heikki Ikola*	GDR 2:04:08.61 *Karl-Heinz Menz* *Frank Ullrich* *Manfred Beer* *Manfred Geyer*	4. FRG Mehringer/Winkler/ Keck/Gehrke 2:04:11.86	5. NOR Hovda/Hanssen/ Engen/Svendsberget 2:05:10.28	6. ITA Jordan/Clementi/ Weiss/Bertin 2:06:16.55

BOBSLED

	Gold	Silver	Bronze	4.	5.	6.
BOBSLED TWO-MAN	GDR 3:44.42 *Meinhard Nehmer* *Bernhard Germeshausen*	FRG 3:44.99 *Wolfgang Zimmerer* *Manfred Schumann*	SUI 3:45.70 *Erich Schärer* *Josef Benz*	4. AUT Sperling/Schwab 3:45.74	5. FRG Heibl/Ohlwärter 3:46.13	6. AUT Delle Karth/Köfel 3:46.37
FOUR-MAN	GDR 3:40.43 *Meinhard Nehmer* *Bernhard Germeshausen* *Jochen Babock* *Bernhard Lehmann*	SUI 3:40.89 *Erich Schärer* *Josef Benz* *Ulrich Bächli* *Rudolf Marti*	FRG 3:41.37 *Wolfgang Zimmerer* *Peter Utzschneider* *Bodo Bittner* *Manfred Schumann*	4. GDR Schönau/Bernhard/ Seifert/Bethge 3:42.44	5. FRG Heibl/Morant/ Radant/Ohlwärter 3:42.47	6. AUT Delle Karth/Schwab/ Breg/Köfel/Krenn 3:43.21

FIGURE SKATING

	Gold	Silver	Bronze	4.	5.	6.
SINGLES	GBR 192.74 *John Curry*	URS 187.64 *Vladimir Kovalev*	CAN 187.38 *Toller Cranston*	4. GDR Jan Hoffman 187.34	5. URS Sergei Volkov 184.08	6. USA David Santee 184.28
SINGLES	USA 193.80 *Dorothy Hamil*	HOL 190.24 *Dianne de Leeuw*	GDR 188.16 *Christine Errath*	4. GDR Anett Pötzsch 187.42	5. FRG Isabel de Navarre 182.42	6. USA Wendy Burge 182.14
PAIRS	URS 140.54 *Irina Rodnina* *Aleksandr Zaytsev*	GDR 136.35 *Romy Kermer* *Rolf Oesterreich*	GDR 134.57 *Manuela Gross* *Uwe Kagelmann*	4. URS Vorobieva/Vlasov 134.52	5. USA Babilonia/Gardner 134.24	6. GDR Stolfig/Kempe 129.57
DANCE	URS 209.92 *Lyudmila Pakhomova* *Aleksandr Gorshkov*	URS 204.88 *Irina Moiseeva* *Andrei Minenkov*	USA 202.64 *Colleen O'Conner* *James Millns*	4. URS Linichuk/Karponosov 199.10	5. HUN Regöczy/Sallay 195.92	6. ITA Ciccia/Ceserani 191.46

HOCKEY

	Gold	Silver	Bronze	4.	5.	6.
FINAL STANDINGS	URS	TCH	FRG	4. FIN	5. USA	6. POL

LUGE

	Gold	Silver	Bronze	4.	5.	6.
SINGLE	GDR 3:27.688 *Dettlef Günther*	FRG 3:28.196 *Josef Fendt*	GDR 3:28.574 *Hans Rinn*	4. GDR H. Wickler 3:29.454	5. AUT Manfred Schmid 3:29.511	6. FRG Anton Winkler 3:29.520

TWO-SEATER	GDR 1:25.604 Hans Rinn Norbert Hahn	FRG 1:25.889 Hans Brandner Balthasar Schwarm	AUS 1:25.919 Rudolf Schmid Franz Schachner	4. FRG Hölzlwimmer/ 1:26.238 Grösswang 5. AUT Schmid/Sulzbacher 1:26.424 6. TCH Zeman/Resl 1:26.826
SINGLE	GDR 2:50.621 Margit Schumann	GDR 2:50.846 Ute Rührold	FRG 2:51.056 Elisabeth Demleitner	4. GDR Eva-Maria Wernicke 2:51.262 5. AUT Antonia Mayr 2:51.360 6. AUT Margit Graf 2:51.459

SKIING, ALPINE

DOWNHILL	AUT 1:45.73 Franz Klammer	SUI 1:46.06 Berhard Russi	ITA 1:46.59 Herbert Plank	4. SUI Philippe Roux 1:46.69 5. CAN Ken Read 1:46.83 6. USA Andy Mill 1:47.06
SLALOM	ITA 2:03.29 Piero Gros	ITA 2:03.73 Gustav Thöni	LIE 2:04.28 Willy Frommelt	4. SUI Walter Tresch 2:05.26 5. FRG Christian Neureuther 2:06.56 6. FRG Wolfgang Junginger 2:07.08
GIANT SLALOM	SUI 3:26.97 Henri Hemmi	SUI 3:27.17 Ernst Good	SWE 3:27.41 Ingemar Stenmark	4. ITA Gustav Thöni 3:27.67 5. USA Phillip Mahre 3:28.20 6. SUI Engelhard Pargätzi 3:28.76
DOWNHILL	FRG 1:46.16 Rosi Mittermaier	AUT 1:46.68 Brigitte Totschnigg	USA 1:47.50 Cynthia Nelson	4. AUT Nicola-Andrea Spiess 1:47.71 5. FRA Danièlle Debernard 1:48.48 6. FRA Jacqueline Rouvier 1:48.58
SLALOM	FRG 1:30.54 Rosi Mittermaier	ITA 1:30.87 Claudia Giordani	LIE 1:32.20 Hanni Wenzel	4. FRA Danièlle Debernard 1:32.24 5. FRG Pamela Behr 1:32.31 6. USA Linda Cochran 1:33.24
GIANT SLALOM	CAN 1:29.13 Kathy Kreiner	FRG 1:29.25 Rosi Mittermaier	FRA 1:29.95 Danièlle Debernard	4. SUI Lise-Marie Morerod 1:30.40 5. SUI Marie-Theres Nadig 1:30.44 6. AUT Monika Kaserer 1:30.49

SKIING, NORDIC

15 KILOMETERS	URS 43:58.47 Nikolai Bazhukov	URS 44:01.10 Yevgeny Beliaev	FIN 44:19.25 Arto Koivisto	4. URS Ivan Garanin 44:41.98 5. NOR Ivar Formo 45:29.11 6. USA William Koch 45:32.22
30 KILOMETERS	URS 1:30:29.38 Sergei Saveliev	USA 1:30:57.84 William Koch	URS 1:31:09.29 Ivan Garanin	4. FIN Juha Mieto 1:31:20.39 5. URS Nikolai Bazhukov 1:31:33.14 6. GDR G. Klause 1:32:00.91
50 KILOMETERS	NOR 2:37:30.05 Ivar Formo	GDR 2:38:13.21 Gert-Dietmar Klause	SWE 2:39:39.21 Benny Södergren	4. URS Ivan Garanin 2:40:38.94 5. GDR Gerhard Grimmer 2:41:15.46 6. NOR Per Knut Aaland 2:41:18.06
4 x 10-KILOMETER RELAY	FIN 2:07:59.72 Matti Pitkänen Juha Mieto Pertti Teurajärvi Arto Koivisto	NOR 2:09:58.36 Pål Tyldum Einar Sagstuen Ivar Formo Odd Martinsen	URS 2:10:51.46 Yevgeny Beliaev Nikolai Bazhukov Sergei Saveliev Ivan Garanin	4. SWE Södergren/Johansson/2:11:16.88 Wassberg/Lundbäck 5. SUI Renggli/Hauser/ 2:11:28.53 Gähler/Kälin 6. USA Peterson/Caldwell/ 2:11:41.35 Koch/Yaeger
COMBINED	GDR 423.39 Ulrich Wehling	FRG 418.90 Urban Hettich	GDR 417.47 Konrad Winkler	4. FIN Rauno Miettinen 411.30 5. GDR Claus Tuchscherer 409.51 6. URS Nikolai Nagovitzin 406.44
5 KILOMETERS	FIN 15:48.69 Helena Takalo	URS 15:49.73 Raisa Smetanina	URS 16:12.82 Nina Baldycheva	4. FIN Hilkka Kuntola 16:17.74 5. SWE Eva Olsson 16:27.15 6. URS Zinaida Amosova 16:33.78
10 KILOMETERS	URS 30:13.41 Raisa Smetanina	FIN 30:14.28 Helena Takalo	URS 30:38.61 Galina Kulakova	4. URS Nina Baldycheva 30:52.58 5. SWE Eva Olsson 31:08.72 6. URS Zinaida Amosova 31:11.23
4 x 5-KILOMETER RELAY	URS 1:07:49.75 Raisa Smetanina Nina Baldycheva Zinaida Amosova Galina Kulakova	FIN 1:08:36.57 Marjatta Kajosmaa Hilkka Kuntola Liisa Suihkonen Helena Takalo	GDR 1:09:57.95 Barbara Petzold Monika Debertshäuser Sigrun Krause Veronika Schmidt	4. SWE Carlzon/Partapuoli/1:10:14.68 Johansson/Olsson 5. NOR Kvello/Myrmael/ 1:11:09.08 Johannessen/Kummen 6. TCH Pasiárová/Sekajová/1:11:27.83 Bartošová/Paulů

SKI JUMPING

SMALL HILL	GDR 252.0 H. Aschenbach	GDR 246.2 Jochen Danneberg	AUT 242.0 Karl Schnabl	4. TCH Jaroslav Balcar 239.6 5. SUI Ernst von Grüningen 238.7 6. AUT Reinhold Bachler 237.2

LARGE HILL	AUT 234.8 KARL SCHNABL	AUT 232.9 ANTON INNAUER	GDR 221.7 HENRY GLASS	4. GDR Jochen Danneberg 221.6 5. AUT Reinhold Bachler 217.4 6. AUT Hans Wallner 216.9

SPEED SKATING

500 METERS	URS 39.17 YEVGENY KULIKOV	URS 39.25 VALERY MURATOV	USA 39.54 DANIEL IMMERFALL	4. SWE Mats Wallberg 39.56 5. USA Peter Mueller 39.57 6. HOL Jan Bazen 39.78
1,000 METERS	USA 1:19.32 PETER MUELLER	NOR 1:20.45 JÖRN DIDRIKSEN	URS 1:20.57 VALERY MURATOV	4. URS Aleksandr Safronov 1:20.84 5. HOL Hans van Helden 1:20.85 6. CAN Gaétan Boucher 1:21.23
1,500 METERS	NOR 1:59.38 JAN EGIL STORHOLT	URS 1:59.97 YURI KONDAKOV	HOL 2:00.87 HANS VAN HELDEN	4. URS Sergei Riabev 2:02.15 5. USA Daniel Carroll 2:02.26 6. HOL Piet Kleine 2:02.28
5,000 METERS	NOR 7:24.48 STEN STENSEN	HOL 7:26.47 PIET KLEINE	HOL 7:26.54 HANS VAN HELDEN	4. URS Victor Varlamov 7:30.97 5. GDR Klaus Wunderlich 7:33.82 6. USA Daniel Carroll 7:36.46
10,000 METERS	HOL 14:50.59 PIET KLEINE	NOR 14:53.30 STEN STENSEN	HOL 15:02.02 HANS VAN HELDEN	4. URS Victor Varlamov 15:06.06 5. SWE Örjan Sandler 15:16.21 6. AUS Colin Coates 15:16.80
500 METERS	USA 42.76 SHEILA YOUNG	CAN 43.12 CATHY PRIESTNER	URS 43.17 TATYANA AVERINA	4. USA Leah Poulos 43.21 5. URS Vera Krasnova 43.23 6. URS Lyubov Sachikova 43.80
1,000 METERS	URS 1:28.43 TATYANA AVERINA	USA 1:28.57 LEAH POULOS	USA 1:29.14 SHEILA YOUNG	4. CAN Sylvia Burka 1:29.47 5. FRG Monika Holzner-Pflug 1:29.54 6. CAN Cathy Priestner 1:29.66
1,500 METERS	URS 2:16.58 GALINA STEPANSKAYA	USA 2:17.06 SHEILA YOUNG	URS 2:17.96 TATYANA AVERINA	4. NOR Lisbeth Korsmo 2:18.99 5. GDR Karin Kessow 2:19.05 6. USA Leah Poulos 2:19.11
3,000 METERS	URS 4:45.19 TATYANA AVERINA	GDR 4:45.23 ANDREA MITSCHERLICH	NOR 4:45.24 LISBETH KORSMO	4. GDR Karin Kessow 4:45.60 5. GDR Ines Bautzmann 4:46.67 6. SWE Sylvia Filipsson 4:48.15

NATIONAL MEDAL COUNT

COMPETITORS   COUNTRIES: 37   ATHLETES: 1,123   MEN: 892   WOMEN: 231

	GOLD	SILVER	BRONZE	TOTAL
URS	13	6	8	27
GDR	7	5	7	19
USA	3	3	4	10
FRG	2	5	3	10

	GOLD	SILVER	BRONZE	TOTAL
NOR	3	3	1	7
FIN	2	4	1	7
AUT	2	2	2	6
NED	1	2	3	6

	GOLD	SILVER	BRONZE	TOTAL
SUI	1	3	1	5
ITA	1	2	1	4
CAN	1	1	1	3
LIE			2	2

	GOLD	SILVER	BRONZE	TOTAL
SWE			2	2
GBR			1	1
TCH		1		1
FRA			1	1

RECORD OF THE XX OLYMPIAD

AUGUST 26, 1972-JULY 16, 1976

OFFICERS OF THE INTERNATIONAL OLYMPIC COMMITTEE

Michael Morris, the Lord Killanin — President
Count Jean de Beaumont — First Vice President
Jonkheer Herman Adrian
van Karnebeek — Second Vice President
Willi Daume — Third Vice President

Other Executive Members:
Constantin Andrianov
Juan Antonio Samaranch
Sylvio de Magalhaes Padilha
Tsuenoshi Takeda

INTERNATIONAL OLYMPIC COMMITTEE MEMBERSHIP DURING THE XX OLYMPIAD

ARRIVALS: 11

— 1972 —

August 21	Pedro Ramirez-Vasquez	Mexico

— 1973 —

October 5	Anthony Bridge	Jamaica
	Manuel Gonzalez-Guerra	Cuba
	Ashwini Kumar	India
	Keba MíBaye	Senegal

— 1974 —

October 23	Dawee Chullasapya	Thailand
	Eduardo Hay	Mexico
	Julian Kean Roosevelt	USA
	Mohamed Zerguini	Algeria
	David McKenzie	Australia

— 1975—

May 21	Epaminondas Petralias	Greece

DEPARTURES: 8

— 1973 —

October 5	Avery Brundage	USA
December 15	Segura Marte Gomez*	Mexico

— 1974 —

October 21	Lewis Luxton	Australia
	Mario Luis Negri	Argentina
	King Constantine	Greece
	Prabhas Charusathiara	Thailand

— 1975 —

March 6	Hugh Richard Weir*	Australia
May 6	Alfredo Inciarte	Uruguay

* Died in office; all others resigned

Net increase in the IOC membership: 3

Total IOC membership by the end of the XX Olympiad: 77

OFFICERS OF THE UNITED STATES OLYMPIC COMMITTEE

13th USOC Quadrennial, April 19, 1969, to February 9, 1973

Franklin L. Orth
Orth was elected president of the USOC on April 19, 1969. His term was to span the XIX and XX Olympiads, but he died on January 4, 1970.

Clifford H. Buck
Buck ascended to the USOC presidency on April 18, 1973, following the death of Franklin L. Orth. He completed his term on February 9, 1973.

Other elected officers:

Philip O. Krumm	First Vice President
Robert J. Kane	Second Vice President
Henry W. Buse Jr.	Secretary
Julian K. Roosevelt	Treasurer
Patrick H. Sullivan	Counselor
Arthur G. Lentz	Executive Director

14th USOC Quadrennial, February 9, 1973, to April 29, 1977

Philip O. Krumm
Krumm was elected president of the USOC on February 9, 1973. His term spanned the XX and XXI Olympiads.

Other elected officers:

Robert J. Kane	Executive Vice President
John B. Kelly Jr.	Second Vice President
Al O. Duer	Third Vice President
E. Newbold Black IV	Secretary
Julian K. Roosevelt	Treasurer
Patrick H. Sullivan	Counselor
Col. F. Don Miller	Executive Director

HONORARY PRESIDENTS OF THE UNITED STATES OLYMPIC COMMITTEE

Starting with President Grover Cleveland, who accepted the honorary presidency of what was then the American Olympic Association in December 1895, every United States president has agreed to serve in this capacity. During the XX Olympiad, President Richard M. Nixon was the honorary president of the USOC until his resignation on August 8, 1974. President Gerald Ford became the honorary president for the remainder of the Olympiad.

OLYMPIC AWARDS

THE OLYMPIC CUP

Beginning in 1906, the Olympic Cup was awarded annually to a person, institution, or association that had contributed significantly to sport or to the development of the Olympic movement. The Olympic Cup was kept at the IOC; honorees received a reproduction. The award was originally conceived by Baron Pierre de Coubertin.

RECIPIENTS

1972	National Olympic Committee of Turkey	
	City of Sapporo	
1973	City of Munich	
1974	National Olympic Committee of Bulgaria	
1975	National Olympic Committee of Italy	

OLYMPIC DIPLOMA OF MERIT

The Olympic Diploma of Merit, created in 1905 during the third Olympic Congress in Brussels, was awarded to an individual who had been active in the service of sport and/or had contributed substantially to the Olympic movement.

RECIPIENTS

1972	Andres Merce Varela	Spain
1973	Frederick Ruegsegger	USA
	Epaminonda Petralias	Greece
	Otl Aicher	Germany
1974	Sir Stanley Rous	Great Britain
	Lord Philip Noel-Baker	Great Britain
	Jean Borotra	France
1975	not attributed	

SIR THOMAS FEARNLEY CUP

The Fearnley Cup, donated in 1950 by Sir Thomas Fearnley, former member of the International Olympic Committee in Norway from 1927 to 1950, was awarded to a sports club or a local sports association practicing meritorious achievement in the service of the Olympic movement.

RECIPIENTS

1972	The Guayas Sports Federation of Ecuador
1973	Not attributed
1974	Not attributed
1975	Not attributed

THE OLYMPIC ORDER

The Olympic Order, created in 1974, is awarded to a person who has expressed the Olympic ideal through his or her action, who has attained remarkable accomplishment in sport, or who has rendered outstanding service to the Olympic cause either through personal achievement or contribution to the development of sport. The award has three degrees: gold, silver, bronze.

RECIPIENTS

THE GOLD OLYMPIC ORDER

1975	Avery Brundage	USA

THE SILVER OLYMPIC ORDER

1975	Ryotaro Azuma	Japan
	Rudyard Russell	Great Britian
	Miguel de Capriles	USA

THE BRONZE OLYMPIC ORDER

1975	Charles Debeur	Belgium
	Gyula Hegyi	Hungary

John Kasyoka   Kenya
Lia Manoliu   Romania
Ellen Müller-Preiss   Austria
Jacques Thiebault   France

OFFICIAL PUBLICATIONS OF THE INTERNATIONAL OLYMPIC COMMITTEE

THE OLYMPIC CHARTER

The Olympic Charter provides the official rules, procedures, and protocols of the IOC, which are periodically updated by vote of the membership at an IOC Session. Six editions were issued during the XX Olympiad.

Edition 17   Issued August 1971
         (In French and English)

Edition 17.1   Issued August 1972
         (In German only)

Edition 17.2   Issued August 1972
         (In German only)

Edition 18   Issued October 1973
         (In French and English)

Edition 19   Issued October 1974
         (In French and English)

Edition 20   Issued May 1975
         (In French and English)

THE OLYMPIC REVIEW

The *Olympic Review* (*Revue Olimpique*) - In January 1970 the IOC began to produce a monthly Olympic magazine that kept members updated on meetings and Olympic news in a more timely fashion than the quarterly information letter that had been published since 1968. The *Olympic Review* was the eleventh version of the International Olympic Committee magazine and is still published today.

#59	October 1972
#60-#61	November-December 1972
#62-#63	January-February 1973
#64-#65	March-April 1973
#66-#67	May-June 1973
#68-#69	July-August 1973
#70-#71	September-October 1973
#72-#73	November-December 1973
#74-#75	January-February 1974
#76-#77	March-April 1974
#78-#79	May-June 1974
#80-#81	July-August 1974
#82-#83	September-October 1974
#84	October 1974
#85-#86	November-December 1974
#87-#88	January-February 1975
#89-#90	March-April 1975
#91-#92	May-June 1975
#93-#94	July-August 1975
#95-#96	September-October 1975
#97-#98	November-December 1975
#99-#100	January-February 1976
#101-#102	March-April 1976
#103-#104	May-June 1976

THE IOC HANDBOOK

This publication lists the names and addresses of the members of the IOC, the NOCs, and the IFs, as well as information on Olympic-related associations. The IOC decided in 1967 that the IOC Handbook was to be published after each IOC Session. Issues during the XX Olympiad included:

1972 IOC Handbook
1973 IOC Handbook
1974 IOC Handbook
1975 IOC Handbook

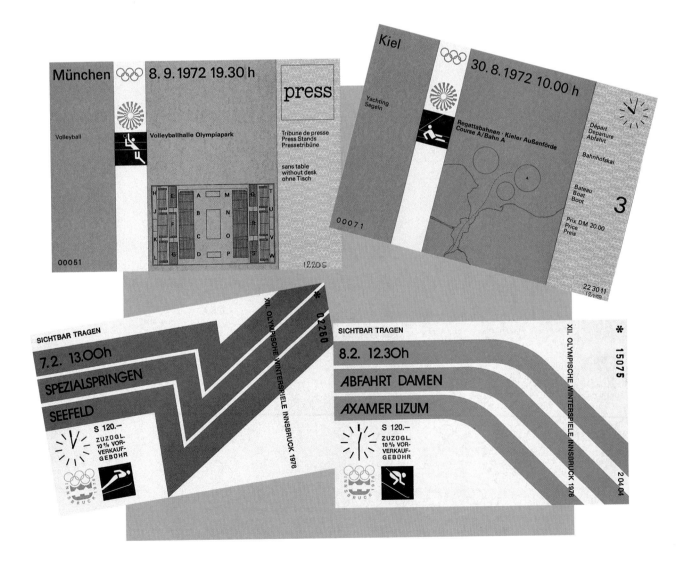

ACKNOWLEDGMENTS

The publisher would like to thank the following for their invaluable assistance to 1st Century Project and World Sport Research & Publications: Gov. Francisco G. Almeda (Philippine Olympic Committee, Manila); Sheik Fahad Al-Ahmad Al-Sabah (Olympic Committee of Kuwait); Don Anthony; Maj. Gen. Charouck Arirachakaran (Olympic Committee of Thailand, Bangkok); Bibliothèque National de France (Paris); Marie-Charlotte Bolot (University of the Sorbonne Cultural Library and Archives, Paris); Boston Public Library; British Museum and Library (London); Gail Britton; Richard L. Coe; Anita DeFrantz (IOC Member in the United States); Margi Denton; Carl and Lieselott Diem - Archives/Olympic Research Institute of the German Sport University Cologne; Edward L. Doheny, Jr. Library (University of Southern California, Los Angeles); Robert G. Engel; Miguel Fuentes (Olympic Committee of Chile, Santiago); National Library of Greece (Athens); Hollee Hazwell (Columbiana Collection, Columbia University, New York); Rebecca S. Jabbour and Bill Roberts (Bancroft Library, University of California at Berkeley); Diane Kaplan (Manuscripts and Archives, Sterling Library, Yale University, New Haven); David Kelly (Sport Specialist, Library of Congress, Washington, D.C.); Fékrou Kidane (International Olympic Committee, Lausanne); Peter Knight; Dr. John A. Lucas; Los Angeles Public Library; Blaine Marshall; Joachaim Mester, President of the German Sport University Cologne; Ed Mosk; Geoffroy de Navacelle; New York Public Library; Olympic Committee of India (New Delhi); Richard Palmer (British Olympic Association, London); C. Robert Paul; University of Rome Library and Archives; Margaret M.

Sherry (Rare Books and Special Collections, Firestone Library, Princeton University); Dr. Ruth Sparhawk; Gisela Terrell (Special Collections, Irwin Library, Butler University, Indianapolis); Walter Teutenberg; The Officers, Directors and Staff (United States Olympic Committee, Colorado Springs); University Research Library, (University of California at Los Angeles); John Vernon (National Archives, Washington, DC); Emily C. Walhout (Houghton Library; Harvard University); Herb Weinberg; Dr. Wayne Wilson, Michael Salmon, Shirley Ito (Paul Ziffren Sports Resource Center Library, Amateur Athletic Foundation of Los Angeles); Patricia Henry Yeomans; Nanci A. Young (Seeley G. Mudd Manuscript Library, Princeton University Archives); Dr. Karel Wendl, Michéle Veillard, Patricia Eckert, Simon Mandl, Ruth Perrenoud, Nikolay Guerguiev, Fani Kakridi-Enz, Laura Leslie Pearman, and Christine Sklentzas (International Olympic Committee Olympic Studies and Research Center, Lausanne); and Pat White (Special Collections, Stanford University Library, Palo Alto).

The publishers recognize with gratitude the special contributions made for Volume 18 by Frau Ernst (Süddeutsches Bildarchiv, München); Ian Hanson (Javelin Communications, Sydney Australia); Tom Mills (Track Record Entertainment & So. Cal. Olympians); Charlotte Ibbotson (Librarian, British Olympic Association); Marge and Jack Haynes (Sydney, Australia); Meagan Gorman (Sydney, Australia); Karin Berg & Rune Flatten (Skiforeningen, Oslo, Norway); Anthony Bijkerk (Oosterwolde, Netherlands); Inha Kanerva (Sports Library of Finland); Peter Daland (Thousand Oaks,

California); Peter Reichl (Police Munich); Daniel Waeger (Koblenz); Val Ching and Neil Loft (Allsport, Pacific Palisades); Michael Shulman (Archive Photos, New York City); Hanns-Peter Lochmann and Wulf-Bert Beil (dpa/Zentralbild, Berlin); Andy Kiss (Duomo, New York City); Tsutomu Kishimoto and Shigeaki Matsubara (Photo Kishimoto, Tokyo); Ian Blackwell and Andrew Wrighting (Popperfoto, Overstone); Phillipe Renard (Presse Sports, Issy-Les-Moulineau); Prem Kalliat (Sports Illustrated Picture Sales, New York City); Deborah Goodsite and Jocelyn Clapp (The Corbis-Bettmann Archive, New York City); Alexandra Leclef Mandl (The International Olympic Committee, Lausanne); Patricia Olkiewicz (United States Olympic Committee, Colorado Springs); and Frank Hörmann (Fotoagentur Sven Simon, Essen)

The Publishers would also like to thank the following individuals, institutions and foundations for providing initial funding for the project: The Amelior Foundation (Morristown, New Jersey); Roy and Mary Cullen (Houston); The English, Bonter, Mitchell Foundation (Ft. Wayne, Indiana); Adrian French (Los Angeles); The Knight Foundation (Miami); The Levy Foundation (Philadelphia); and, Jonah Shacknai (New York). And for completion funding: Michael McKie, Optimax Securities, Inc. (Toronto); Graham Turner, Fraser & Beatty (Toronto); and Century of Sport Partnership (Toronto).

And a special thanks to Barron Pittenger (Assistant Executive Director, United States Olympic Committee, September 1981 to August 1987 and Executive Director, August 1987 to December 1989).

BIBLIOGRAPHY

Anonymous. "The Russian Dash Man." *World Sports*, April 1972.

Anonymous. "The Olympics: 'Political Blackmail'." *Newsweek*, September 4, 1972.

Associated Press. *Pursuit of Excellence: The Olympic Story.* Danbury, Connecticut: Grolier, 1979.

Allen, Neil. "Pay Up, Pay Up, and They'll Play the Game." *World Sports*, February 1972.

Besford, Pat. "Gould Girl!" *World Sports*, February 1972.

Bornstein, Larry. *After Olympic Glory: The Lives of Ten Outstanding Medalists.* New York: Frederick Wane, 1978.

Brasher, Christopher. *Munich '72.* London: Stanley Paul and Company, 1972.

Bryden, Wendy. *Canada at the Olympic Winter Games.* Edmonton: Hartig Publishers, 1988.

Buchanon, Ian. *British Olympians: A Hundred Years of Gold Medallists.* Enfield, Guinness, 1988.

Carlson, Lewis H. and John J. Fogarty. *Tales of Gold: An oral History of the Summer Olympic Games told by America's Gold Medal Winners.* Chicago: Contemporary Books, 1987.

Chavoor, Sherman and Bill Davidson. *The 50-Meter Jungle.* New York: Coward, McCann, Geoghan Inc., 1973.

Colwin, Cecil M., *Swimming into the 21st Century.* Champaign, IL.: Human Kinetics Publishers, 1992.

Condon, Robert J., *Great Women Athletes of the 20th Century.* Jefferson, NC: McFarland Press, 1991.

Coote, James & John Goodbody. *The Olympics 1972.* London: Robert Hale Company, 1972.

Crossman, Jim. *Olympic Shooting.* Washington, D.C.: National Rifle Association, 1978.

Daume, Willi. "Games of the XXth Olympiad." *Olympic Review*, October 1977.

Denver Olympic Committee Official Report, December 1972.

Die Spiele. The Official Report of the Organizing Committee for the Games of the XXth Olympiad Munich 1972. Munich: pro Sport München, 1972.

Duncanson, Neil. *The Fastest Man on Earth: The 100m Olympic Champions.* London: Willow Books, 1988.

Duncanson, Neil and Patrick Collins. *Tales of Gold.* London: McDonald Queen Anne Press, 1992.

Espy, Richard. *The Politics of the Olympic Games.* Berkeley, CA: University of California Press, 1979.

Gammon, Clive. "Lord of the Games." *Sports Illustrated.* February 9, 1976.

Gardner, Doug (ed.). *Official Report of the Olympic Games 1972: British Olympic Association.* London: Sportsworld, 1972.

Gardner, Doug. "Bed and Bored in Munich." *World Sports*, October 1971.

Gardner, Doug. "Putting the lid on the Olympics." *World Sports*, October 1971.

Gilbert, Doug. *The Miracle Machine*. New York: Coward, McCann & Geoghegan, 1980.

Giller, Norman. *The Marathon: The Runners of the Race*. Secaucus, New Jersey: Chartwell Books Inc., 1983.

Goodbody, John. *The Illustrated History of Gymnastics*. London: Stanley Paul, 1982.

Gordon, Harry. *Australia at the Olympic Games*. St. Lucia, Queensland: University of Queensland Press, 1994.

Grombach, John V. *The 1976 Olympic Guide*. Chicago: Rand McNally and Co., 1975.

Groussard, Serge. *The Blood of Israel*. New York: William Morrow & Company Inc., 1975.

Guttman, Allen. *The Games Must Go On: Avery Brundage and the Olympic Movement*. New York: Colombia University Press, 1984 .

Guttman, Allen. *The Olympics: A History of the Modern Games*. Urbana and Chicago: University of Illinois Press, 1992.

Howell, Reet & Max. *Aussie Gold: The Story of Australia at the Olympics*. Melbourne: Australian Brooks Waterloo, 1988.

Hendershott, Jon, *Tracks Greatest Women*. Los Altos, California: Tafnews Press, 1987.

Henry, Bill. *An Approved History of the Olympic Games*. Los Angeles: Southern California Committee for the Olympic Games,1981.

Innsbruck '76: XII Olympische Winterspiele. Innsbruck: Organisationskomitee der XII Olympischen Winterspiele 1976 Innsbruck, Juli 1976.

Jerome, John. "Goodbye, Denver Olympics." *Skiing*, February 1973.

Johnson, William O. "Avery Brundage: The Man Behind the Mask." *Sports Illustrated*. August 4, 1980.

Kamper, Erich and Bill Mallon. *The Golden Book of the Olympic Games*. Milan, Italy: Vallardi and Associati Editrice, 1992 .

Kirkpatrick, Curry. "Babes Who Are Going Gunning." *Sports Illustrated*, August 3, 1972.

Kirshenbaum, Jerry. "A Sanctuary Violated." *Sports Illustrated*, September 18, 1972.

Kirshenbaum, Jerry. "The Golden Days of Mark the Shark." *Sports Illustrated*, September 11, 1972.

Kirshenbaum, Jerry. "Mexico to Munich: Mark Spitz Quest for Gold." *Sports Illustrated*, September 4, 1972.

Kirshenbaum, Jerry. "They're Sure A Winning Toothsome." *Sports Illustrated*. August 28, 1972.

Kirshenbaum, Jerry. "Buzz Before the Curtain." *Sports Illustrated*, August 28, 1972.

Kirshenbaum, Jerry. "Mark of Excellence." *Sports Illustrated*, August 14, 1972.

Kirshenbaum. Jerry. "Voting to Snuff the Torch." *Sports Illustrated*, November 20, 1972.

Klammer, Franz. "Downhill All the Way." *Sports Illustrated*, March 12, 1979.

Kutzer, William F. *The History of Olympic Weightlifting in the United States*. Salt Lake City: Bringham Young University Ed. D., 1979.

Lucas, John. *The Modern Olympic Games*. London: Thomas Yoseloff Ltd., 1976.

Mandell, Richard D. *The Olympics of 1972: A Munich Diary*. Chapel Hill, North Carolina: The University of North Carolina Pres, 1991.

Manning, J.L. "Amateur-The Word That's Gone from Games." *World Sports*, May 1971.

Manning, J.L. "Accounting Expenses." *World Sports*, May 1971.

Manning, J.L. "Princess Anne-Heiress to the Olympic Throne?" *World Sports*, June 1971.

McKay, Jim. *My Wide World*. New York: Macmillan Publishing Co., 1973.

McMillan, Tom. *Out of Bounds*. New York: Simon and Schuster, 1973.

Moore, Kenny. "An Enigma Wrapped in Glory." *Sports Illustrated*, June 27, 1977.

Moore, Kenny. "There Have Been Shootings in the Night." *Sports Illustrated*, September 18, 1972.

Mora, Lynn. "Dedicated to Olga! With Love," *International Gymnast*, April 1978.

Naughton, Lindie and Watterson, Johnny. *Irish Olympians*. Dublin: Blackwater Press, 1992.

Olympia- Mannschaft der Deutschen Demokratischen Republik, *Presse Information*, Olympische Sommerspiele 1972, Nationales Olympishes Komitee der Deutschen Demokratischen Republik, Dresden.

Olympia- Mannschaft der Deutschen Demokratischen Republik, *Presse Information*, Olympische Winterspiele 1976, Nationales Olympishes Komitee der Deutschen Demokratischen Republik, Dresden.

Page, James A. *Black Olympian Medalists*. Denver, Colorado: Libraries Unlimited, Inc., 1991.

Paul, Robert Jr., *Games of the XXI Olympiad/XII Winter Games*. Munich: Roland Wolf, 1976.

Peters, Mary with Ian Wooldridge. *Mary P.: Autobiography*. London: Stanley Paul, 1974.

Pilley, Phil. "State Aid, Amateurism and All That." *World Sports*, November 1960.

Pilley, Phil. "Halt this Olympic Show." *World Sports*, April 1960.

Porter, David L. (ed.) *Biographical Dictionary of American Sports*. New York: Greenwood Press, 1988.

Pozzoli, Peter. *Irish Women's Athletics*. London: Women's Track and Field World, 1977.

Prokop, David (ed.). *The African Running Revolution*. London: World Publications, 1975.

Putnan, Pat. "Saved by Very Fast Wottle." *Sports Illustrated*, September 11, 1972.

Putnam, Pat. "Olympic Overture: Flags and Flak." *Sports Illustrated*, September 4, 1972.

Putnam, Pat. "Experience May Not BE Necessary." *Sports Illustrated*, August 28, 1972.

Putnam, Pat. "The High and the Mighty." *Sports Illustrated*, July 14, 1972.

Putnam, Pat. "Just A Guy Having Some Fun." *Sports Illustrated*, July 10, 1972.

Raevoom, Antero and Haikkola, Rolf. (transl. by Matti Hannus) *Lasse Viren Olympic Champion*. Portland, OR: Continental Pu blishing House, 1978.

Rapoport. Roger. "Olympian snafu at Sniktau." *Sports Illustrated*, February 15, 1971.

Seagrave, Jeffrey D. and Donald Chu. *The Olympic Games in Transition*. Champaign IL: Human Kinetic Books, 1988.

Shorter, Frank with Marc Bloom. *Olympic Gold: A Runner's Life and Times*. Boston: Houghton Mifflin Company, 1984.

Sport in the USSR. November 1979.

Sport in the USSR. January 1967.

Steinbach, Valeri. *638 OLYMPIC CHAMPIONS*. Moscow: Raduga Publishers, 1980.

Track and Field News. September 1972.

Track and Field News. November 1972.

Verscoth, Anita. "Sugar and Spice and Iron." *Sports Illustrated*, August 21, 1972.

Wallechinsky, David. *The Complete Book of the Summer Olympics*. Boston: Little, Brown and Company, 1996.

Wallechinsky, David. *The Complete Book of the Winter Olympics*. Brown: Little, Brown and Company, 1994.

Watman, Mel. *Athletics at the Olympic Games*. Cambridge, UK: Cantabria, 1992.

Welch, Paula. "Cute Little Creatures." *Olympic Review*, September/October 1988.

Whall, Hugh D. "Their Finish Line was C Day." *Sports Illustrated*, July 10, 1972.

Wilson, Neil (ed.) *Olympics 1976: British Olympic Association Official Report 1976*. London: West Nally Ltd., 1976.

Women's Track and Field World. September/October 1972.

PHOTO CREDITS

Every effort has been made to locate the holders of the rights to the pictures in this book.

INDEX

THE OLYMPIC WORLD
INNSBRUCK 1976 WINTER GAMES

PARTICIPATING COUNTRIES

North America

CAN . . . . CANADA
USA. UNITED STATES OF AMERICA

South America

ARG . . . . ARGENTINA
CHI. . . . . CHILE

Europe

AND . . . . ANDORRA
AUT. . . . . AUSTRIA
BEL . . . . BELGIUM
BUL . . . . BULGARIA
CHE. . . . . CZECHOSLOVAKIA
ESP. . . . . SPAIN
FIN . . . . FINLAND

FRA. . . . . FRANCE
FRG. . . . . WEST GERMANY
GBR . . . . GREAT BRITAIN
GDR . . . . EAST GERMANY
GRE . . . . GREECE
HOL. . . . . THE NETHERLANDS

HUN. . . . . HUNGARY
ISL . . . . ICELAND
ITA . . . . ITALY
LIE . . . . LIECHTENSTEIN
NOR . . . . NORWAY
POL . . . . POLAND